Timo Warns

Structural Failure Models for Fault-Tolerant Distributed Computing

VIEWEG+TEUBNER RESEARCH

Software Engineering Research

Herausgeber/Editor:

Prof. Dr. Wilhelm Hasselbring

Im Software Engineering wird traditionell ein Fokus auf den Prozess der Konstruktion von Softwaresystemen gelegt. Der Betrieb von Systemen, die kontinuierlich Dienste mit einer geforderten Qualität bieten müssen, stellt eine ebenso große Herausforderung dar. Ziel der Reihe Software Engineering Research ist es, innovative Techniken und Methoden für die Entwicklung und den Betrieb von nachhaltigen Softwaresystemen vorzustellen.

Traditionally, software engineering focuses on the process of constructing and evolving software systems. The operation of systems that are expected to continuously provide services with required quality properties is another great challenge. It is the goal of the Series Software Engineering Research to present innovative techniques and methods for engineering and operating sustainable software systems.

Timo Warns

Structural Failure Models for Fault-Tolerant Distributed Computing

With a foreword by Prof. Wilhelm Hasselbring

VIEWEG+TEUBNER RESEARCH

Bibliographic information published by the Deutsche Nationalbibliothek
The Deutsche Nationalbibliothek lists this publication in the Deutsche Nationalbibliografie; detailed bibliographic data are available in the Internet at http://dnb.d-nb.de.

Dissertation Universität Oldenburg, 2009

1st Edition 2010

Editorial Office: Ute Wrasmann | Anita Wilke

Vieweg+Teubner Verlag is a brand of Springer Fachmedien.
Springer Fachmedien is part of Springer Science+Business Media.
www.viewegteubner.de

Cover design: KünkelLopka Medienentwicklung, Heidelberg
Printed on acid-free paper
Printed in Germany

ISBN 978-3-8348-1287-2

Foreword

Despite means of fault prevention such as extensive testing or formal verification, errors inevitably occur during system operation. To avoid subsequent system failures, critical distributed systems, therefore, require engineering of means for fault tolerance. Achieving fault tolerance requires some redundancy, which, unfortunately, is bound to limitations. Appropriate fault models are needed to describe which types of faults and how many faults are tolerable in a certain context. Previous research on distributed systems has often introduced fault models that abstract too many relevant system properties such as dependent and propagating component failures. In this research work, Timo Warns introduces new structural failure models that are both accurate (to cover relevant properties) and tractable (to be analyzable). These new failure models cover dependent failures (for instance, failure correlation by geographic proximity) and propagating failures (for instance, propagation by service utilization). To evaluate the new failure models, Timo Warns shows how some seminal problems in distributed systems can be solved with improved resilience and efficiency, as compared to existing solutions.

Particularly, the textbook-style introduction to distributed systems and the rigorous presentation of the new failure models and their evaluation may serve as an example for other software engineering research projects – which is why this book is a valuable addition to both a researcher's and a student's library.

Wilhelm Hasselbring

Acknowledgments

A PhD thesis – as every result of research – is embedded in a scientific and in a personal context. Let me express my gratitude to a few people who have contributed in these contexts to my work in one or another way. While I do not name everyone who would deserve it I will remember each of them and their support.

First of all, I would like to thank Willi Hasselbring for the open and friendly environment I was able to work in and for his confidence in me. His support – both professional and personal – and the freedom to develop and elaborate my own ideas have been more than what a PhD student can ask for.

During the last year of being a PhD student, I worked in the group of Oliver Theel, whom I would like to thank for cordially accepting me in his group. He taught me a lot about research and has considerably improved the quality of my scientific work. His diverting stories have always been an incredible moral support.

Very special thanks go to Felix Freiling for his advice and insights not limited to distributed computing. Working with him was a substantial source of motivation and has significantly shaped different contributions of the thesis. His friendliness, perspicacity, and balance in academia have been a role model.

Working in different contexts with different people has been a particular privilege that I appreciate. I would like to thank the members of the Software Engineering Group, of the System Software and Distributed Systems Group, and of the graduate school TrustSoft of the University of Oldenburg. They made the time more instructive and more enjoyable by numerous and multifaceted discussions.

While there are too many people to mention them individually, I would like to thank some of them in particular. Special thanks go to Christian Storm, Matthias Rohr, Marko Bošković, Jens Happe, Heiko Koziolek, Roland Meyer, and Henrik Lipskoch for more than working on joint papers, co-organizing workshops, sharing an office room, a lot of humour, and becoming or remaining best friends. I sincerely appreciate the assistance and continuous good will of Ira Wempe and Manuela Wüstefeld who have relieved me of many disturbances. Particular thanks also go to Christian Storm, André van Hoorn, and Kinga Kiss-Jakab for proofreading the thesis.

Very sincere thanks go to my mum, Elisabeth Warns, who has always had confidence in me and has supported me all along the way.

The contribution of my girlfriend, Alexandra Kroll, to finishing the thesis can hardly be overestimated. I would like to thank her for sharing the good times and for helping me through the bad times in the last couple of years.

Timo Warns

Abstract

The dependability of distributed systems strongly depends on the occurrence of faults and on the ability of a system to cope with them. A fault-tolerant system is capable of providing service as expected even if some components have failed. Unfortunately, no system can tolerate arbitrary severe and arbitrary many faults. Engineering a fault-tolerant system, therefore, requires a fault model that describes the faults to tolerate. A good fault model must be accurate for the relevant aspects of faults, but abstract away irrelevant details. There is empirical evidence that, in particular, dependences and propagation of faults are relevant in real-world systems. In this thesis, we address the questions of how to model such faults and how to tolerate them.

For a fault model, we distinguish *functional* from *structural failure models*. A functional failure model describes how a component that is failed may behave. A structural failure model describes the extent of component failures. We investigate different classes of nonprobabilistic structural failure models and, in particular, introduce two new ones: *set-based models* for dependent faults and *sequence-based models* for dependent and propagating faults. Both classes close a gap between probabilistic models that cover dependent and propagating faults and previous nonprobabilistic models that do not. The new classes and several previous ones are compared with respect to their expressiveness resulting in a comprehensive hierarchy of nonprobabilistic structural failure models. All of the considered previous classes are strictly less expressive than the new set-based class, which is strictly less expressive than the new sequence-based class.

For many problems of distributed computing, there exist solutions that rely on quorums and, in particular, on highly available coteries to achieve fault tolerance. We illustrate how to solve distributed computing problems under the new model classes using *highly available coteries* and *probing* quorums. More precisely, we give characterisations of highly available coteries that show how to construct such a coterie from a set-based model if a highly-available coterie exists. Considering sequence-based models, we introduce the quality measure *refined probe complexity* that gives a tight bound on the number of required probes to find a quorum of noncrashed processes or to reveal that no such quorum exists. Additionally, we present a new *probe strategy* that is defined for all quorum sets and is more efficient in the number of required probes than previous strategies.

The considerations of quorums are independent of a particular fault tolerance problem. As a concrete problem, we show how to *reach consensus* in the presence of faults. In particular, we demonstrate that the new model classes do not require solutions developed from scratch: Adapting and transforming previous solutions for previous model classes suffice to reach consensus. Using the new model classes turns out to be beneficial as it allows more resilient and/or more efficient solutions.

Zusammenfassung

Die Verlässlichkeit verteilter Systeme wird stark vom Auftreten von Fehlern und von der Fähigkeit eines Systems, mit ihnen umzugehen, bestimmt. Ein fehlertolerantes System ist auch dann noch in der Lage seinen Dienst wie gewünscht zu erbringen, wenn einige Komponenten ausfallen. Leider kann kein System beliebig schwerwiegende und beliebig häufige Fehler tolerieren. Für die Entwicklung eines fehlertoleranten Systems wird daher ein Fehlermodell benötigt, das die zu tolerierenden Fehler beschreibt. Ein gutes Fehlermodell muss in den relevanten Aspekten von Fehlern genau sein, aber von unwichtigen Details abstrahieren. Empirische Studien haben gezeigt, dass Abhängigkeiten und die Fortpflanzung von Fehlern relevante Aspekte in realen Systemen sind. Diese Arbeit beschäftigt sich damit, wie diese Aspekte modelliert werden und die dadurch ausgedrückten Fehler toleriert werden können.

In der Arbeit werden *funktionale* und *strukturale* Fehlermodelle unterschieden. Ein funktionales Fehlermodell beschreibt, wie sich eine ausgefallene Komponente verhalten kann. Ein strukturales Fehlermodell beschreibt das Ausmaß von Komponentenausfällen (z.B. wie viele Komponenten ausfallen können). Die Arbeit untersucht verschiedene Klassen von nicht-probabilistischen strukturalen Modellen und stellt insbesondere zwei neue Klassen vor: *mengenbasierte Modelle* für abhängige Fehler und *folgenbasierte Modelle* für abhängige und sich fortpflanzende Fehler. Beide Klassen schließen eine Lücke zwischen probabilistischen Modellen, die abhängige und sich fortpflanzende Fehler abdecken, und bereits existierenden nicht-probabilistischen Modellen, die das nicht tun. Die neuen und verschiedene bereits existierende Klassen werden miteinander bzgl. ihrer Ausdrucksmächtigkeit verglichen. Dabei entsteht eine umfassende Hierarchie von nicht-probabilistischen strukturalen Fehlermodellen. Alle der betrachteten bereits existierenden Klassen sind echt weniger ausdrucksmächtig als die neue mengenbasierte Klasse, die wiederum echt weniger ausdrucksmächtig ist als die neue folgenbasierte Klasse.

Für viele Probleme verteilter Systeme gibt es Lösungen, die sich auf Quoren und insbesondere hoch verfügbare Coterien verlassen, um Fehlertoleranz zu erreichen. Die Arbeit zeigt Lösungen für die neuen Modellklassen, die *hoch verfügbaren*

Coterien und *Prüfungen* von Quoren verwenden. Genauer werden Charakterisierungen von hoch verfügbaren Coterien und deren Konstruktion aus mengenbasierten Modellen vorgestellt. Bzgl. der folgenbasierten Modelle wird die Qualitätsmetrik der *verfeinerten Prüfkomplexität* vorgestellt. Sie gibt eine enge Schranke für die Anzahl der Prüfungen an, die notwendig sind, um ein Quorum von nicht ausgefallenen Prozessen zu finden (bzw. um herauszufinden, dass es kein solches Quorum gibt). Zusätzlich wird eine neue *Prüfstrategie* präsentiert, die für alle Quorenmengen definiert und effizienter in der Anzahl der benötigten Prüfungen als bisherige Strategien ist.

Die Untersuchung von Quoren in der Arbeit ist unabhängig von einem bestimmten Fehlertoleranz-Problem. Als ein konkretes Problem wird gezeigt, wie man *Konsensus erreicht*, wenn Fehler auftreten können. Insbesondere machen die neuen Modellklassen es nicht notwendig, vollständig neue Lösungen zu entwickeln: Die Anpassung und Transformation bestehender Lösungen für bisherige Modellklassen reichen aus, um das Problem zu lösen. Die Nutzung der neuen Modellklassen stellt sich dabei als vorteilhaft heraus, da sie widerstandsfähigere und/oder effizientere Lösungen ermöglichen.

Contents

List of Figures and Tables

1 Introduction

1.1 Motivation

Dependable Distributed Systems Distributed systems have become crucial in most application domains of computing systems. Their success stems from, for example, being more cost-efficient, more powerful, and more scalable than stand-alone systems. Distributed systems are characterised by consisting of active components that are spatially distributed and share information via some means of communication. The components are active in the sense that they perform computations that are of interest for the user of the system. The range of the components' spatial distribution is wide, from micro-scale embedded systems-on-a-chip to globally – and possibly further – distributed systems.

As distributed systems more and more pervade our daily life, we increasingly depend on their correct service. Many distributed systems deliver critical services, whose failures are not acceptable. Prominent examples include air traffic control systems, power grid systems, and patient monitoring systems. Failures of such systems may entail excessive costs or even cause loss of life. Hence, the *dependability* of distributed systems is essential for their acceptance in the future.

Dependability is a fundamental property of computing systems besides, for example, performance and costs. Avižienis et al. [2004] have spent significant effort on a comprehensive dependability taxonomy over the past two decades. They describe dependability as the ability of a system to deliver service that can justifiably be trusted. Dependability is a general concept that subsumes different more specific attributes such as *availability*, *reliability*, and *integrity*. For example, availability deals with the "readiness for correct service," reliability with the "continuity of correct service," and integrity with the "absence of improper system alterations." These attributes are threatened by *faults*, *errors*, and *failures*. A failure is an event that occurs when the delivered service of a system deviates from correct service. An error is a part of the system state that may lead to a failure. A fault is the cause of an error.

Means of Fault Tolerance With raising needs for dependable distributed systems, the demand for means to attain dependability increases. Avižienis et al. [2004] divide such means into four classes: *fault forecasting*, *fault prevention*, *fault* *removal*, and *fault tolerance*. Despite all efforts of prevention and removal, each distributed system consists of components that are bound to fail eventually. Means of fault tolerance allow to avoid that component failures – being system faults – lead to system failures; a dependable system can be built from undependable components. Ideally, a system should completely mask the occurrence of faults from external observers of the system. However, other forms (e.g., remaining in a safe state despite faults) may be acceptable while being more cost-efficient.

A prerequisite for any type of fault tolerance is some form of redundancy [Gärtner, 1999]: A fault-tolerant design must incorporate some entities that are not required per se to deliver the desired service. These entities are only added for the sake of fault tolerance. A simple example is a checksum that is added to some data for purposes of error detection and correction. Another example is to have an algorithm executed by different processors and vote on the result to mask a failed processor. The extent of such redundancy in a system determines the costs of the system and the resilience of the system to faults.

The Need for Models While designing and evaluating a distributed system are already complex tasks, fault tolerance makes the tasks even more complex. If these tasks are not done properly, the fault tolerance mechanisms themselves can become the source of failures. For example, Mackall [1988] has reported that the fault detection logic in a flight-crucial control system caused failures of an aircraft: Each of overall three communication channels declared the other two channels as failed although no actual hardware failure occurred. Only a manual selection of a backup system allowed to land the aircraft safely. Such examples illustrate that designing and evaluating fault tolerance mechanisms are complex as well as critical tasks and, therefore, require a rigorous treatment.

Models as means of abstraction are crucial for a rigorous treatment and are the key to master the complexity of fault-tolerant distributed systems. For example, Bolosky et al. [2007] have reported that formal modelling was essential for designing the distributed directory service of a distributed file system. While this task took several months and 19 design iterations, it would have required even more time without formal modelling.

A model is an abstract representation of an object of interest. A good model describes the relevant aspects of the object but abstracts away the irrelevant ones. Schneider [1993a] explains that the challenge in finding a good model lies in finding a model that is both, *accurate* and *tractable*. A model is accurate if evaluations based on the model yield results that do not only hold for the model, but also for the actual object. A model is tractable if evaluations are possible at all. A model that is not accurate or not tractable is useless, because it yields invalid results or does not allow to obtain any results.

Fault Assumptions No matter to which extent a fault-tolerant design incorporates redundancy, no system can tolerate arbitrary faults. If faults are too severe or occur too frequently, then the redundancy required for fault tolerance will get exhausted: The system fails. For example, if all components of a system fail with an arbitrary behaviour, the system cannot behave as desired anymore. Therefore, it is essential for the design and the evaluation of a fault-tolerant system to make a *fault assumption* on the faults to tolerate.

Fault assumptions are represented by fault models that – for the sake of tractability – rely on simplifying assumptions. For example, such assumptions include:

- At most t components may fail.
- Component failures are identically distributed for all components.
- Component failures are stochastically independent.
- There is no propagation of failures among components.

Of course, such assumptions must be justified for the sake of accuracy. If a system is designed or evaluated under invalid assumptions, the system may fail even if its correctness has been formally verified. For example, Mackall [1988] has reported that, for the flight-crucial control system mentioned above, dual simultaneous component failures had been ruled out as impossible. Hence, the design of the system did not account for them. However, such faults did occur during a testing phase. The assumption that at most one component fails was not valid leading to a failure of the overall system.

While simplifications as listed above are frequently found in the literature, there is empirical evidence that they are not valid in many real-world systems. For example, Tang and Iyer [1992] evaluated two DEC VAX-cluster systems and found correlated failures due to errors in shared resources. Dobson et al. [2004, 2005] argue that large-scale blackouts of power grids are typically caused by propagating failures. It is likely that propagating failures in power grids manifest as propagating failures in distributed systems that are connected to these grids.

Dependent and Propagating Faults Correlated and, therefore, dependent component failures occur over the whole range of spatial distribution. For example, failure correlation coefficients up to 0.92 have been found in the globally distributed PlanetLab system [Warns et al., 2008]. If the failures had been stochastically independent, the coefficients would have been approximately equal to 0.

Likewise, Bakkaloglu et al. [2002] found correlated failures when measuring the availability of globally distributed web servers. Amir and Wool [1996] have found strongly correlated failures when evaluating quorum systems on 14 computers located in two geographical sites with a 50 km distance between both sites. With an increasing integration density of embedded systems, faults such as electric discharges are more likely to affect several neighboured components at the same time and cause dependent failures [Limbourg et al., 2007].

The impact of correlated failures is significant. Although the average failure correlation coefficient in the study on PlanetLab is rather low with 0.06, a prediction underestimates the probability that exactly one node fails (in the next 5 minutes) by four orders of magnitude under the assumption that failures are independent. Likewise, Yalagandula et al. [2004] have provided empirical evidence that correlated failures significantly hurt the availability of a system. Tang and Iyer [1993] have shown that this is the case even if the correlation coefficients are low.

Fault Models for Dependence and Propagation The relevance of dependent and propagating component failures has raised the interest for suitable fault models. Fault models that address the extent of faults are called *structural failure models*. Most of these models are probabilistic and, for example, rely on correlation coefficients as input parameters. Some examples are the models of Tang and Iyer [1992] and Bakkaloglu et al. [2002]. Other models cover dependences by explicitly considering the causes for dependent faults. For example, Limbourg et al. [2007] make the assumption that the spatial arrangement of components has an impact on fault dependences. They construct a probabilistic fault model by explicitly considering the spatial arrangement. Junqueira [2006] has presented a model for dependent faults that associates a set of attributes to each process of a distributed system. Intuitively, these attributes capture causes for process failures: If an attribute "is activated", all processes that have this attribute fail.

Despite such efforts, threshold models are predominant in the literature on fundamentals of fault-tolerant distributed computing. Describing the extent of faults by a simple threshold eases the design and the evaluation of a system and allows to refrain from a probabilistic system model. Considering probabilistic behaviour introduces additional complexities.

As Keidar and Marzullo [2002] have criticised, threshold models only allow to model identically distributed and independent faults. Due to the relevance of dependence and propagation in practice, such phenomena deserve to be considered when studying the fundamentals of fault-tolerant distributed computing. Hence, there is a need for simple fault models that allow to describe dependent and propagating faults.

1.2 Objectives

The objectives of this thesis are twofold: (i) to identify tractable structural failure models that cover relevant aspects of the real world and (ii) to show how to design fault tolerance mechanisms under these models. More precisely, we are looking for classes of nonprobabilistic structural failure models that allow to accurately describe dependent and propagating component failures for the domain of fault-tolerant distributed computing. We take threshold models – being prevalent in this domain – and other nonprobabilistic models as references for our models. It may be suspected that designing and evaluating fault-tolerant systems under the new models become intractable due to the increased accuracy. We demonstrate that, on the contrary, these tasks are hardly more complex. With these objectives, the thesis contributes to a more comprehensive understanding of the fundamentals of fault-tolerant distributed computing.

1.3 Outline

The thesis is organised into six chapters as follows.

Chapter 2 – Modelling Fault-Tolerant Distributed Systems After the introductory Chapter 1, Chapter 2 presents the system model that will be used throughout the thesis. Distributed systems are formalised by process models in terms of states, traces, and properties. The chapter gives elementary definitions for these terms and also addresses the fundamental aspects of interprocess communication, faults, and timing. The contribution of this chapter lies in providing the foundation for the rest of the thesis.

Chapter 3 – Modelling Fault Assumptions with Structural Failure Models Chapter 3 addresses the question of how to formalise fault assumptions in terms of functional and structural failure models. We give formal definitions for these models and show how to describe process, channel, and hybrid failure models in terms of functional and structural failure models. In the literature, it has been suspected that process failure models are incomplete, that is, some fault assumptions cannot be modelled using process failure models. We show that this suspicion is wrong under reasonable assumptions: Process failure models are complete if channels do not have externally visible states. In this case, any fault assumption for our system model can be given by a process failure model.

While functional failure models have been investigated in detail in the literature, structural failure models have received less attention so far. We formalise different fault assumptions taken from the literature by structural failure models and compare the resulting model classes with respect to their expressiveness. The resulting hierarchy is the most comprehensive classification of structural failure models so far. We introduce two new classes, namely the class of Didep models and the class of sequence-based structural failure models. The class of Didep models is strictly more expressive than the class of threshold models and covers dependent faults. The class of sequence-based models is strictly more expressive than the class of Didep models and additionally covers propagating faults. We close the chapter with showing how to map probabilistic fault models to Didep models and sequence-based models.

Chapter 4 – Constructing Coteries Static and dynamic coteries are fundamental means to implement coordination and agreement in fault-tolerant distributed systems. Chapter 4 demonstrates that Didep models and sequence-based models are tractable by relating them to static and dynamic coteries. Additionally, the chapter shows that these models allow more resilient and/or more efficient solutions.

More precisely, we give constructive characterisations of highly available static coteries in terms of Didep models. The results cover both, crash and Byzantine failures (i.e., prematurely halting and arbitrary failures). In particular, Didep models allow to achieve high availability when being impossible with threshold models. For crash failures, we additionally give a constructive characterisation of highly available dynamic coteries. For Byzantine failures, we show that dynamic coteries do not bear advantages over static coteries with respect to high availability.

Besides high availability, we address the quality measure of probe complexity. We refine the notion of probe complexity by explicitly considering sequence-based structural failure models. In contrast to the original probe complexity, the refined one gives a tight bound for a quorum set. It is significantly smaller than the original probe complexity under many failure models. Additionally, we give a universal probe strategy that meets the refined probe complexity. The probe strategy requires a number of probes equal to the refined probe complexity in the worst case due to exploiting the knowledge provided by a failure model.

Chapter 5 – Reaching Consensus In Chapter 5, we use the problem of reaching consensus as a "benchmark problem" to demonstrate that Didep models are tractable. We show how to reach consensus under Didep models by reusing and transforming existing algorithms. This approach illustrates that using Didep models does not require completely new solutions. Some of the algorithms are quorum-based allowing us to reuse the construction of highly available coteries from the previous chapter.

Another aspect to demonstrate is that Didep models can be combined with different functional failure models and different synchrony assumptions. Covering a wide range of possible assumptions, we exemplarily consider benign as well as malicious failures, transient and permanent failures, and synchrony assumptions ranging from asynchronous systems to synchronous systems.

If a less expressive model (e.g., a threshold model) "under-approximates" a fault assumption, using a Didep model allows to obtain a higher assumption coverage and, therefore, a more resilient solution. If a less expressive model "over-approximates" a fault assumption, using a Didep model allows to obtain a more efficient solution. We assess these aspects by evaluating the resilience and the efficiency of our solutions to consensus.

Chapter 6 – Conclusion and Future Work Chapter 6 summarises the results of the thesis and gives an outlook on topics for future work that arised from the thesis.

1.4 Remarks on Notation

Structured Proofs We formulate our proofs as structured proofs to ease their readability. As introduced by Lamport [1993], each structured proof is a sequence of hierarchically numbered steps. Each step has a proof on its own that may include additional steps on a lower level. The notation for the number of a step gives its level and its rank within its level. For example, a step numbered $\langle 1 \rangle 2$ is the second step on the first level. The hierarchical structure provides the general outline of the proof on high levels; the details are on low levels. Readers who are not interested in the details of a proof can skip the lower levels.

Bulleted Formulae List We use the bulleted-list notation of TLA [Lamport, 2002] for conjunctions and disjunctions to make complicated formulae more readable. A list of formulae that are bulleted with $\wedge$ or $\vee$ equals the conjunction or disjunction of the formulae. The $\wedge$ or $\vee$ symbols in a bulleted-list must line up exactly and indentation is used to eliminate (some) parentheses. For example, the list

$$\begin{aligned}
&\vee\ Answer = 42 \\
&\vee \wedge CountingNumber = 3 \\
&\quad \wedge NumberCount = 3 \\
&\vee\ Pages \leq 200
\end{aligned}$$

denotes the formulae

$$Answer = 42 \vee (CountingNumber = 3 \wedge NumberCount = 3) \vee Pages \leq 200.$$

2 Modelling Fault-Tolerant Distributed Systems

A distributed system can be modelled on different levels of abstraction, from high-level specifications of its properties to low-level descriptions of its implementation. We describe distributed systems by *process models* that represent a system by concurrent executions of sequential processes. Sequential processes represent the active entities that perform the computations in a distributed system, for example, processors, operating system processes, or threads. The most fundamental concerns on such a level of abstraction are the method of *interprocess communication* and the *timing model*. The method of interprocess communication determines how different processes in a system communicate. Prominent examples include communication via message passing or by accessing shared memory. The timing model relates events in a system to the passage of time. For example, a timing model may state upper bounds on the period it takes to deliver a message.

Semantically, we model distributed systems and their components by describing their possible behaviour. Such behaviour is represented by *traces*, that is, sequences of *states*. A *property* is a set of such traces. It represents a component or a distributed system as a whole. Component properties can be composed to a distributed system property with set intersection as (parallel) composition. As explicitly writing down sequences of states is inconvenient, we exemplarily show how a variant of temporal logic, namely the *Temporal Logic of Actions (TLA)*, allows to describe properties concisely. We use TLA and pseudo-code as abstract notations for describing systems and their components.

Modelling a fault-tolerant system raises the question of how to represent faults. A *fault model* describes the faults that may occur in a system. Usually, it describes faults in the same terms as normal system behaviour is described. A system is fault-tolerant if it is able to cope with the modelled faults and implements some high-level specification even if some of its components become faulty. Different forms of fault tolerance can be distinguished depending the specification that is implemented. For example, if faults are completely hidden from an external observer, a system is *masking fault-tolerant*. A weaker form is *nonmasking fault tolerance*: A system is *nonmasking fault-tolerant* if it does not hide the occurrence of faults, but eventually behaves permanently as desired if faults are transient.

Contribution In this chapter, we introduce our system model that forms the foundation for the rest of the thesis. We give a brief overview of the different concerns of modelling fault-tolerant distributed systems. Basic terms (e.g., state, trace, and property) are formally defined for distributed systems and their components. Note that our system model is not particularly new: Variants of this model are common in the literature on fault-tolerant distributed computing. Therefore, the results that are obtained under our model also hold in settings addressed by previous models (or can be easily adapted). In particular, our system model is derived from the models of Abadi and Lamport [1991, 1995], and Lamport [1994], which also serve as the semantic model for TLA. Restricting their models, we limit ourselves to interleaving properties and closed systems, which are sufficient for our purposes.

Overview In Section 2.1, we describe how processes communicate by passing messages over channels. Section 2.2 gives formal definitions for states, traces, and properties that are used to describe the behaviour of distributed systems. TLA is briefly summarised in Section 2.3. Fault models and fault tolerance are formally defined in Section 2.4 and Section 2.5, respectively. Section 2.6 gives an overview of different timing models, before we summarise this chapter in Section 2.7.

2.1 Interprocess Communication

Processes Distributed systems are generally described by *process models* that represent a system by concurrent executions of sequential processes [Lamport and Lynch, 1990]. Sequential processes model "active" entities of a system that perform computations. For example, a process may represent a computing system, a processor, or an operating system thread depending on the distributed system to be modelled. For our system model, we assume that a distributed system consists of a finite set of processes, denoted by $\Pi = \{p_1, \ldots, p_n\}, n > 1$.

Interprocess Communication Different process models can be distinguished by their style of interprocess communication. For example, processes may communicate via *shared memory*, *remote procedure calls*, or *message passing*. For our system model, we assume communication via message passing. This style of communication is fundamental for distributed system. For example, Lamport and Lynch [1990] consider a process model to be distributed iff its interprocess communication can be implemented using message passing.

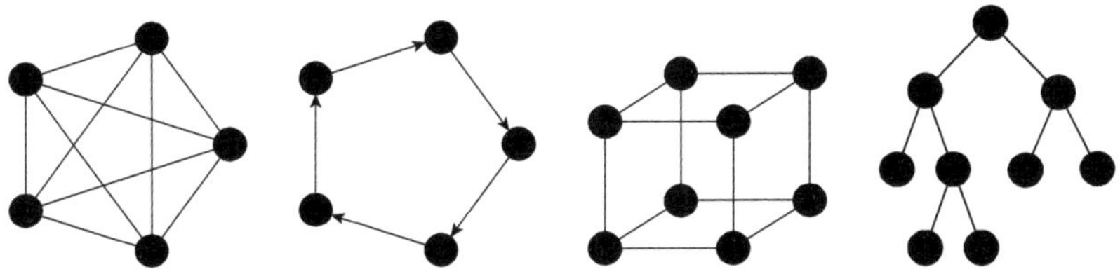

(a) Complete graph (b) Directed Ring (c) Cube (d) Tree

Figure 2.1: Examples for network topologies. Each node represents a process. Each directed edge represents a channel. Each undirected edge between two nodes represents two directed edges with opposite directions between the two nodes.

Channels In a message passing model, processes communicate by sending and receiving messages over *channels*. The channels model entities that support communication among the entities modelled by processes. For example, a channel may represent a twisted pair cable, a TCP/IP connection, or a UNIX named pipe.

We adopt a message passing model, in which pairs of processes communicate via unidirectional point-to-point channels. A process p_i can directly send a message to a process p_j iff there is a channel from p_i to p_j. If there is no channel from p_i to p_j, p_i cannot directly send a message to p_j (but may be able to do so indirectly with the help of other processes). We denote the set of channels in a distributed system by $\Xi = \{c_1, \ldots, c_m\}$. In particular, we assume that at least one channel exists (i.e., $\Xi \neq \emptyset$) and that channels and processes are different entities (i.e., $\Xi \cap \Pi = \emptyset$). As we will often treat processes and channels alike, we speak of a *component* if we mean a process or a channel.

A distributed system that consists of processes and unidirectional channels can be represented by a directed graph, where the nodes of the graph represent processes and the edges represent channels. In principle, different topologies of processes and channels are possible. For example, Fig. 2.1a shows a complete graph: In the system, each process can directly send a message to each other process. Figure 2.1b to Figure 2.1d show systems, in which the processes and channels form a ring, a cube, and a tree, respectively. In the following, however, we will restrict ourselves to complete graphs and only consider *reliable channels*.

Intuitively, a reliable channel does not lose messages, does not change them, and does not invent new ones on its own (cf., for example, Lynch [1996]). More precisely, a reliable channel c from a process p_i to a process p_j is characterised by three properties:

Reliable delivery If p_i sends a message m to p_j over c, then c eventually delivers m to p_j.

No duplication Every message is delivered to p_j by c at most once.

No creation If a message m is delivered to p_j by c, then m was sent by p_i.

Note that reliable channels do not necessarily preserve the order in which message are sent. A channel that delivers messages in the order they were sent is called a *first-in, first-out (FIFO) channel.*

2.2 States, Traces, Properties

Distributed systems often show unanticipated behaviour due to subtle complications. Dealing with such systems, therefore, requires a rigorous treatment. We continue with introducing a formal system model that represents the behaviour of a system in terms of *states*, *traces*, and *properties*.

States The state of a distributed system is composed from the states of the individual components (i.e., the processes and the channels). Each component state consists of an external part and an internal part. The external part is the part that can be observed by an external observer of the system. It is the relevant part for describing behaviour. The internal part is hidden from external observers. It is not strictly necessary for describing a system, but often allows to formulate and understand a system description more easily.

Formally, we assume that all components are defined over the same fixed sets Σ_{CE} of *external component states* and Σ_{CI} of *internal component states*. A *component state* is a pair of an external and an internal component state. An *internal system state* is a finite sequence of internal component states, one for each component. We denote the set of all finite sequences of length k over elements in a set S by S^k. The set of all internal system states Σ_I equals $\Sigma_{CI}^{|(\Pi \cup \Xi)|}$. Analogously, an *external system state* is a finite sequence of external component states, one for each component, with $\Sigma_E = \Sigma_{CE}^{|(\Pi \cup \Xi)|}$ denoting the set of all external system states.

A *system state* is a pair of an external and an internal system state with $\Sigma = \Sigma_E \times \Sigma_I$ denoting the set of all system states. We define a projection π_E that maps a system state to its external system state with $\pi_E(\langle e, i \rangle) = e$ for any $\langle e, i \rangle \in \Sigma$ and a projection π_M that maps a component $m \in (\Pi \cup \Xi)$ and a system state $s \in \Sigma$ to the component state of m in s. If clear from context or irrelevant, we omit the terms "system" and "component" and just write "state" instead of "system state" or "component state."

Traces The behaviour of a system is represented by an infinite sequence of system states. For an arbitrary set S, we denote the set of all infinite sequences over elements in S by S^∞. A *trace* is an infinite sequence of system states in Σ^∞. It represents a possible execution of a system. For a terminating system, an infinite sequence of states is obtained by repeating the final state of the system forever. We extend the projection π_E from states to traces: For $\tau = \langle s_0, s_1, \ldots \rangle \in \Sigma^\infty$, we define $\pi_E(\tau)$ as the sequence $\langle \pi_E(s_0), \pi_E(s_1), \ldots \rangle \in \Sigma_E^\infty$. We call a sequence in Σ_E^∞ an *external trace*[1].

Note that it may be impossible for an external observer to differentiate some system states. For example, consider a system that cycles among three different system states s_0, s_1, and s_2 starting with s_0. Such a behaviour is represented by the trace $\tau = \langle s_0, s_1, s_2,\ \ s_0, s_1, s_2, \ldots \rangle$. If $s_0 = \langle e_0, i_0 \rangle$, $s_1 = \langle e_1, i_1 \rangle$, and $s_2 = \langle e_1, i_2 \rangle$, then the external trace $\pi_E(\tau)$ is $\langle e_0,\ e_1,\ e_1,\ e_0,\ e_1,\ e_1,\ \ldots \rangle$. Hence, an external observer can only distinguish two different externally visible states, although the system cycles among three different system states.

Traces can be classified into *interleaving* and *noninterleaving* traces. Informally, an interleaving trace only allows steps (i.e., state transitions) that change the component state of *at most one* component. Noninterleaving traces allow steps that change the component state of *more than one* component. Such steps represent simultaneous (i.e., parallel) operations of different components. Formally, a *step* is a pair of system states $\langle s, s' \rangle$ and is called a *stuttering step* iff $s = s'$. For a component $m \in (\Pi \cup \Xi)$, a step $\langle s, s' \rangle$ *is an* m*-step* iff $\pi_M(m, s) \neq \pi_M(m, s')$; that is, an m-step changes the component state of m. A trace $\langle s_0, s_1, \ldots \rangle$ is called *interleaving* iff, for each $i \geq 0$, $\langle s_i, s_{i+1} \rangle$ is a stuttering step or is an m-step for exactly one component $m \in (\Pi \cup \Xi)$. A trace is *noninterleaving* iff it is not interleaving.

Stuttering Stuttering steps are an important concept for the verification of distributed systems as they allow to refine a system model [Lamport, 1983a]. For an arbitrary set S, a sequence $\langle s_0, s_1, \ldots \rangle \in S^\infty$ is called *stutter-free* iff, for each $i \geq 0$, either $s_i \neq s_{i+1}$ or, to allow terminating systems, $s_j = s_{j+1}$ for all $j \geq i$. For $\tau = \langle s_0, s_1, \ldots \rangle \in S^\infty$, the *stutter-free form* of τ is defined as the sequence that is obtained from τ by replacing every maximal finite subsequence $\langle s_i, s_{i+1}, \ldots, s_j \rangle$ of identical elements by s_i. Two sequences $\tau, \zeta \in S^\infty$ are *equivalent up to stuttering* iff their stutter-free forms are equal.

[1] We accept the nuisance that, formally, an external trace is not a trace. Abadi and Lamport [1991], for example, avoid this by additionally considering external system states as system states. However, such an approach would complicate the presentation and does not yield relevant advantages for our purposes.

For a subset P of S^∞, we define the *stuttering closure* $\kappa_S(P)$ as the set of all infinite sequences over S that are equivalent up to stuttering to some sequence in P. Formally,

$$\kappa_S(P) = \{\zeta \in S^\infty : \exists \tau \in P : \zeta \text{ and } \tau \text{ are equivalent up to stuttering}\}.$$

P is called *closed under stuttering* iff $P = \kappa_S(P)$.

Properties Distributed systems are represented by *properties* being sets of traces that are closed under stuttering. Intuitively, a property represents all possible executions of a system. An *external property* is defined as a set of external traces that is closed under stuttering and represents all executions that can be seen by an external observer.

We extend the projection π_E from traces to sets of traces by defining $\pi_E(P) = \{\pi_E(\tau) \in \Sigma_E^\infty : \tau \in P\}$ for a set of traces $P \subseteq \Sigma^\infty$. Note that $\pi_E(P)$ may not be closed under stuttering even if P is a property[2]. The external property *induced* by a property P is defined by $\kappa_S(\pi_E(P))$.

We extend the notion of interleaving to properties: A property is interleaving iff it only contains interleaving traces. Otherwise, it is noninterleaving. As interleaving properties are more easy to reason about, we represent distributed systems only by interleaving properties. A property is a *distributed system property* iff it is an interleaving property. We do not consider the restriction to interleaving properties a severe limitation, because the choice between interleaving and noninterleaving is merely one of convenience [Lamport, 2002, Sect. 10.5.2]. On a sufficiently detailed level of abstraction, any system can be represented by interleaving traces [Abadi and Lamport, 1995].

Describing distributed systems by writing down sets of infinite sequences is inconvenient. More abstract formalisms are required to describe a property more concisely. Well-known and useful examples of such formalisms are Guarded Commands [Dijkstra, 1975], temporal logic [Pnueli, 1977], and CSP [Hoare, 1978, 1985]. We do not care which particular formalism is used to describe a system, but assume that each system description defines a distributed system property. For illustration purposes, we will rely on TLA and pseudo-code when describing distributed systems.

---

[2] The underlying reason is that the projection yields "new" stuttering steps: Consider a trace $\tau = \langle\langle e_0, i_0\rangle, \langle e_0, i_1\rangle, \langle e_1, i_2\rangle, \ldots\rangle$ with $i_0 \neq i_1$ and a property P with $\tau \in P$, but without any trace of the form $\langle\langle e_0, i_3\rangle, \langle e_1, i_4\rangle, \ldots\rangle$. Then, $\pi_E(\tau) = \langle e_0, e_0, e_1, \ldots\rangle$ is in $\pi_E(P)$, but $\langle e_0, e_1, \ldots\rangle$ is not in $\pi_E(P)$ although both are equivalent up to stuttering.

Correctness Verifying the correctness of a distributed system means to show that the system implements a given specification that describes the properties required from the system. As a system itself may also serve as a specification for another system, we do not formally distinguish systems and specifications and represent both by properties. In abuse of terminology, we use the term specification also for the property that is defined by a specification. For example, we say that a specification is a distributed system specification if the property defined by the specification is a distributed system property.

For correctness, only the behaviour that is externally visible is relevant. Internal states are only used for convenience. Formally, we say that a property P_1 *implements* a property P_2 iff the external property induced by P_1 is a subset of the external property induced by P_2. Hence, if P_1 implements P_2, all behaviour permitted by P_1 – as can be seen by an external observer – is also permitted by P_2. If P_1 implements P_2 and P_2 implements P_1, we call them *equivalent*, denoted by $P_1 \equiv P_2$.

Safety and Liveness Lamport [1977] has identified two important classes of properties, *safety* and *liveness*. Their relevance stems from requiring different verification techniques and from the result of Alpern and Schneider [1985] that every property equals an intersection of a safety property and a liveness property.[3] In particular, a criterion for considering a distributed system specification being well-written is that safety and liveness are explicitly separated.

Informally, a safety property states that something "bad" never happens. Formally, a property P is a safety property iff, for each trace τ that is not in P, there is a prefix of τ such that all traces with the same prefix are not in P [Alpern and Schneider, 1985]. Intuitively, the end of the prefix marks the point in time when something bad happens that is not permitted by P.

A liveness property states that something "good" must eventually happen. Formally, a property P is a liveness property iff, for each finite sequence τ of states, there is a trace in P that has τ as a prefix. Intuitively, the end of the finite sequence marks the point when something good happens that is required by P.

For example, consider the problem of reaching consensus, which we will address in detail in Chapter 5. To reach consensus, each process initially *proposes* a value and is supposed to eventually *decide* for a commonly agreed value. The problem is defined by the intersection of two safety properties, *uniform agreement* and *validity*, and a liveness property, *uniform termination*. These properties are defined as follows:

[3] Less well known, they have also shown that each property that is defined over more than one state equals an intersection of two liveness properties.

Uniform Termination Every process eventually decides on some value.

Uniform Agreement No two processes decide differently.

Validity If a process decides a value v, then v was proposed by some process.

The "bad thing" for uniform agreement happens when two processes decide differently. For validity, it happens when a process decides a value that has not been proposed. The "good thing" for uniform termination happens when each process decides on a value.

Safety properties are generally proved using assertional methods [Keller, 1976, Ashcroft, 1975, Owicki and Gries, 1976, Lamport, 1977]. For such methods, a state invariant is found that implies the safety property to be proven. This invariant is proven by induction on the number of performed steps. For the base case, the invariant is shown to hold in the initial state (no step has been performed yet). For the induction step, it is shown that, if the invariant holds in a state, then the invariant holds after any step performed by the system. By induction, the invariant holds in any state.

A classical method for proving liveness properties relies on well-founded sets and convergence functions. A well-founded set is a set S with a partial order $\succ$ on the set such that any sequence $\langle e_0, e_1, \ldots \rangle$ with $e_i \succ e_{i+1}, e_i \in S$, and $i \geq 0$ is finite. For example, the set $\mathbb{N}$ of natural numbers with the common "greater than" relation $>$ is a well-founded set. The convergence function (also called "ranking function" or "progress function" [Manna and Pnueli, 1982, Lynch, 1996]) maps from states to the well-founded set. Proving that something "good" eventually happens means to show that (a) something "good" happens when the value of the convergence function reaches a minimum of the well-founded set and that (b) the value of the progress function monotonically decreases with each performed step.

Liveness and safety properties can also be proven by using *temporal logic*, a modal logic with symbols for temporal notions like "always" and "eventually" [Pnueli, 1977, Owicki and Lamport, 1982, Lamport, 1994]. We look into temporal logic in more detail in Sect. 2.3 when we give an overview of TLA.

Component Properties Analogously to modelling distributed systems, we also represent the components of a distributed system by properties. To represent a component m and only m, a property must describe the behaviour of m, but must not restrict the behaviour of the environment of m (e.g., other processes and channels). Informally, such a property allows the environment of m to perform an arbitrary step whenever m does not perform a step.

Formally, a step $\langle s, s' \rangle$ is called an *m-environment step* iff

$$\pi_M(m,s) = \pi_M(m,s')$$

for a component $m \in (\Pi \cup \Xi)$. That is, an m-environment step does not change the state of m. A property P is a *component property for* m iff, for each trace $\langle s_0, s_1, \ldots \rangle$ in P, each state $s \in \Sigma$, and each $i \geq 0$, there is a trace $\langle t_0, t_1, \ldots \rangle \in P$ with $\langle t_0, \ldots, t_i \rangle = \langle s_0, \ldots, s_i \rangle$ and $t_{i+1} = s$ if $\langle s_i, s_{i+1} \rangle$ and $\langle s_i, s \rangle$ are m-environment steps. That is, a component property allows an *arbitrary* m-environment step $\langle s_i, s \rangle$ whenever it allows an m-environment step $\langle s_i, s_{i+1} \rangle$. Note that a component property contains noninterleaving traces. However, each step either changes the state of m, changes the state of m's environment, or is a stuttering step. Such traces are interleaving in the sense that each step is either an m-step or an m-environment step.

Decomposed System Specifications Although a component property contains noninterleaving traces, a composition of properties for all components of a system must result in a distributed system property, which only contains interleaving traces. The following lemma shows that, with set intersection as (parallel) composition, the composition of component properties indeed results in a distributed system property.

Lemma 2.1
If P_m is a component property for component $m \in (\Pi \cup \Xi)$, the property

$$P = \bigcap_{m \in (\Pi \cup \Xi)} P_m$$

is a distributed system property.

PROOF: We need to show that P is a set of interleaving traces and is closed under stuttering. We prove this separately.

$\langle 1 \rangle 1$. P is a set of interleaving traces.

PROOF: P is a set of traces as each $P_m \subseteq \Sigma^\infty$. For each P_m holds that each step permitted by P_m is either an m-step or an m-environment step. Hence, each step permitted by P is a stuttering step or an m-step for a single component $m \in (\Pi \cup \Xi)$.

$\langle 1 \rangle 2$. P is closed under stuttering.

PROOF: By $\langle 1 \rangle 1$, P is a set of traces. If a trace τ is in P, then τ is in each $P_m, m \in (\Pi \cup \Xi)$. As each component property is closed under stuttering, all traces that are equivalent to τ up to stuttering are also in each P_m and, therefore, also in P.

$\langle 1 \rangle 3.$ Q.E.D.
PROOF: By $\langle 1 \rangle 1$ and $\langle 1 \rangle 2$.

Decomposing a system specification into component specifications often eases the understanding and the verification of a specification. We now show that such decompositions are, in principle, possible for any distributed system in our system model: The model allows to compose every distributed system property from component properties.

Lemma 2.2
If P is a distributed system property, there exist component properties P_m for each component $m \in (\Pi \cup \Xi)$ such that

$$P = \bigcap_{m \,\in\, (\Pi \cup \Xi)} P_m.$$

PROOF: We obtain a component property P_m for $m \in (\Pi \cup \Xi)$ from P by adding all traces that have the same prefix as a trace $\tau \in P$ and only continue with m-environment steps if τ continues with an m-environment step.

ASSUME: For $m \in (\Pi \cup \Xi)$, let $P_m = P \cup P_{env}(m)$ with

$$\begin{aligned} P_{env}(m) = \kappa_S(\{\langle s_0, s_1, \ldots \rangle \in \Sigma^\infty :\ & \\ \exists \langle t_0, t_1, \ldots \rangle \in P, i \in \mathbb{N} :\ & \\ & \wedge \langle t_0, \ldots, t_i \rangle = \langle s_0, \ldots s_i \rangle \\ & \wedge \langle t_i, t_{i+1} \rangle \text{ is an } m\text{-environment step} \\ & \wedge \forall j \geq i : \langle s_j, s_{j+1} \rangle \text{ is an } m\text{-environment step}\}). \end{aligned}$$

PROVE: P_m is a component property for m and $P = \bigcap_{m \in (\Pi \cup \Xi)} P_m$.

$\langle 1 \rangle 1.$ P_m is a component property for m.
PROOF: P_m is a property as P and $P_{env}(m)$ are sets of traces that are closed under stuttering: If two sets of traces are closed under stuttering, their union is closed under stuttering as well. P_m is a component property for m as P_m allows an arbitrary m-environment step whenever it allows an m-environment step.

$\langle 1 \rangle 2.$ $P \subseteq \bigcap_{m \in (\Pi \cup \Xi)} P_m$
PROOF: $P \subseteq P_m$ for each component $m \in (\Pi \cup \Xi)$ by the construction of P_m.

$\langle 1 \rangle 3.$ $\bigcap_{m \in (\Pi \cup \Xi)} P_m \subseteq P$
PROOF: The proof is by induction over prefixes of a trace, with the base case proved in step 1 and the induction step in step 2.
ASSUME: $\langle s_0, s_1, \ldots \rangle \in \bigcap_{m \in (\Pi \cup \Xi)} P_m$
PROVE: $\langle s_0, s_1, \ldots \rangle \in P$

$\langle 2 \rangle 1.$ There is a trace in P with the prefix $\langle s_0 \rangle$.
PROOF: Otherwise, there would be no $\langle s_0, s_1, \ldots \rangle$ in $\bigcap_{m \in (\Pi \cup \Xi)} P_m$.

$\langle 2 \rangle 2.$ If there is a trace in P with the prefix $\langle s_0, \ldots, s_i \rangle$, then there is a trace in P with the prefix $\langle s_0, \ldots, s_{i+1} \rangle$.

PROOF:
⟨3⟩1. CASE: $\langle s_i, s_{i+1} \rangle$ is a stuttering step
PROOF: By the induction hypothesis and as P is closed under stuttering.
⟨3⟩2. CASE: $\langle s_i, s_{i+1} \rangle$ is an m-step for a component $m \in (\Pi \cup \Xi)$
PROOF: By the induction hypothesis and as, otherwise, there would be no trace with the prefix $\langle s_0, \ldots, s_{i+1} \rangle$ in P_m by the construction of $P_{env}(m)$.
⟨3⟩3. Q.E.D.
PROOF: By ⟨3⟩1 and ⟨3⟩2.
⟨2⟩3. Q.E.D.
PROOF: By ⟨2⟩1, ⟨2⟩2, and mathematical induction.
⟨1⟩4. Q.E.D.
PROOF: ⟨1⟩1 – ⟨1⟩3

2.3 Temporal Logic of Actions

Our results do not depend on a particular formalism to express a property. Nevertheless, we exemplarily show how such an formalism, namely the *Temporal Logic of Actions (TLA)* from Lamport [1994], allows to present properties concisely. Temporal logic in general provides useful means to specify and reason about concurrent systems [Lamport, 1983a]. TLA is a variant of temporal logic for specifying and verifying concurrent systems in terms of their actions. The main differences to the well-known temporal logic of Pnueli [1977] are invariance under stuttering, support for temporal existential quantification, and allowing action formulae as atomic formulae.

Unlike other formalisms, both, systems and their specifications, are represented in the same logic. A system implements its specification iff the logic formula that describes the system implies the formula that describes its specification, where "implies" means logical implication. Structural relations among components are also represented by logical operators. For example, logical conjunction is parallel composition.

We now briefly summarise the syntax and the semantics of TLA. Refer to Lamport [1994], Abadi and Merz [1996], and Lamport [2002] for more detailed presentations.

Syntax Syntactically, TLA formulae are built from constant symbols, variable symbols, and the special symbols $\neg, \wedge, \Box, \exists, \boldsymbol{\exists}, ', (,),$ and $=$. The variables are partitioned into sets of *rigid variables*, whose values are state-independent, and *flexible variables*, whose values are state-dependent.

An *action* is a first-order predicate over the constant and variable symbols, for example, $y = x' + 1$. With *free variables* defined as in first-order logic, a *state function* is a first-order expression over the constant and variable symbols without free primed variables, for example, $x + y - 1$. Analogously, a *predicate* is an action without free primed variables, for example, $y = x + 1$.

We define *substitution* for actions, state functions, and predicates as in first-order logic and write, for example, $A\{a/x\}$ for the results of substituting the first-order expression (over constant and variable symbols) a for the free occurrences of variable x in action A. For any state function (or predicate) p, p' is defined as the state function (or predicate) obtained by priming the free flexible variables. For example, $(x + y - 3)'$ equals $(x' + y' - 3)$.

A TLA *formula* is built from predicates and formula of the form $\Box[A]_f$, where A is an action, f is a state function, and $[A]_f$ is an abbreviation for $(A \vee (f' = f)$. Additionally, $\Box F$ is a formula if F is one. For example, $\Box(y = x + 1)$ and $\Box[x' = x + 1]_x$ are formulae.

In addition to common abbreviations such as $\vee, \Rightarrow$, and $\equiv$ or the temporal operator $\Diamond$, the following abbreviations are defined:

- $\langle A \rangle_f \triangleq A \wedge (f' \neq f)$,
- $\text{UNCHANGED}\ f \triangleq f' = f$,
- if $x_1, \ldots, x_n$ are the free variables of A, then $\text{ENABLED}\ A \triangleq \exists x'_1, \ldots, x'_n : A$,
- if x is the tuple $\langle x_1, \ldots, x_n \rangle$, then $\exists\!\!\exists\, x : F \triangleq \exists\!\!\exists\, x_1 : \ldots \exists\!\!\exists\, x_n : F$
- a weak fairness operator $\text{WF}_f(A) \triangleq \Diamond\Box\text{ENABLED}\ \langle A \rangle_f \Rightarrow \Box\Diamond\langle A \rangle_f$, and
- a strong fairness operator $\text{SF}_f(A) \triangleq \Box\Diamond\text{ENABLED}\ \langle A \rangle_f \Rightarrow \Box\Diamond\langle A \rangle_f$,

where $x, x_1, \ldots, x_n$ are variables, A is an action, and f a state function.

Semantics The meaning of TLA formulae is defined over a set of *values*. We assume a fixed set of values that includes all required values. A *state* is a mapping from the set of flexible variables to the set of values. The *internal state* is given by the mapping from the set of hidden flexible variables (see below) to the set of values; the *external state* by the mapping from free flexible variables to values. As in the previous section, a *trace* is an infinite sequence of states.

The meaning of a state function is a mapping from the set of states to the set of values. Analogously, a predicate is either true or false for a state. A state *satisfies* a predicate iff the meaning of the predicate is true for the state. A predicate P is called *valid*, denoted by $\models P$, iff every state satisfies the predicate. The meanings of common operators such as $\wedge, \neg$, and $\exists x : F$ are standard.

The semantics of actions is defined for pairs of states, where the unprimed variables refer to the first state and the primed variables to the second one. For example, $y' = x + 1$ is true at a pair of states $\langle s, t \rangle$ iff the value of y in t equals the value of x plus 1 in s. A pair of states *satisfies* an action iff the meaning of the action is true for the pair of states. A pair of states that satisfies an action A is called an A *step*. An action A is called *valid*, denoted by $\models A$, iff every step is an A step.

Analogously to state predicates, a formula is either true or false for a trace. A trace *satisfies* a formula iff the meaning of the formula is true for the trace. A formula F is called *valid*, denoted by $\models F$, iff every trace satisfies the formula. Each formula represents a set of traces, namely the set of all traces that satisfy the formula. As such, a formula can describe a property and, therefore, specify a distributed system. The meaning of a formula is defined inductively as follows. A state predicate is true for a trace iff it is true of its first state. Derived from temporal logic, $\Box$ denotes the *always* operator; $\Box F$ means that F is always true in the future. The operator $\boldsymbol{\exists}$ denotes *temporal existential quantification*; the formula $\boldsymbol{\exists}\, x : F$ means that there exists a sequence of values for x such that F holds. Intuitively, $\boldsymbol{\exists}$ hides variables from external observers: x is called an internal or hidden variable of $\boldsymbol{\exists}\, x : F$. Such a variable x is part of the domain for the mapping that defines the internal state.

Specifications In TLA, a specification is expressed by a formula that has the "canonical form"

$$\boldsymbol{\exists}\, x : \mathit{Init} \wedge \Box[\mathit{Next}]_v \wedge L,$$

where *Init* is a state predicate, *Next* is an action describing possible steps of the system, L is a conjunction of fairness conditions, x is a variable, and v a state function. The formula is true for all those traces, whose initial state satisfies *Init*, where every step is a *Next* step or leaves v unchanged, and where L holds. Note that each TLA formula defines a property, namely the set of all traces that satisfy the formula, as each TLA formula is invariant under stuttering [Lamport, 1994, Abadi and Merz, 1996].

TLA is an expressive formalism that allows to describe different kinds of specifications. For example, it supports interleaving and noninterleaving specifications and allows to represent closed as well as open systems. Intuitively, an *open system* interacts with its environment (being beyond the control of the system). A *closed system* is self-contained: it does not interact with its environment, but its external state may be inspected by an external observer. We restrict ourselves to closed system specifications as these are more easy to reason about and as, for our purposes, it suffices to model inputs to a system as being nondeterministically generated by the system itself.

Decomposed System Specifications Semantically, a state is a mapping from flexible variables to values in TLA. We assume that the flexible variables of a distributed system specification can be partitioned among the components. A component can only change its own variables, which cannot be changed by any other component. The internal local state of a component m is then given by the mapping from the set of hidden flexible variables of m to the set of values. The external local state of m is given by the mapping from the set of free flexible variables of m to the set of values.

Component specifications arise when composing a system from reusable components or decomposing a given system into its components. We only deal with system specifications that are decomposed into component specifications such that the environment of each component is known.[4] For a component $m \in (\Pi \cup \Xi)$, we assume that the tuple o of *output variables* is the tuple of the free flexible variables of m and that the tuple e of *environment variables* is the tuple of the flexible variables of all other components. A component specification then has the canonical form

$$\exists\!\!\!\exists\, x : \mathit{Init} \wedge \Box[\mathit{Next}]_{\langle x,o\rangle} \wedge L$$

with:

- x is the tuple of all internal variables of the component. The set of variables in x are precisely the domain of the mapping that defines the internal local state of the component.

- The state predicate *Init* specifies the initial values of the component's internal variables x and output variables o.

- The action Next allows steps of the component that change the value of an output variable of o with $\mathit{Next} \Rightarrow e' = e$.

- L is a conjunction of fairness conditions. Each fairness condition must be of the form $\mathit{WF}_{\langle x,o\rangle}(A)$ or $\mathit{SF}_{\langle x,o\rangle}(A)$, where A is an action.

The formula $\Box[\mathit{Next}]_{\langle x,o\rangle}$ allows the environment to do anything but change the component's internal or output variables. Due to $\mathit{Next} \Rightarrow e' = e$, the values of the

[4] In particular, we do not consider *assume/guarantee specifications* of the form $E \stackrel{+}{\rhd} M$, which assert that a component satisfies a guarantee M as long as the environment satisfies an assumption E [Abadi and Lamport, 1995]. Such specifications allow to describe reusable components for unknown environments.

$$
\begin{aligned}
o &\triangleq \langle in\_ack, out\_sig, out\_msg \rangle \\
Init &\triangleq \land\, in\_ack \in \text{BOOLEAN} \land in\_ack = in\_sig \\
&\quad\ \land\, out\_sig \in \text{BOOLEAN} \land out\_sig = out\_ack \\
&\quad\ \land\, buffer = \emptyset \\
AckSend &\triangleq \land\, in\_ack \neq in\_sig \\
&\quad\ \land\, buffer' = buffer \cup \{in\_msg\} \\
&\quad\ \land\, in\_ack' = \neg in\_ack \\
&\quad\ \land\, \text{UNCHANGED } \langle e, out\_sig, out\_msg \rangle \\
Deliver(m) &\triangleq \land\, m \in buffer \land out\_sig = out\_ack \\
&\quad\ \land\, out\_sig' = \neg out\_sig \\
&\quad\ \land\, out\_msg' = m \\
&\quad\ \land\, buffer' = buffer \setminus \{m\} \\
&\quad\ \land\, \text{UNCHANGED } \langle e, in\_ack \rangle \\
Next &\triangleq AckSend \lor \exists m : Deliver(m) \\
L &\triangleq WF_{\langle buffer, o \rangle}(Next) \\
Spec &\triangleq \boldsymbol{\exists}\, buffer : Init \land \Box[Next]_{\langle buffer, o \rangle} \land L
\end{aligned}
$$

Figure 2.2: A TLA specification of a reliable channel (cf. Abadi and Lamport [1995]).

component's and its environment variables cannot change simultaneously. Hence, the specification defines a component property.

Example 2.1 (TLA Component Specification)
An example of a TLA component specification is given in Fig. 2.2. The formula *Spec* specifies a reliable channel in terms of three output variables, in_ack, out_sig, and out_msg, and one internal variable, *buffer*. Additionally, the specification refers to three environment variables, in_sig, in_msg, and out_ack. These variables belong to the processes that are connected by the channel: in_sig and in_msg to the sender process and out_ack to the receiver process. Figure 2.3 shows a schematic view on the specification.

As an abbreviation the output variables are joined in the sequence o. The internal variable *buffer* (hidden by temporal existential quantification) holds the set of messages that are currently buffered by the channel, that is, messages sent by the sender process, but not yet delivered to the receiver process. Initially, *buffer* is empty.

The Boolean variables in_sig and in_ack are used to implement a simple handshake protocol between the channel and the sender process. Initially, $in\_sig = in\_ack$, which

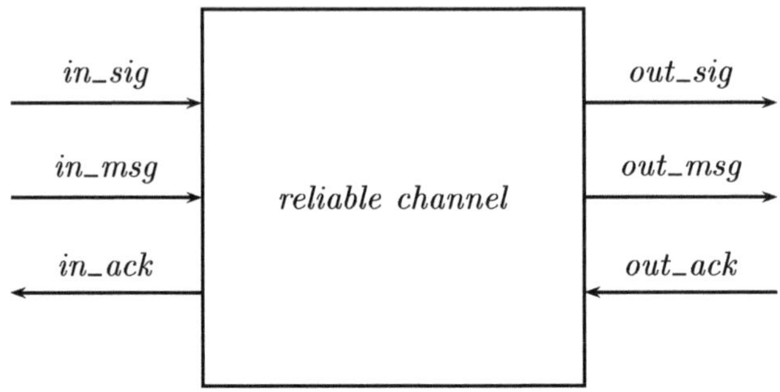

Figure 2.3: A schematic view on a reliable channel.

models that no new message is to be sent. The sender process sends a message m as follows: It puts m into in_msg and signals the new message by negating in_sig. The channel handles m by acknowledging the sending with the action $AckSend$. A precondition (or "guard") for $AckSend$ is that $in\_ack \neq in\_sig$, that is, the sender process must have signalled a new message. The message is added to $buffer$ and in_ack is negated to signal that the channel is ready for the next message.

Delivering a message to the receiving process is performed similarly by the $Deliver$ action: The message m to deliver must be in $buffer$. The channel removes m from $buffer$ and puts it into out_msg. The channel signals the new message by negating out_sig. The receiving process can take the message from out_msg and acknowledges that it is ready for further messages by negating out_ack.

Both actions, $AckSend$ and $Deliver$, are subsumed by the $Next$ action for the final specification. To ensure that a sent message is indeed delivered, the specification includes a liveness formula L defined by weak fairness over the $Next$ actions.

Verification Using TLA Being a logic, TLA includes axioms and proof rules for proving formulae. If a formula F is provable by the axioms and rules of the logic, denoted by $\vdash F$, then F is also valid as TLA is a sound logic. For verification, a specification S_1 implements another specification S_2 iff $S_1 \Rightarrow S_2$; that is, logical implication is implementation. As we use TLA just for presenting specifications, but not for verification, we do not further discuss the axioms and proof rules of TLA. Refer to Lamport [1994] for a detailed description and to Lamport and Merz [1994] for an elaborate example of how to verify a fault-tolerant distributed system using TLA.

2.4 Fault Model

Despite interprocess communication, the *fault model*, the formalisation of a fault assumption, is another important concern of modelling fault-tolerant distributed systems. No system can tolerate arbitrary severe faults. Any consideration of fault tolerance requires a decision, which faults to tolerate, resulting in a fault assumption.

For a rigorous treatment of fault tolerance, a fault assumption must be formalised in terms of the respective system model. The common approach has been to represent a fault assumption as a mapping (or "transformation") that augments a specification by faults. We follow this approach and define a fault model as a mapping of distributed system properties. Refer to Gärtner [1999] for a survey of the wide range of approaches that rely on mappings for the specification and verification of fault-tolerant systems.

Fault Actions and Variables The key for formalising fault assumptions is the observation of Cristian [1985] that a system changes its state either due to a normal system step or due to a *fault step*. This observation allows a simple representation of faults: syntactically, they are represented in the same way as normal system steps. For example, if a system is specified by a TLA formula, which describes steps by actions, then faults can be modelled by augmenting the formula with additional *fault actions*.

While not strictly necessary [Gärtner, 2002], it is often convenient to augment a specification by *fault variables*. Fault variables indicate the manifestation of faults and help to structure a specification. They make a specification easier to understand. For example, with a Boolean fault variable f, the manifestation of a fault is indicated by setting f from FALSE to TRUE. If $\neg f$ is added as a conjunct to each normal action and f to each fault action, normal actions are disabled and fault actions are enabled by the manifestation of a fault. These additional conjuncts help to easily separate normal from fault actions.

Consider the TLA specification in Fig. 2.4a. The specification contains a single variable v, which initially equals 0. Each step either leaves v unchanged or increments v by 1. Now consider a fault that prevents any further increase of v, but decreases v. Such a fault is formalised in Fig. 2.4b. The manifestation of a fault is represented by the *Fail* action that sets the fault variable f, which is initially FALSE, to TRUE. If f is TRUE, the normal action *Inc* is disabled, whereas the fault action *Dec* is enabled. While the original specification is only true for traces, where the value of v increases with every step that changes v, the transformed specification is also true for traces, in which the value of v increases for some time, but then permanently decreases.

$$\begin{aligned} Init &\triangleq v = 0 \\ Inc &\triangleq v' = v + 1 \\ Next &\triangleq Inc \\ L &\triangleq WF_v(Next) \\ Spec &\triangleq Init \land \Box[Next]_v \land L \end{aligned}$$

(a) Example specification

$$\begin{aligned} Init &\triangleq v = 0 \land f = \text{FALSE} \\ Inc &\triangleq \land \neg f \\ &\quad\; \land v' = v + 1 \land \text{UNCHANGED}\, f \\ Dec &\triangleq \land f \\ &\quad\; \land v' = v - 1 \land \text{UNCHANGED}\, f \\ Fail &\triangleq f' = \text{TRUE} \land \text{UNCHANGED}\ v \\ Next &\triangleq Inc \lor Dec \lor Fail \\ L &\triangleq WF_v(Next) \\ Spec &\triangleq Init \land \Box[Next]_v \land L \end{aligned}$$

(b) Specification with fault actions and variables

Figure 2.4: Example of augmenting a TLA specification with fault actions and variables.

The approach of modelling faults by additional actions and variables (or equivalent approaches) is common in the literature [Liu and Joseph, 1992, Arora and Gouda, 1993, Arora and Kulkarni, 1998a, Gärtner, 1998, 1999] across different system models (e.g., CSP [Nordahl, 1992, 1993] or Petri nets [Völzer, 1998]). Closely related to our TLA example, Liu and Joseph [1992, 1995, 1996, 1999, 2006] also use TLA for specifications and model faults by fault actions and variables.

Fault Models Due to faults, an external observer may see behaviour that would not have been possible without faults. A fault model allows a system to show additional externally visible behaviour. Semantically, we define a fault model as a mapping that weakens a distributed system property.

Definition 2.1 (Fault Model)
A fault model α is a mapping from a distributed system property P to a distributed system property $\alpha(P)$ such that P implements $\alpha(P)$.

If a distributed system property P implements $\alpha(P)$, then any externally visible trace permitted by P is also permitted by $\alpha(P)$. This reflects that a fault model only describes *possible* manifestations of faults, but does not make them obligatory.

Defining fault models as mappings of properties bears advantages for comparing the severeness of different fault models. Consider a distributed system property P and two fault models α_i and α_j. If $\alpha_i(P)$ implements $\alpha_j(P)$, then α_j allows at least the same additional behaviour as α_i and possibly more behaviour with respect to P. If $\alpha_i(P)$ implements $\alpha_j(P)$ for any distributed system property, then α_j can be considered to describe "more severe" faults as α_i.

Faults as Component Failures We do not consider stuttering steps as fault steps, because, otherwise, each distributed system would include fault steps. As our system model allows to attribute each nonstuttering step to a single component, each fault step can be assigned to a single component as well. We, therefore, call a fault step that is an m-step for a component $m \in (\Pi \cup \Xi)$, an *m-failure step*. This terminology reflects that we change our view on faults from system- to component-level: A system contains (system) faults that must be tolerated; system faults are component failures.

We partition the states into *failed* and *nonfailed* states for each component m. Intuitively, a state is a failed state for a component m iff m suffered from a failure and cannot perform "useful" work at the moment. Formally, we assume a state predicate failed_m that is invariant under m-environment steps and is true for any state that immediately results from an m-failure step. If failed_m is true in a state, we call m *failed* in this state and, otherwise, *nonfailed*. A component may *recover* from a failed state and continue to perform useful work. A *component recovery* of m is an m-step that leads from a state, where failed_m is true, to a state, where failed_m is false.

Let $\tau = \langle s_0, s_1, \ldots \rangle \in \Sigma^\infty$ be a trace. A component $m \in (\Pi \cup \Xi)$ is considered *correct* in τ iff failed_m is false for each state $s_i, i \geq 0$. Hence, an m-failure-step invalidates the correctness of m. Even if a component is not correct, it may perform useful work if it recovers and remains nonfailed. We call such components *nonfaulty*. More precisely, a component is *nonfaulty* in τ iff there is an $j \geq 0$ such that $\mathit{failed}_m(s_i)$ is false for each $i \geq j$. As a special case any correct component is nonfaulty. If a component is not *nonfaulty*, we call the component *faulty*. Note that m is faulty iff failed_m is infinitely often true such that m may not be able to perform any useful work. Figure 2.5 illustrates the terms correct, faulty, and nonfaulty.

We assume that each m-failure step is externally visible, that is, changes the external system state of component m. Such a requirement is useful for high-level specifications that refer to the occurrence of component failures. For example, some properties give requirements that have to be satisfied by nonfaulty components. Having externally visible m-failure steps eases the specification of such requirements.

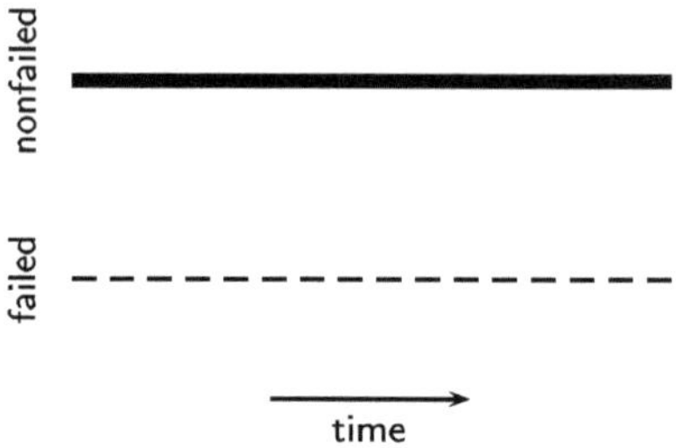

(a) A correct component.

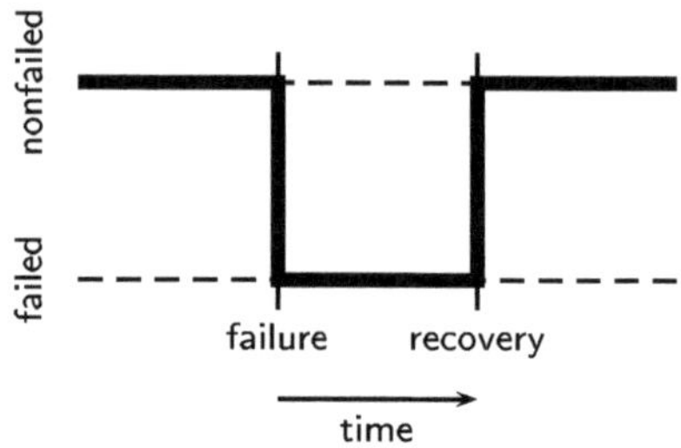

(b) A nonfaulty component.

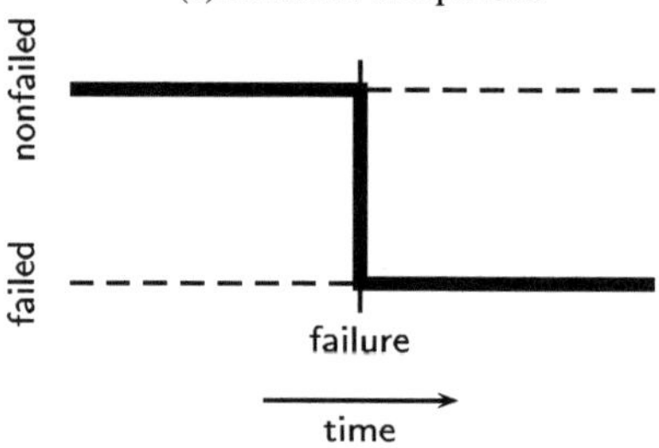

(c) A faulty component (without recovery).

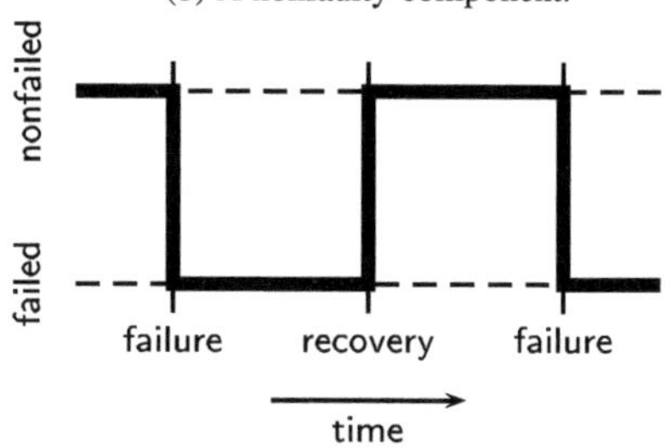

(d) A faulty component (with intermittent recovery).

Figure 2.5: Correct, faulty, and nonfaulty components. A correct component is always nonfailed. A nonfaulty component is eventually permanently nonfailed. A faulty component fails infinitely often.

We denote the faulty components of a trace τ by $F(\tau)$; More precisely, we define

$$F(\tau) = \{m \in (\Pi \cup \Xi) : \forall i \in \mathbb{N} : \exists j \geq i : \mathit{failed}_m(s_j) = \text{TRUE}\}$$

for a trace $\tau = \langle s_0, s_1, \ldots \rangle$. We extend F from traces to properties to denote all components that are faulty in some trace of a property:

$$F(P) = \bigcup_{\tau \in P} F(\tau)$$

for a property P.

In particular, F allows to construct a necessary condition for the equivalence of distributed system properties: If the sets of faulty components for two properties are not equal, then the properties are not equivalent. This result will be used later for comparing fault models: If two fault models are applied to the same distributed system property and result in different sets of faulty components, the fault models express different fault assumptions. Let P_i and P_j be two distributed system properties.

Lemma 2.3
If $P_i \equiv P_j$, then $F(P_i) = F(P_j)$.

PROOF: We assume that $P_i \equiv P_j$. As $F(P_i) = \bigcup_{\tau \in P_i} F(\tau)$ and $F(P_j) = \bigcup_{\tau \in P_j} F(\tau)$ by the definition of F, it suffices to prove

$$\bigcup_{\tau \in P_i} F(\tau) = \bigcup_{\tau \in P_j} F(\tau).$$

⟨1⟩1. $\bigcup_{\tau \in P_i} F(\tau) \subseteq \bigcup_{\tau \in P_j} F(\tau)$
PROOF:
⟨2⟩1. $\forall \tau_i \in P_i : \exists \tau_j \in P_j : \pi_E(\tau_i) = \pi_E(\tau_j)$
PROOF: As $P_i \equiv P_j$.
⟨2⟩2. $\forall s, t \in \Sigma, m \in (\Pi \cup \Xi) : \pi_E(s) = \pi_E(t) \Rightarrow \mathit{failed}_m(s) = \mathit{failed}_m(t)$
PROOF: As fault steps are externally visible.
⟨2⟩3. $\forall \tau_i, \tau_j \in \Sigma^\infty : \pi_E(\tau_i) = \pi_E(\tau_j) \Rightarrow F(\tau_i) = F(\tau_j)$
PROOF: If $\pi_E(\tau_i) = \pi_E(\tau_j)$, then $\pi_E(s_0) = \pi_E(t_0), \pi_E(s_1) = \pi_E(t_1), \ldots$ for $\tau_i = \langle s_0, s_1, \ldots \rangle$ and $\tau_j = \langle t_0, t_1, \ldots \rangle$. Then, by ⟨2⟩2, $\mathit{failed}_m(s_0) = \mathit{failed}_m(t_0)$, $\mathit{failed}_m(s_1) = \mathit{failed}_m(t_1), \ldots$ for each $m \in (\Pi \cup \Xi)$. $F(\tau_i) = F(\tau_j)$ follows from the definition of F.
⟨2⟩4. Q.E.D.
PROOF: By ⟨2⟩1 and ⟨2⟩3.
⟨1⟩2. $\bigcup_{\tau_i \in P_i} F(\tau_i) \supseteq \bigcup_{\tau_j \in P_j} F(\tau_j)$
PROOF: Analogously to the proof of ⟨1⟩1.
⟨1⟩3. Q.E.D.
PROOF: By ⟨1⟩1 and ⟨1⟩2.

The definitions of "correct" and "nonfaulty" may seem too strong for real-world systems as no realistic component will be nonfailed forever. We do not consider this a severe limitation, but just a matter of convenience: Any realistic system has an upper bound to fulfill its purpose (e.g., to provide a service). Hence, a component must only be nonfailed up to this upper bound. For convenience, we do not give these bounds explicitly. If necessary, they can be determined for a given system.

2.5 Fault Tolerance

While the notion of fault tolerance was only treated informally so far, we are now ready to formally define what it means for a system to be fault-tolerant. We assume a distributed system that is given by a low-level specification P_l and a fault assumption that is formalised by a fault model α. Furthermore, we assume a high-level specification P_h that captures the desired behaviour of the system such that P_l implements P_h. We adopt the definitions of Arora and Gouda [1993], Arora and Kulkarni [1998a,b], and Gärtner [1999] and distinguish three different forms of fault tolerance: *masking*, *nonmasking*, and *fail-safe fault tolerance*.

Ideally, a system should be able to implement its problem specification despite any assumed fault. This is the most strict form of fault tolerance and called *masking fault tolerance*.

Definition 2.2 (Masking Fault Tolerance)
A distributed system given by a property P_l is *masking fault-tolerant* for a specification P_h and a fault model α iff $\alpha(P_l)$ implements P_h.

Masking fault tolerance is the most desirable form of fault tolerance as faults do not affect at all whether a system implements its specification or not. In this sense, the system "masks" the manifestation of faults.

Unfortunately, it may not be possible or too costly to achieve masking fault tolerance. In such cases, it may be feasible and acceptable to implement a weaker variant of the original problem specification: P_h is weakened to a specification P'_h (P_h implements P'_h) and only P'_h is required to be implemented. Weakenings for nonmasking and fail-safe fault tolerance rely on the result that each property can be written as the intersection of a safety and a liveness property (see Sect. 2.2). While fail-safe fault tolerance requires to implement the safety part of a problem specification and allows to violate liveness, nonmasking fault tolerance requires to implement the liveness part and allows to violate safety requirements for a finite amount of time.

Definition 2.3 (Fail-Safe Fault Tolerance)
A distributed system given by a property P_l is *fail-safe fault-tolerant* for a specification $P_h \equiv S \cap L$ and a fault model α iff $\alpha(P_l)$ implements S, where S is a safety property and L is a liveness property.

For example, consider the problem of reaching consensus. If a system only decides agreed upon values that were indeed proposed despite faults, then it implements the safety properties of consensus (i.e., agreement and validity). If the faults prevent processes from deciding, the system violates liveness (i.e., termination). Hence, the system may fail, but fails safely; it is fail-safe fault-tolerant.

From a theoretical point of view, another form of fault tolerance could be defined that only requires to implement the liveness part of a problem specification. However, such a *fail-live* variant has been basically neglected in the literature as it seems to lack reasonable applications [Gärtner, 2001]. Other variants, for example, implementing some liveness properties of a problem that is given as the intersection of liveness properties have not been addressed yet as well. A stricter variant of *fail-live*, namely nonmasking fault tolerance, is more popular and has found various applications.

Definition 2.4 (Nonmasking Fault Tolerance)
A distributed system given by a property P_l is *nonmasking fault-tolerant* for a specification $P_h \equiv S \cap L$ and a fault model α iff $\alpha(P_l)$ implements L and $\alpha(P_l)$ implements a distributed system property S' with

$$\forall \langle s_0, s_1, \ldots \rangle \in S' : \exists \langle t_0, t_1, \ldots \rangle \in S, i, j \geq 0 : \langle s_i, s_{i+1}, \ldots \rangle = \langle t_j, t_{j+1}, \ldots \rangle,$$

where S is a safety property and L is a liveness property.

Intuitively, a nonmasking fault-tolerant system implements the liveness property of its original problem specification and, eventually, also implements the safety property; the system is allowed to violate the safety property for a finite period of time. Prominent examples of nonmasking fault tolerance are *self-stabilising systems* [Dijkstra, 1974, Schneider, 1993b, Dolev, 2000]: P_l is self-stabilizing for P_h and α iff α models arbitrary, transient faults and P_l is nonmasking fault-tolerant for P_h and α. Note that another variant of nonmasking fault tolerance could be defined that allows to violate safety in space (instead of in time).

2.6 Timing Model

A timing model captures timing assumptions by relating the behaviour of a system to the passage of time. As we will use different timing models throughout the thesis, we now give a brief overview of the spectrum of timing models ranging from *asynchronous* to *synchronous* models. We also give a brief overview of *failure detectors* as means of abstracting away timing assumptions. Refer to Veríssimo and Raynal [2000] and Gärtner [2001] for surveys of timing models and to Freiling et al. [2006] for a survey on failure detectors.

Asynchronous Systems Assuming an asynchronous system means to make as few assumptions about timing of computation and communication as reasonably possible. More precisely, relative process speeds and message delivery times are assumed to be unbounded, but finite. As such a timing model does not have a concept of real-time, it is also called a "time-free" model [Cristian and Fetzer, 1999, Charron-Bost et al., 2000].

Due to unbounded relative process speeds, the progress of different processes may differ arbitrarily. For any bound δ, a process may not perform a single step within a period of δ. If time is measured in numbers of (nonstuttering) steps, a process may perform an arbitrary (but finite) number of steps before another process performs its next step. As message delivery times are unbounded, it may take an arbitrary period of time to receive a message: If a message is sent at time t, it will eventually be received (if channels are reliable and no failures occur), but one cannot find a bound Δ such that the message is guaranteed to be received before time $t + \Delta$.

The asynchronous timing model bears the advantage that it makes less assumptions than guaranteed by real-world systems. The assumption of asynchrony holds for any reasonable system. No validation of this assumption is required. Hence, a system that is developed under this timing model can be easily implemented in the real-world. Another advantage is that no care needs to be taken about timing issues when modelling an asynchronous system, which may significantly simplify specifications.

On the downside, having no information about timing makes it hard or even impossible to solve fundamental problems. For example, reaching consensus is impossible in an asynchronous system if a single process may fail by crashing (i.e., prematurely halting) [Fischer et al., 1985]. The underlying reason for this result is that a process cannot distinguish a slow running process from a crashed one. Another disadvantage is that the asynchronous timing model does not allow timeliness specifications. For example, it is impossible to state that a system terminates within a certain period of time. Hence, real-time systems that must satisfy timing constraints cannot be modelled with the asynchronous timing model.

Synchronous Systems Assuming a synchronous system means to assume synchronous computation and communication with known upper bounds on relative process speeds and message delivery times. If δ is an upper bound for the relative process speed, every process must perform at least one step in a period of δ. If time is measured in (nonstuttering) steps, every process performs at least one step if an arbitrary process performs δ steps. If Δ is an upper bound for message delivery times, a message sent by a process $p \in \Pi$ at time t must be received before time $t + \Delta$. When measuring time in number of steps, the message is received before p performs Δ steps after sending the message.

The synchronous model allows to solve some problems that are impossible to solve without timing assumptions. For example, consensus can be solved in a synchronous model even if some processes crash. The underlying reason why consensus can be solved in a synchronous system – but not in an asynchronous one – is that processes can use time-outs to detect whether another process has crashed: If a correct process p_i sends a message to process p_j, p_j will receive the message within a period of Δ if p_j is not crashed. It takes at most a period of δ for p_j to handle the message and send an answer, which takes at most a period of Δ to be received by p_i. So, p_i can safely assume that it will receive an answer to its message within a period of $2\Delta + \delta$ if p_j is not crashed. If the answer is not received within this period, p_i can be sure that p_j has crashed.

If a problem cannot be solved in a synchronous model, it can neither be solved in weaker models such as the asynchronous model. In other words, impossibility results carry over to weaker timing models. Additionally, the synchronous timing model bears the advantage that it allows timeliness specifications. For example, it allows to specify that a system terminates within a given period of time.

The synchronous model has the disadvantage that the assumed bounds must be validated to hold in the real system. If they do not hold, the results obtained with the model will not correspond to reality. Unfortunately, there are only few real-world systems that indeed give the guarantees required by the synchronous model. Hence, implementing a system that is designed under a synchronous model may be hard if not impossible. For example, message delivery times cannot be bound for applications that rely on the Internet for communication due to arbitrary delays introduced by queueing and routing.

Another disadvantage is that systems may be less efficient than possible if they exploit the information provided by the timing model. The upper bounds δ and Δ for relative process speeds and message delivery times are worst-case assumptions and may be significantly larger than the normal-case values. The performance of a system depends on δ and Δ if the system exploits such worst-case assumptions. Hence, the performance may degrade with increasing upper bounds even when the average-case remains the same. Reasonable performance can then only be achieved if the upper bounds are small.

Partially Synchronous Systems The asynchronous and synchronous models mark the boundaries for the spectrum of timing models. Other models in-between have been proposed for different trade-offs among, for example, the possibility to solve problems, and the specification of timeliness [Dolev et al., 1987, Dwork et al., 1988, Chandra and Toueg, 1996, Cristian and Fetzer, 1999, Veríssimo and Almeida, 1995, Veríssimo and Casimiro, 2002, Fetzer et al., 2005]. Such models have in common that synchrony is not completely invariant as in the synchronous model, but varies with time or space.

For example, Dwork et al. [1988] have introduced different timing models under the term *partial synchrony*. They distinguish *partially synchronous communication* and *partially synchronous processes*. Communication is partially synchronous iff the message delivery times are bounded by Δ and (i) Δ is unknown or (ii) Δ is known but only holds eventually. The latter is an example of synchrony varying in time. Processes are partially synchronous iff relative process speeds are bounded by δ and (i) δ is unknown or (ii) δ is known but only holds eventually. Dwork et al. [1988] define different timing models by different combinations of synchronous and partially synchronous communication and processes. For example, one of their models relies on partially synchronous channels and asynchronous processes and, therefore, is an example of synchrony varying in space.

The partially synchronous model bears the advantages that it is a very realistic one and that it allows to solve fundamental problems. It is realistic since many real-world systems obey certain time bounds although these bounds are not known. Dwork et al. [1988] have investigated different variants of partially synchronous systems. For example, they have shown that a timing model with partially synchronous communication and processes suffices to reach consensus in the presence of crash failures.

On the downside, specifications explicitly address timing when using a partially synchronous model, which may significantly complicate a specification. In particular, if a system uses timing assumptions only for failure detection, the specification may become unnecessarily complicated. This observation lead to the seminal approach of *failure detectors*: Failure detectors abstract away timing assumption by providing a high-level interface for the detection of failures.

Unreliable Failure Detectors Chandra and Toueg [1996] have introduced the notion of *unreliable failure detectors* that encapsulate the detection of failures. An unreliable failure detector is an abstract device that provides some information about component failures, but hides how this information is obtained (which generally involves timing assumptions).

Each failure detector consists of a number of local failure detector modules, one for each process. A module informs its process about failures by *suspecting* other components (e.g., by adding them to a list of suspects). An unreliable failure detector is not perfect, but may make mistakes. For example, a module of a process may suspect another process to be failed although it is not failed as illustrated in Fig. 2.6. The module may correct this mistake by *unsuspecting* the erroneously suspected component (e.g., by removing it from the list of suspects).

A failure detector indicates component failures, but abstracts away how this information is obtained. Hence, different implementations of a failure detector are possible. For example, a failure detector for process crash failures can be implemented by periodic "heartbeat" (or "push") messages and time-outs in a synchronous system: Each failure detector module periodically sends out heartbeat messages and awaits heartbeat messages from other failure detector modules. If the module of another process does not send a heartbeat message within a certain period, this process will be suspected. Another implementation could rely on "pull" messages: Each module periodically sends a request message to each other module and awaits a response within a certain period. Any process that does not respond within this period will be suspected.

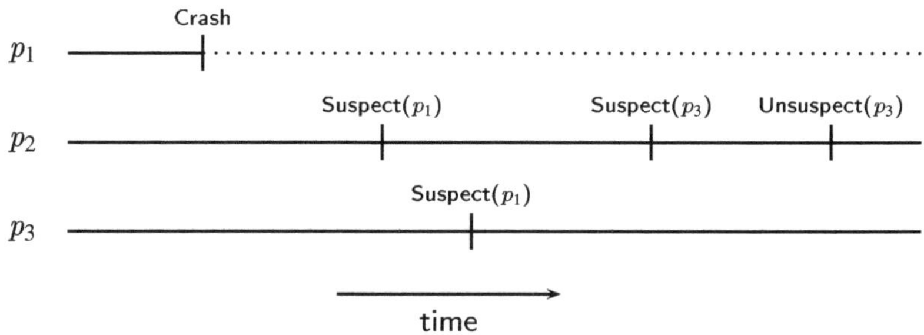

Figure 2.6: Illustration of an unreliable failure detector with 3 processes. Process p_1 crashes and is suspected by both, process p_2 and p_3. As the detector is unreliable it may make mistakes: p_2 erroneously suspects p_3, which is later corrected by unsuspecting p_3.

For process crashes, Chandra and Toueg [1996] characterise failure detectors in terms of *completeness* and *accuracy* properties. Informally, completeness describes that a failure detector eventually suspects every crashed process. Accuracy restricts the number of mistakes that the detector may make. Let $\mathit{Correct} \subseteq \Pi$ be a state function that gives the set of processes that are correct in the current trace. Let $\mathit{Faulty} = \Pi \setminus \mathit{Correct}$ be a state function that gives the processes that are faulty.[5] Note that both functions are invariant in a trace. Furthermore, let $\mathit{Suspects}(q)$ be a state function that gives the set of processes that are currently suspected by process q in the state.

Chandra and Toueg [1996] distinguish two particular completeness properties, strong and weak completeness. Informally, *strong completeness* denotes that, eventually, every process that crashes is permanently suspected by *every* correct process, formally expressed by

$$\forall p \in \mathit{Faulty}, q \in \mathit{Correct} : \Diamond\Box\,(p \in \mathit{Suspects}(q))\,.$$

Weak completeness only requires this for *some* correct process:

$$\forall p \in \mathit{Faulty} : \exists q \in \mathit{Correct} : \Diamond\Box\,(p \in \mathit{Suspects}(q))\,.$$

Chandra and Toueg [1996] have shown that completeness alone does not sufficiently specify a failure detector. For example, a failure detector with local modules that always suspect every process trivially implements strong completeness,

[5] As crash failures are permanent (i.e., processes do not recover), each process that is not correct is faulty.

Table 2.1: Classes of failure detectors [Chandra and Toueg, 1996]. The table shows different classes of failure detectors characterised by completeness and accuracy properties.

Completeness	Accuracy			
	Strong	**Weak**	**Eventual Strong**	**Eventual Weak**
Strong	Perfect $\mathscr{P}$	Strong $\mathscr{S}$	Eventually Perfect $\Diamond\mathscr{P}$	Eventually Strong $\Diamond\mathscr{S}$
Weak	$\mathscr{L}$	Weak $\mathscr{W}$	$\Diamond\mathscr{L}$	Eventually Weak $\Diamond\mathscr{W}$

but is useless for failure detection. A failure detector additionally needs to implement some accuracy property that restricts the mistakes.

Four variants of accuracy properties are distinguished: strong, weak, eventually strong, and eventually weak accuracy defined as follows. Let *Crashed* be a state function that denotes the set of processes that did already crash. Intuitively, *strong accuracy* describes that *no* process is suspected before it crashes, formally expressed by,

$$\Box\,(\forall p, q \in \Pi \setminus \mathit{Crashed} : p \notin \mathit{Suspects}(q))\,.$$

Weak accuracy only requires that *some* correct process is never suspected:

$$\exists p \in \mathit{Correct} : \Box\,(\forall q \in \Pi \setminus \mathit{Crashed} : p \notin \mathit{Suspects}(q))\,.$$

If the failure detection is based on time-outs in a partially synchronous system, even weak accuracy is difficult to achieve: If bounds only hold eventually, then time-outs may occur for every correct process before the bounds hold. This issue is addressed by *eventual strong accuracy* and *eventual weak accuracy*. They only require that strong / weak accuracy hold eventually. A simplified but equivalent definition of eventual strong accuracy requires that, eventually, correct processes are permanently not suspected by any correct process:

$$\Diamond\Box\forall p, q \in \mathit{Correct} : p \notin \mathit{Suspects}(q).$$

For *eventual weak accuracy*, this only holds for some correct process:

$$\Diamond\exists p \in \mathit{Correct} : \Box\,(\forall q \in \mathit{Correct} : p \notin \mathit{Suspects}(q))\,.$$

Chandra and Toueg [1996] have obtained eight different classes of failure detectors by combining different completeness and accuracy properties as shown in Table 2.1. For example, the class of *perfect failure detectors*, denoted by $\mathscr{P}$, is defined by strong completeness and strong accuracy. The class of *eventually strong failure detectors*, denoted by $\diamond\mathscr{S}$, is defined by strong completeness and eventual weak accuracy.

A system that is augmented by a failure detector can be implemented under a system model if the failure detector can be implemented under this system model. Chandra and Toueg [1996] have shown, for example, that a $\mathscr{P}$ failure detector can be implemented in a synchronous system and an $\diamond\mathscr{P}$ failure detector in a partially synchronous system. Note that, however, an asynchronous model with a failure detector is generally not equivalent to a model with time bounds. For example, Charron-Bost et al. [2000] show that the synchronous model is stronger than the asynchronous model with a $\mathscr{P}$ failure detector even if only time-free specifications are considered.

The major benefit of failure detectors is that they allow to encapsulate and hide timing assumptions (if timeliness of a system is not required except for failure detection). For example, if a fault-tolerant system does not need to satisfy real-time constraints, timing assumptions can be completely omitted from the system specification using a failure detector. Such an omission may significantly shorten and simplify a specification. For example, Bernstein et al. [1987] have shown how to solve the problem of *nonblocking atomic commit* making extensive use of time-outs. Guerraoui [2002] has given a solution that is significantly easier to evaluate due to using failure detectors. Moreover, failure detectors allow to obtain conservative results: System models with more restrictive timing assumptions do not allow less efficient or less resilient systems.

2.7 Summary

In this chapter, we have presented the system model that will be used throughout this thesis. We consider distributed systems on an abstraction level, where they are composed from processes and channels. Processes communicate among each other by passing messages over channels. As we will use different timing models, we have given a brief overview of these models, ranging from asynchronous to synchronous models, with failure detectors as a means of encapsulating timing assumptions.

Formally, we represent both, high-level specifications and low-level implementations, by properties that describe a system by sets of possible behaviour. Verifying an implementation reduces to showing that a subset relation on the externally visible behaviour holds. We also represent processes and channels by properties and have shown that each distributed system property can be decomposed into component properties. This result will be used later to show that any fault model can be given by a component failure model. As an example for a concise notation language for properties, we have presented a variant of temporal logic, the Temporal Logic of Actions.

As this thesis is concerned with modelling faults and tolerating them, the definition of fault models is of particular relevance for further chapters. A fault model is defined as a weakening of a property. A weakened property permits more behaviour, namely behaviour due to faults. While this notion is well accepted in the literature, it allows arbitrary complex fault models leading to intractable models. Next, we will address the question how to separate different concerns of fault models to obtain abstract and, therefore, more tractable models.

3 Modelling Fault Assumptions with Structural Failure Models

By formalising fault assumptions, fault models are essential for engineering fault-tolerant systems: A fault-tolerant system is designed and evaluated to tolerate all faults that are described by a fault model. The accuracy of a fault model is of particular importance. An inaccurate fault model results in a system that is either not as resilient as expected or less efficient than possible. Unfortunately, many fault models used in the literature abstract away aspects that are relevant in realistic systems. For example, the prevalent threshold models abstract away dependences of faults although there is empirical evidence that dependent faults are relevant in real-world systems [Tang and Iyer, 1992, 1993, Long et al., 1995, Amir and Wool, 1996, Weatherspoon et al., 2002, Bakkaloglu et al., 2002, Yalagandula et al., 2004, Warns et al., 2008]. Abstracting away dependent and, therefore, correlated faults is particularly disturbing as even small correlations have a significant impact on the dependability of a system [Tang and Iyer, 1992, Weatherspoon et al., 2002, Warns et al., 2008]. Likewise, threshold models hide the propagation of faults. As propagating faults have been observed in electric power transmission systems [Dobson et al., 2004, 2005], they are likely to occur in distributed computing systems as well.

We consider distributed systems on an abstraction level, where they are composed from processes and channels. This composition is exploited for formalising fault assumptions: We describe faults by component failures. The resulting fault models are called *component failure models*. In particular, we identify two basic building blocks for fault models, *functional* and *structural failure models*, that allow to specify different variants of component failure models. Informally, a functional failure model describes how a component that is failed may behave. A structural failure model describes system-wide constraints of faults.

While significant effort has been spent on assumptions that describe faulty component behaviour, system-wide constraints of faults have received considerably less attention. We identify and evaluate different classes of structural failure models that, in particular, allow to model dependent and propagating faults.

Contribution In this chapter, we address the question of how to formalise fault assumptions by functional and structural failure models. We use these models to define three classes of fault models: *process*, *channel*, and *hybrid failure models*. They represent fault assumptions by attributing faults to the components of a distributed system. Process failure models attribute all faults to the processes of a system, channel failure models to the channels, and hybrid failure models to both, processes and channels.

With respect to accuracy, we show that the class of process failure models is complete under reasonable assumptions: Any fault model for our system model can be represented by a process failure model if channels do not have externally visible states. Completeness of hybrid failure models follows trivially as each process failure model is a special case of a hybrid failure model. The class of channel failure models, however, is not complete: Some fault models for a given system cannot be represented by attributing faults to channels.

As the completeness results indicate, functional and structural failure models are not tractable in general. While tractable subclasses of functional failure models have been investigated in the literature extensively, we address tractable subclasses of structural failure models that are accurate for aspects that are relevant in real-world systems. In particular, we consider set-based and sequence-based structural failure models for dependent and propagating faults.

Overview This chapter is organised as follows. We distinguish related work from our contributions in Section 3.1. In Section 3.2, we define our notion of functional failure models and illustrate that these models capture common assumptions on faulty component behaviour. Analogously, we define structural failure models and illustrate that these models capture, for example, the prevalent threshold assumptions in Section 3.3. Section 3.4 defines process failure models, channel failure models, and hybrid failure models in terms of functional and structural failure models. It includes the completeness result for process failure models. In Section 3.5 and 3.6, we present the classes of set- and sequence-based structural failure models for dependent and propagating faults. Section 3.5 gives a classification of structural failure models with respect to their expressiveness. In Section 3.7, we discuss the relation between (nonprobabilistic) structural failure models and probabilistic fault models before we conclude in Section 3.8.

3.1 Related Work

While we focus on modelling faults by component failures, other approaches have been suggested by Santoro and Widmayer [1989, 2005] and, for example, adopted by Hutle and Schiper [2007], and Biely et al. [2007]. Santoro and Widmayer [1989, 2005] have suggested to model faults by *transmission failures*: All faults are modelled by erroneous transmissions of messages between processes and not assigned to any particular component. While our fault models can be combined with arbitrary timing assumptions, the transmission failure model is defined in terms of a synchronous system model. It is, therefore, restricted to synchronous systems. In the context of transmission failure models, process failure models have been criticised for not being appropriate for transient and dynamic faults [Santoro and Widmayer, 1989, Charron-Bost and Schiper, 2007]. Our completeness result on process failure models shows that, from a theoretical perspective, process failure models allow to formalise all kinds of fault assumptions.

Our notion of functional and structural failure models is inspired by the notion of functional and structural failure considerations of Echtle [1990]. A *functional failure consideration* describes how failures affect the functioning of a component. This notion corresponds to *local failure assumptions* of Nordahl [1992, 1993], which state how a component fails. Closely related, Völzer [1998] defines *fault impact models*, which are Petri nets representing a fault assumption.

Echtle [1990] defines a *structural failure consideration* to describe which components are faulty. While Echtle [1990] focusses on a binary model that defines for every component over time whether it is failed or not, our definition allows both, more and less abstract models. For example, the examples for threshold assumptions and eventual absence of failed components (given below) are more abstract models as they are not concerned with the details of when a component fails, but only distinguish whether a component is faulty or not. Example 3.8 gives a model that is orthogonal to the binary model of Echtle as it is not concerned with the time when processes fail, but covers more than one failure mode.

Structural failure models correspond to *global failure assumptions* of Nordahl [1992, 1993], which "typically state how many (and which) components may fail simultaneously." Closely related, Völzer [1998] has used *rely specifications* to express such assumptions. Völzer [1998] does not encode rely specifications into the formalism – Petri nets – that he uses to model the behaviour of systems, but leaves them as extra specifications consisting of temporal propositions. These propositions are considered as axioms during verification. When using TLA, the same formalism is used to model systems and to express structural failure models. As the structural failure models are described by temporal formulae this leaves the possibility to use them as axioms during verification. In contrast to the work of Echtle [1990], Nordahl [1992, 1993], and Völzer [1998], we classify previous fault models in terms of functional and structural failure models and compare them in terms of their expressiveness.

Closely related to our set-based structural failure models, various approaches in the literature model dependent faults by sets of components [Hirt and Maurer, 1997, Junqueira and Marzullo, 2003a, Malkhi and Reiter, 1997, Junqueira and Marzullo, 2005a,c]. In contrast, we (i) characterise what kind of dependent faults these models address and (ii) compare all of these models with respect to their expressiveness. In particular, we find that none of these models is able to express all kinds of dependent faults and introduce a new class that is able to do so. Furthermore, we introduce more expressive sequence-based models that allow to describe propagating faults in distributed systems.

In contrast to dependent faults, propagating faults have hardly been addressed in the context of fault-tolerant distributed computing. Cristian [1991] has described propagation faults in distributed systems, but considers propagation of faults along the hierarchy of hierarchically composed components, that is, how a fault propagates within a component. In contrast, we consider propagation of faults on one level of a hierarchy, that is, how a fault propagates among different components.

3.2 Functional Failure Models

Describing fault assumptions in terms of component failures has been a common approach in the literature. For example, Cristian et al. [1985] have summarised a number of popular assumptions on faulty component behaviour (e.g., crash, omission, Byzantine). We formalise this approach by so called *functional failure models* that weaken single component properties instead of system properties as a whole.

Informally, a *functional failure model* describes how a component that is failed may behave. By allowing additional (externally visible) behaviour – behaviour that occurs when the component fails – it weakens the component's specification. Formally, we define a functional failure model ϕ as a mapping between component properties such that a component property m implements $\phi(m)$.

Definition 3.1 (Functional Failure Model)
A functional failure model ϕ is a mapping from a component property P_m for a component $m \in (\Pi \cup \Xi)$ to a component property $\phi(P_m)$ for m such that P_m implements $\phi(P_m)$.

We consider functional failure models a natural building block for component failure models as fault assumptions often explicitly state how components behave when being failed (e.g., "processes may fail by crashing"). For illustration, we now define some common fault assumptions by functional failure models: crash, crash-recovery, and Byzantine failures. Let P_m be a component property for a component $m \in (\Pi \cup \Xi)$. We give a functional failure model ϕ for the different fault assumptions, respectively. For illustration, we also show how these functional failure models could be applied syntactically to TLA specifications. Let M be a TLA component specification of the canonical form that represents the property P_m, where the tuple o of output variables includes a failure variable f with $\models$ $\mathit{Init} \Rightarrow f = \text{FALSE}$ and $\models \mathit{Next} \Rightarrow f = f'$.

Example 3.1 (Crash Assumption)
Consider the crash assumption as, for example, assumed by Fischer et al. [1985] and Chandra and Toueg [1996]. A component that crashes prematurely halts and stops to make any progress. This can be modelled by ϕ_C with

$$\begin{aligned}\phi_C(P_m) = P_m \cup \{\, \langle s_0, s_1, \ldots \rangle \in \Sigma^\infty :&\\ &\exists \langle t_0, t_1, \ldots \rangle \in P_m, i \in \mathbb{N} :\\ &\quad \wedge \langle s_0, \ldots, s_i \rangle = \langle t_0, \ldots, t_i \rangle\\ &\quad \wedge \forall j \geq i : \langle t_j, t_{j+1} \rangle \text{ is an } m\text{-environment step}\}.\end{aligned}$$

ϕ_C augments P_m by traces that have the same prefix as a trace in P_m, but continue without any m-step. Hence, m behaves as usual, but may eventually stop performing any step.

Syntactically, the crash model can be applied as follows:

$$\begin{aligned} M_C &\triangleq \exists x : \mathit{Init} \wedge \Box[\mathit{FNext}]_{\langle x, o \rangle} \wedge (L \vee \Diamond f),\\ \mathit{FNext} &\triangleq \neg f \wedge (\mathit{Next} \vee \mathit{Fail}),\\ \mathit{Fail} &\triangleq f' = \text{TRUE} \wedge \text{UNCHANGED } \langle x, \bar{o}, e \rangle,\end{aligned}$$

where $\bar{o}$ is the tuple of all variables in o except f. The component may proceed as usual as long as not being failed, but additionally fail at any point in time. As soon as it is failed, the state of the component does not change anymore. It does not make any further progress. Note that the fairness conditions need to be weakened as well, because, if the component is failed, no Next action will be performed anymore even if permanently enabled.

Example 3.2 (Byzantine Failures)
A component that fails arbitrarily can be modelled by ϕ_B with

$$\begin{aligned}\phi_B(P_m) = P_m \cup \{\, \langle s_0, s_1, \ldots \rangle \in \Sigma^\infty :&\\ &\exists \langle t_0, t_1, \ldots \rangle \in P_m, i \in \mathbb{N} :\\ &\quad \wedge \langle s_0, \ldots, s_i \rangle = \langle t_0, \ldots, t_i \rangle\\ &\quad \wedge \forall j \geq i : \langle t_j, t_{j+1} \rangle \text{ is either an } m\text{-environment step}\\ &\qquad\qquad \text{or an arbitrary } m\text{-step}\}.\end{aligned}$$

P_m is augmented with traces that have the same prefix as a trace in P_m, but continue with arbitrary m- and m-environment steps. Hence, m may behave as usual or eventually starts to show arbitrary behaviour. The term *Byzantine failures* for such an assumption has been introduced by Lamport et al. [1982]: An agreement problem was given in terms of *Byzantine generals*, who are supposed to agree on attacking even if some of them are traitorous. A traitorous general may behave completely arbitrarily.

Syntactically, the fault model can be applied as follows:

$$\begin{aligned}
M_B &\triangleq \exists x : \mathit{Init} \wedge \Box[\mathit{FNext}]_{\langle x,o\rangle} \wedge (L \vee \Diamond f),\\
\mathit{FNext} &\triangleq \vee \neg f \wedge (\mathit{Next} \vee \mathit{Fail})\\
&\quad\;\; \vee f \wedge \text{UNCHANGED } \langle f, e\rangle,\\
\mathit{Fail} &\triangleq f' = \text{TRUE} \wedge \text{UNCHANGED } \langle x, \bar{o}, e\rangle,
\end{aligned}$$

with $\bar{o}$ being the tuple of all variables in o except f. Analogously to crash failures, a component may proceed as usual and, additionally, fail at any point in time. If failed, each step of the process may arbitrarily perturbate the state of the process except for the fault variable f.

Example 3.3 (Crash-Recovery Assumption)
The crash-recovery assumption allows a component to crash and to recover subsequently. When a component recovers, it continues to make progress. For this fault assumption, we only give a TLA specification as a description in terms of sets of traces is lengthy and hard to comprehend. Consider the following TLA formula

$$\begin{aligned}
M_{CR} &\triangleq \exists x : \mathit{Init} \wedge \Box[\mathit{FNext}]_{\langle x,o\rangle} \wedge (L \vee \Box\Diamond f),\\
\mathit{FNext} &\triangleq \vee \neg f \wedge (\mathit{Next} \vee \mathit{Fail})\\
&\quad\;\; \vee f \wedge \mathit{Recover},\\
\mathit{Fail} &\triangleq f' = \text{TRUE} \wedge \text{UNCHANGED } \langle x, \bar{o}, e\rangle,\\
\mathit{Recover} &\triangleq \mathit{Init}',
\end{aligned}$$

where $\bar{o}$ is the tuple of all variables in o except f. Then, M_{CR} allows crash failures of a component with possible recovery. When the component is failed, no Next-step can occur. The component can, however, recover when being failed, which resets the local state to an initial state in this case. As $\mathit{Init} \Rightarrow f = \text{FALSE}$, Next-actions can be taken again. As the fairness conditions L should hold after recovery, they are weakened. A violation of L is only allowed if the process is infinitely often failed.

Note that the definition of M_{CR} prevents message losses by the component (except for the first message after the crash). Usually, processes and channels interact with a handshake mechanism for sending and delivering messages: A process that sends a message over a channel c awaits an acknowledgement from c before sending the next message. The acknowledgement indicates that the channel has received the message. Analogously, a channel that delivers a message to a process p awaits an acknowledgement from p before trying to deliver the next message. The acknowledgement indicates that the process received the message. With our definition of M_{CR}, a crashed process or channel does not acknowledge any received message[1]. However, the crash-recovery assumption that is common in the literature includes that messages in transit may be lost while a component is crashed. This issue can be easily solved by changing M_{CR}: A component is allowed to acknowledge the reception of messages while being crashed.

As the state is reset to an initial state for recovery, a component is not aware of recovering. It cannot distinguish whether it just started or recovered from a crash. However, it needs to be aware of recovering if it ought to invoke additional recovery actions. For example, such actions include informing other components about the recovery and retrieving some previously recorded values. Such special recovery actions are not a part of the fault assumption, but must be included in the original component specification. If recovery is indicated by a variable r analogously to the failure variable f, awareness of recovery can be easily included in M_{CR} by setting r appropriately in the *Recovery* action.

Example 3.4 (Multiple Failure Modes)
So far, we have only assumed single failure modes neglecting that a component may fail in more than one way. Distinguishing different failure modes may lead to more efficient and more resilient implementations [Thambidurai and Park, 1988, Meyer and Pradhan, 1991, Lincoln and Rushby, 1993]. Functional failure models allow to cover such assumptions (sometimes called *hybrid failure models* [Lincoln and Rushby, 1993]) easily by set unions. For example, consider a fault assumption that allows processes to either fail by crashing or completely arbitrary. Using the functional failure models ϕ_C and ϕ_B from the previous examples, this can be formalised by

$$\phi_{CB}(P_m) = \phi_B(P_m) \cup \phi_C(P_m).$$

Syntactically, we have only used boolean failure variables so far. For multiple failure modes, variables that indicate the failure mode are more convenient and make specifications more comprehensible. For example, consider the following TLA specification, where the value of f – if not FALSE – indicates the failure mode.

$$\begin{aligned}
M_{CB} &\triangleq \exists x : Init \wedge \Box[FNext]_{\langle x,o\rangle} \wedge (L \vee \Diamond failed),\\
FNext &\triangleq \vee \neg failed \wedge (Next \vee Fail)\\
&\quad\;\; \vee crashed \wedge \text{UNCHANGED}\ \langle x,o,e\rangle\\
&\quad\;\; \vee byz \wedge \text{UNCHANGED}\ \langle f,e\rangle,\\
failed &\triangleq f \neq \text{FALSE},\\
crashed &\triangleq f = \text{"}CRASH\text{"},\\
byz &\triangleq f = \text{"}BYZ\text{"},\\
Fail &\triangleq \left(crashed' \vee byz'\right) \wedge \text{UNCHANGED}\ \langle x,\bar{o},e\rangle,
\end{aligned}$$

[1] Except for the recovery. A recovery might acknowledge one message.

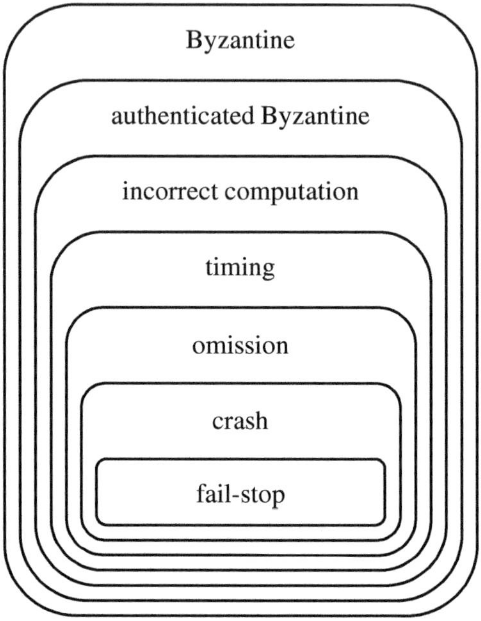

Figure 3.1: Hierarchy of functional failure model classes from Barborak et al. [1993]. The set of a class A is a proper subset of the set of class B iff all behaviour of a process under the latter failure class is also possible under the former.

If the component m fails, the failure mode is indicated by the value of f (either "$CRASH$" for crash failures or "BYZ" for Byzantine failures). Depending on the failure mode, the variables of m either may change arbitrarily or do not change anymore.

Classification As illustrated by the examples, functional failure models capture the process failure classes identified by Cristian et al. [1985], for example, crash, omission, and Byzantine process failures. These failure classes are ordered in a hierarchy, where the (partial) order is given by an inclusion relation. Cristian et al. [1985] define a failure class to *include* another if all behaviour of any process under the latter failure class is also possible under the former. For example, the crash failure class is included in the Byzantine failure class as Byzantine failures allow a process to stop making progress. The hierarchy has been extended by different other authors. For example, Figure 3.1 gives the hierarchy presented by Barborak et al. [1993] in a survey paper on the problem of consensus.

For functional failure models, we can formally express the inclusion relation by our implementation relation: a functional failure model ϕ_1 includes another ϕ_2 if $\phi_2(P)$ implements $\phi_1(P)$ for any component property P. For example, it is easy to see that ϕ_B includes ϕ_C for every component property P.

In addition to stating how components behave when being failed, fault assumptions usually also include system-wide constraints. For example, a common fault assumption is "at most t out of n processes may fail by crashing," which asserts that failures are partial: The number of processes that are faulty is bounded. Although possible, we do not include such system-wide constraints into functional failure models for a separation of concerns. We introduce a second building block, structural failure models, for constraints that define which components may be faulty. While functional failure models address the behaviour of failed components, structural failure model address the extent of faults.

3.3 Structural Failure Models

A *structural failure model* describes system-wide constraints of faults. For example, such a model could describe that a certain number of components is faulty at most or that components fail in a certain order. While a functional failure model allows additional behaviour by *weakening* component properties (and therefore weakening the overall system property), a structural failure model restricts the possible behaviour by *strengthening* a system property. As such, functional and structural failure models should be completely orthogonal. To ensure orthogonality, we require that a structural failure model differentiates traces only based on the $failed_m$ predicates (see page 27). As an abbreviation, we define a state function *Failed* that maps a system state to the set of components that are failed in the state:

$$Failed(s) = \{m \in (\Pi \cup \Xi) : failed_m(s)\}.$$

Moreover, we extend *Failed* to traces by

$$Failed(\langle s_0, s_1, \ldots \rangle) = \langle Failed(s_0), Failed(s_1), \ldots \rangle.$$

Definition 3.2 (Structural Failure Model)
A structural failure model σ is a mapping from a distributed system property P to a distributed system property $\sigma(P)$ such that $\sigma(P)$ implements P and, for all distributed system properties P_i and P_j,

$$\forall \tau_i \in P_i, \tau_j \in P_j : \left(\tau_i \in \sigma(P_i) \wedge Failed(\tau_i) = Failed(\tau_j)\right) \Rightarrow \tau_j \in \sigma(P_j).$$

Hence, a structural failure model distinguishes different traces only based on when which components are failed. Like functional failure models, we consider structural failure models a natural building block for component failure models, because common fault assumptions explicitly state the extent of faults (e.g., "at most t of n processes fail"). For illustration, we now give some common fault assumptions in terms of structural failure models. Again, we additionally give the corresponding TLA specifications to demonstrate how structural failure models could be applied syntactically. Let P_S be a distributed system property and S a corresponding TLA specification of the canonical form. Furthermore, let failed_m be a TLA state predicate that is true for a state iff component $m \in (\Pi \cup \Xi)$ is failed in the state. The predicate could be defined, for example, by checking the value of a failure variable (e.g., $\mathit{failed}_m \triangleq f_m \neq \text{FALSE}$ if f_m is a boolean failure variable for component m).

Example 3.5 (Threshold Assumption)
The fault assumption stating that at most t components are faulty is often made in the literature [Fischer et al., 1985, Chandra and Toueg, 1996, Dwork et al., 1988]. The assumption can be given by the structural failure model σ_t that restricts a property to traces with less than or equal to t faulty components. Formally,

$$\sigma_t(P_S) = P_S \cap \{\tau \in \Sigma^\infty : |F(\tau)| \leq t\},$$

where $F(\tau)$ denotes the set of faulty processes in τ.

A corresponding TLA specification is

$$S_t \triangleq S \wedge |\{m \in (\Pi \cup \Xi) : \Box\Diamond \mathit{failed}_m\}| \leq t.$$

The resulting specification asserts that less or equal to t components are infinitely often failed (i.e., $\leq t$ components are faulty, see p. 27).

Example 3.6 (Majority Clique)
Consider a fault assumption stating that, despite faulty channels, a majority of processes is completely connected by correct channels. That is, a majority of processes P induces a complete graph (a *clique*) if we consider each process as a node and each pair of correct channels between two processes as an undirected edge. For example, such an assumption has been used by Lamport [1978a] for the implementation of reliable distributed systems. The assumption can be formalised by

$$\begin{aligned}\sigma_{MC}(P_S) = \{\langle s_0, s_1, \ldots\rangle \in P_S :\ & \\ & \exists M \subseteq \Pi : |M| > \frac{n}{2} \wedge \forall p_i, p_j \in M : p_i \neq p_j \Rightarrow \\ & \quad \exists c \in \Xi : \mathit{rcv}(c) = p_i \wedge \mathit{snd}(c) = p_j \wedge \forall i \in \mathbb{N} : \neg \mathit{failed}_c(s_i)\},\end{aligned}$$

where $\mathit{snd}(c) = p_i$ and $\mathit{rcv}(c) = p_j$ for a channel c from process p_i to p_j.

A corresponding TLA specification is

$$S_{MC} \triangleq S \wedge \exists M \subseteq \Pi : |M| > \frac{n}{2} \wedge \forall p_i, p_j \in M : p_i \neq p_j \Rightarrow$$
$$\exists c \in \Xi : rcv(c) = p_i \wedge snd(c) = p_j \wedge \Box(\neg failed_c).$$

Example 3.7 (Eventual Absence of Failed Components)
A self-stabilising system converges to a "legal state" in the presence of transient failures. Hence, fault assumptions for self-stabilising systems often include that, eventually, all components are permanently nonfailed [Schneider, 1993b, Dolev, 2000]. This assumption can be given by the structural failure model

$$\sigma_{EAF}(P_S) = \{\langle s_0, s_1, \ldots \rangle \in P_S : \exists i \in \mathbb{N} : \forall j \geq i, m \in (\Pi \cup \Xi) : \neg failed_m(s_j)\}.$$

A corresponding TLA specification is

$$S_{EAF} \triangleq S \wedge \Diamond\Box(\forall m \in (\Pi \cup \Xi) : \neg failed_m).$$

Example 3.8 (Multiple Failure Modes)
So far, we have only considered structural failure models that do not distinguish different failure modes. Consider the fault assumption that at most c components fail by crashing and at most b components by Byzantine failures. The structural constraint can be expressed, for example, by the TLA specification

$$S_{CB} \triangleq S \wedge |\{m \in (\Pi \cup \Xi) : \Diamond crashed_m\}| \leq c \wedge |\{m \in (\Pi \cup \Xi) : \Diamond byz_m\}| \leq b,$$

where $crashed_m$ is a state predicate that indicates that component m has crashed and byz_m is a state predicate that indicates that component m failed arbitrarily.

Classification In the literature, models that describe how components behave when being failed (covered by functional failure models) have been investigated extensively. For example, Thambidurai and Park [1988], Cristian et al. [1985], and Powell [1992] have proposed classifications of such models and discuss the relation between different classes. Models for system-wide constraints of faults (covered by structural failure models) have received significantly less attention. While, for example, Fitzi and Maurer [1998] and Junqueira and Marzullo [2003b] have identified classes for dependent faults, we are not aware of a classification that is as comprehensive as, for example, the classification of Cristian et al. [1985] for process failure behaviour.

In Section 3.5 and Section 3.6, we present a classification of structural failure models and examine the relation among different classes. Analogously to the inclusion relation of Cristian et al. [1985] for process failure classes, we define a partial order on classes of structural failure models that allows to compare different classes.

Definition 3.3 (Less-Expressive-Than Relation)
A class Σ_1 of structural failure models is *less expressive* than a class Σ_2 of structural failure models iff, for every distributed system property P and each structural failure model $\sigma_1 \in \Sigma_1$, there exists a structural failure model $\sigma_2 \in \Sigma_2$ with $\sigma_1(P) \equiv \sigma_2(P)$.

Intuitively, any fault assumption that can be given by a model of Σ_1 can also be given by a model of Σ_2 if Σ_1 is less expressive than Σ_2. However, Σ_2 may include additional models. We say that Σ_1 and Σ_2 are *equivalent* iff Σ_1 is less expressive than Σ_2 and Σ_2 is less expressive than Σ_1. Σ_1 is *strictly less expressive* than Σ_2 iff Σ_1 is less expressive than Σ_2, but Σ_2 is not less expressive than Σ_1.

Resilience Predicates The relevance of classes of structural failure models stems from affecting resilience predicates. A *resilience predicate* describes which structural failure models can be tolerated when solving a given problem under a given functional failure model. Resilience predicates – also called *replication predicates* [Junqueira and Marzullo, 2005b] – describe the component redundancy that is sufficient to solve a problem. For example, Chandra and Toueg [1996] have presented an algorithm that solves the consensus problem using an $\diamond\mathcal{S}$ failure detector under the assumption that at most t processes crash. They found a resilience predicate of $2t < n$ (i.e., the majority of processes must be correct).

In general, a resilience predicate is expressed in the same terms as the structural failure model. If a structural failure model is given by a threshold, the resilience predicate is usually also given in terms of a threshold. In particular, more expressive structural failure model classes allow to describe resilience predicates more fine-granularly. For example, Chandra and Toueg [1996] also have shown that $2t < n$ is an upper bound on resilience when solving consensus under an $\diamond\mathcal{S}$ failure detector. However, this result only holds when using threshold to describe structural failure models. In Chapter 5, we will see that more expressive classes allow to improve on this bound. This illustrates that results obtained under more expressive classes generalise results obtained under less expressive classes.

Before we investigate structural failure models in more detail, we illustrate that functional and structural failure models are indeed useful building blocks for component failure models by showing that they allow to define different types of component failure models.

3.4 Component Failure Models

Just as we distinguish components of a distributed system into processes and channels, we distinguish component failure models into *process failure models*, *channel failure models*, and *hybrid failure models*. Process failure models describe system faults in terms of process failures, channel failure models in terms of channel failures, and hybrid failure models in terms of both, channel and process failures. We use functional and structural failure models as basic building blocks to formally define these models.

3.4.1 Process Failure Models

Traditionally, fault assumptions have been given by attributing all system faults to the processes of a system. That is, only processes may fail, but channels are assumed to be correct. Often, they even implement strong high-level specifications such as being reliable, delivering in FIFO order, or operating (partially) synchronously. This approach has been followed in many seminal papers and remains prevalent until today. For example, Fischer et al. [1985] and Chandra and Toueg [1996] have assumed that processes may fail by crashing and channels are reliable. In their famous paper on Byzantine generals, Lamport et al. [1982] have assumed that processes (which they call "generals") may behave completely arbitrary when they fail, but channels (called "messengers") are reliable and synchronous. In more recent work, Schiper and Toueg [2006] have assumed "benign" process failures and reliable channels and Hurfin et al. [2002], Gorender et al. [2007] have assumed process crashes and reliable channels.

We formalise such approaches by *process failure models* relying on functional and structural failure models as building blocks. Informally, a process failure model weakens a system property by only weakening its process properties; the channel properties remain as they are. Let $P_S = \bigcap_{m \,\in\, (\Pi \cup \Xi)} P_m$ be a distributed system property, where P_m is a component property for component $m \in (\Pi \cup \Xi)$.

Definition 3.4 (Process Failure Model)
A process failure model ψ is a fault model that is given in terms of a functional failure model ϕ and a structural failure model σ. It maps P_S to a distributed system property $\psi(P_S)$ with

$$\psi(P) = \sigma\left(\bigcap_{p \,\in\, \Pi} \phi(P_p) \cap \bigcap_{c \,\in\, \Xi} P_c\right).$$

For illustration, we formalise some fault assumptions that have been used to obtain seminal results in fault-tolerant distributed computing.

Example 3.9 (Crashes and Thresholds)
Fischer et al. [1985] have shown that consensus is impossible to solve deterministically in an asynchronous system with reliable channels even if only at most one process may crash. We will revisit this result – known as the FLP impossibility result – in Section 5.2.2. This fault assumption can be defined by a process failure model ψ using the functional failure

model ϕ_C for crashes from Example 3.1 (p. 43) and the structural failure model σ_t for threshold assumptions from Example 3.5 (p. 48) with $t = 1$ such that

$$\psi(P_S) = \sigma_t\left(\bigcap_{m \in \Pi} \phi_C(P_m) \cap \bigcap_{m \in \Xi} P_m\right).$$

Example 3.10 (Crashes and Thresholds)
To circumvent the FLP impossibility result, Chandra and Toueg [1996] have proposed to augment an asynchronous system with failure detectors. They have shown that an $\Diamond\mathscr{S}$ failure detector allows to solve consensus deterministically if at most $\lfloor n/2 \rfloor$ processes crash. Analogously to the previous example, this fault assumption can be formalised with ϕ_C and σ_t with $t = \lfloor n/2 \rfloor$.

Example 3.11 (Byzantine Failures and Thresholds)
Lamport et al. [1982] have shown how to solve *interactive consistency* (being closely related to the consensus problem) in a synchronous system even if at most $\lfloor n/3 \rfloor$ processes exhibit Byzantine failures. This fault assumption can be modelled analogously to the assumption of Fischer et al. [1985] using σ_t with $t = \lfloor n/3 \rfloor$ and ϕ_B for Byzantine failures instead of ϕ_C.

Example 3.12 (Eventual Absence of Byzantine Components)
The previous examples dealt with masking fault-tolerant systems. A common fault assumption for nonmasking, self-stabilising systems is that processes may behave arbitrarily when failed, but are eventually permanently nonfailed. This fault assumption can be given by combining a functional failure model for transient Byzantine failures and the structural failure model σ_{EAF} for the eventual absence of failed components.

Although process failure models attribute system faults solely to the processes of a system, this does not necessarily mean that the processes are "responsible" for the faults in the real-world. It has been common practice to model channel failures of the real world by failures of the sending or the receiving process. For example, Walter and Suri [2003] have addressed channel failures, but ascribe them to the sending process. Perry and Toueg [1986] have modelled message omissions of channels by send- and receive-omissions of processes.

Note that artificially attributing failures of a component to other components results in invalid component specifications: The component specifications do not reflect the behaviour of the real-world components. For example, if message losses performed by real-world channels are modelled by send-omissions of processes, the lossy real-world channels can be modelled as nonlossy. However, as long as the resulting overall system specification is valid, invalid component specifications are of minor importance, because the verification of a fault-tolerant system requires to verify the system as a whole. The verification process may even benefit from composing a system specification from invalid component specifications. For example, such a specification may alleviate finding symmetries in components that can be exploited during verification (e.g., to limit state space explosion for model checking).

A criticism on traditional fault models is that they are primarily concerned with permanent and static faults (e.g., crash and Byzantine failures) [Charron-Bost and Schiper, 2007]. Indeed, the important classes of transient and dynamic faults have received significantly less attention. If a fault model only allows to express permanent static faults, it requires to model transient dynamic faults by permanent static faults. Such an approach, however, yields less efficient and overly pessimistic solutions in general. In many cases, it may even be impossible to solve a problem then: If dynamic process failures, which affect every process in a system over time, are approximated by static failures, eventually all process are considered as faulty. No nontrivial problem can be solved under such a fault model.

However, as we will show now, these issues are not an inherent limitation of process failure models. In particular, we will show that process failure models are complete under reasonable assumptions. They are complete in the sense that every fault model for a distributed system composed from given component properties can be given by a process failure model. This result holds as long as a high-level specification permits all kinds of channel behaviour. We consider this assumption reasonable as most problems of fault-tolerant distributed computing are only specified in terms of processes, but not in terms of channels. For example, the problem of consensus requires all processes to agree on a common value, but does not restrict channels (i.e., permits all kinds of channel behaviour). The same also holds for other seminal problems in fault-tolerant distributed computing (e.g., broadcast, atomic commit, termination detection, and mutual exclusion).

The reason for the exposed role of processes is that they model the active entities in a distributed system: They perform the computation yielding the necessary and sufficient behaviour to implement a problem. In contrast, channels model the communication entities, which are required to implement a specification, but should not be unnecessarily restricted by a high-level specification. We formalise the assumption of arbitrary channel behaviour by requiring that channels do not have an externally visible state. Hence, their behaviour is hidden from external observers. This requirement does not imply that channel properties can simply be omitted from a compositional distributed system property. Process properties may restrict the externally visible behaviour depending on the internal part of the system state, which may be restricted by a channel property. Hence, omitting a channel property can permit more behaviour: Possibly more externally visible behaviour is allowed.

Theorem 3.1 (Completeness of Process Failure Models)
Consider a distributed system property $P_S = \bigcap_{m \in (\Pi \cup \Xi)} P_m$, where P_m is a component property for component $m \in (\Pi \cup \Xi)$. For every fault model α, there exists a functional failure model ϕ and a structural failure model σ such that

$$\alpha(P_S) \equiv \sigma\left(\bigcap_{m \in \Pi} \phi(P_m) \cap \bigcap_{m \in \Xi} P_m\right)$$

if channels do not have externally visible states.

PROOF: As an abbreviation, we define

$$P_C = \sigma\left(\bigcap_{m \in \Pi} \phi(P_m) \cap \bigcap_{m \in \Xi} P_m\right).$$

ASSUME: Let σ be the identity mapping and let $\phi(P_m) = P_m \cup \alpha(P_S) \cup P^S_{env}(m)$ with

$$\begin{aligned} P^S_{env}(m) = \kappa_S(\{\langle s_0, s_1, \ldots\rangle \in \Sigma^\infty :\; & \\ \exists \langle t_0, t_1, \ldots\rangle \in \alpha(P_S), i \in \mathbb{N} :\; & \\ \wedge \langle t_0, \ldots, t_i\rangle = \langle s_0, \ldots s_i\rangle & \\ \wedge \langle t_i, t_{i+1}\rangle \text{ is an } m\text{-environment step} & \\ \wedge \forall j \geq i : \langle s_j, s_{j+1}\rangle \text{ is an } m\text{-environment step}\}). & \end{aligned}$$

PROVE:
1. ϕ is a functional failure model
2. σ is a structural failure model
3. $\alpha(P_S) \equiv P_C$

$\langle 1\rangle 1.$ ϕ is a functional failure model

PROOF: We need to show that $\phi(P_m)$ is indeed a component property for m and that P_m implements $\phi(P_m)$. We do this separately in two steps.

$\langle 2\rangle 1.$ $\phi(P_m)$ is a component property for m.

PROOF: $\phi(P_m)$ is a property as P_m, $\alpha(P_S)$, and $P^S_{env}(m)$ are sets of traces that are closed under stuttering. If sets of traces are closed under stuttering, their union is closed under stuttering as well. $\phi(P_m)$ is a component property for m as $\phi(P_m)$ allows an arbitrary m-environment step whenever it allows an m-environment step.

$\langle 2\rangle 2.$ P_m implements $\phi(P_m)$

PROOF: Trivial as $P_m \subseteq \phi(P_m)$.

$\langle 2\rangle 3.$ Q.E.D.

PROOF: By $\langle 2\rangle 1$ and $\langle 2\rangle 2$.

$\langle 1\rangle 2.$ σ is a structural failure model

PROOF: Trivial as σ is the identity mapping.

$\langle 1\rangle 3.$ $\alpha(P_S) \equiv P_C$

PROOF:

⟨2⟩1. $\alpha(P_S)$ implements P_C

PROOF: Consider an arbitrary external trace in the external property induced by $\alpha(P_S)$. We need to show that this trace is also in the external property induced by P_C. It suffices to show that, for any trace $\tau_i \in \alpha(P_S)$, there is a trace $\tau_j \in P_C$ such that $\pi_E(\tau_i) = \pi_E(\tau_j)$. This is the case because, for any trace $\tau \in \alpha(P_S)$, $\bigcap_{m \in \Pi} \phi(P_m)$ permits traces that are equal to τ as can be seen by an external observer with arbitrary channel behaviour, because the P^S_{env} properties allow arbitrary channel behavour. Hence, at least one of these traces is in $\bigcap_{m \in \Xi} P_m$ and, therefore, also in P_C.

⟨2⟩2. P_C implements $\alpha(P_S)$

PROOF: Consider an arbitrary external trace in the external property induced by P_C. We need to show that this trace is also in the external property induced by $\alpha(P_S)$. It suffices to show that, for any trace $\tau_i \in P_C$, there is a trace $\tau_j \in \alpha(P_S)$ such that $\pi_E(\tau_i) = \pi_E(\tau_j)$. This is the case because, by the definition of P_C, a trace τ in P_C

- is in $\alpha(P_S) \cup P^S_{env}(m)$ for each $m \in \Pi$ such that τ is equal to some trace in $\alpha(P_S)$ or
- is in each $P_m, m \in (\Pi \cup \Xi)$ and, therefore, equal to some trace in P_S

for an external observer. In the latter case, τ is also equal to some in $\alpha(P_S)$ as P_S implements $\alpha(P_S)$.

⟨2⟩3. Q.E.D.

PROOF: By ⟨2⟩1 and ⟨2⟩2.

⟨1⟩4. Q.E.D.

PROOF: By ⟨1⟩1 – ⟨1⟩3.

The theorem shows that using process failure models has no disadvantages from a theoretical perspective: Any fault model can be given by a process failure model. More precisely, a fault model can be expressed by a process failure model for given component properties. Hence, using process failure models does not put any restrictions on how to specify the system's components. From a more practical perspective, using process failure models may result in specifications that are hard to understand and/or verify. In particular, if only channel failures are assumed for a system, it may be inconvenient to attribute these failures to processes. In such cases, channel failure models, which we describe next, are better suited.

3.4.2 Channel Failure Models

Instead of modelling fault assumptions by process failures, *channel failure models* alternatively attribute system faults to the channels of a system. This approach also has been studied for fundamental problems of fault-tolerant distributed computing. For example, Abu-Amara and Lokre [1994], Mans and Santoro [1998], and Sayeed et al. [1995] have shown how to solve the problem of *leader election* in the presence of channel failures. While Mans and Santoro [1998] have considered permanent detectable crash failures, Abu-Amara and Lokre [1994] have addressed intermittent message omissions. Sayeed et al. [1995] have assumed Byzantine channels. We formalise channel failure models analogously to process failure models using functional and structural failure models as building blocks. Informally, a channel failure model weakens a system property by only weakening its channel properties; the process properties remain as they are.

Definition 3.5 (Channel Failure Model)
A channel failure model γ is a fault model that is given in terms of a functional failure model ϕ and a structural failure model σ. It maps P_S to a distributed system property $\gamma(P_S)$ with

$$\gamma(P_S) = \sigma\left(\bigcap_{m\,\in\,\Pi} P_m \cap \bigcap_{m\,\in\,\Xi} \phi(P_m)\right).$$

Example 3.13 (Byzantine Failures and Thresholds)
We illustrate channel failure models by formalising the fault assumption of Sayeed et al. [1995]: Leader election can be solved if at most $\lfloor (n-2)/2 \rfloor$ channels fail arbitrarily. Using the functional failure model ϕ_B for Byzantine failures from Example 3.2 (p. 43) and the threshold model σ_t from Example 3.5 (p. 48), this assumption can be modelled by a channel failure model γ with

$$\gamma(P_S) = \sigma_t\left(\bigcap_{m\,\in\,\Pi} P_m \cap \bigcap_{m\,\in\,\Xi} \phi_B(P_m)\right),$$

where t equals $\lfloor (n-2)/2 \rfloor$.

Analogously to process failure models that attribute real-world channel failures to processes, channel failure models attribute real-world process failures to channels. For example, Mans and Santoro [1998] model the crash of a process by crashes of all its incident channels. However, as we will show now, this may not be possible for given component properties in general. Hence, channel failure models are not complete in the same sense as process failure models.

Theorem 3.2 (Incompleteness of Channel Failure Models)
Consider a distributed system property $P_S = \bigcap_{m\,\in\,(\Pi\cup\Xi)} P_m$, where P_m is a component property for m. There is a fault model α for P_S such that

$$\alpha(P) \not\equiv \sigma\left(\bigcap_{m\,\in\,\Pi} P_m \cap \bigcap_{m\,\in\,\Xi} \phi(P_m)\right)$$

for any functional failure model ϕ and any structural failure model σ.

PROOF: We define a distributed system property P_S and a fault model α, assume that α can be given by a channel failure model, and obtain a contradiction.

LET: 1. $e_0, e_1 \in \Sigma_E$ are two externally visible states with $e_0 \neq e_1$.

2. $P_m = \{\langle t_0, t_1, \ldots \rangle \in \Sigma^\infty :$
$\pi_E(t_0) = e_0 \wedge \forall i \in \mathbb{N} : \langle t_i, t_{i+1} \rangle$ is an m-env. step$\}$

3. $P_S = \bigcap_{m \in (\Pi \cup \Xi)} P_m$

4. $Q_m = \{\langle t_0, t_1, \ldots \rangle \in \Sigma^\infty :$
$\pi_E(t_0) = e_1 \wedge \forall i \in \mathbb{N} : \langle t_i, t_{i+1} \rangle$ is an m-env. step$\}$

5. $Q_S = \bigcap_{m \in (\Pi \cup \Xi)} Q_m$

6. $\alpha(P_S) = P_S \cup Q_S$

ASSUME: 1. ϕ and σ are a functional and a structural failure model such that

$$\alpha(P_S) \equiv \sigma\left(\bigcap_{m \in \Pi} P_m \cap \bigcap_{m \in \Xi} \phi(P_m)\right)$$

2. γ is a channel failure model defined by ϕ and σ

PROVE: $\alpha(P_m) \not\equiv \gamma(P_m)$

$\langle 1 \rangle 1.$ P_m and Q_m are component properties.

PROOF: As each step permitted by P_m and Q_m is an m-environment step.

$\langle 1 \rangle 2.$ P_S and Q_S are distributed system properties.

PROOF: By $\langle 1 \rangle 1$ and Lemma 2.1.

$\langle 1 \rangle 3.$ α is a fault model for P_S.

PROOF: By $\langle 1 \rangle 2$, P_S and Q_S are interleaving properties. As the union of two interleaving properties is an interleaving property, $P_S \cup Q_S$ is a distributed system property. As $P_S \subseteq P_S \cup Q_S$, P_S implements $\alpha(P_S)$.

$\langle 1 \rangle 4.$ $\gamma(P_S)$ implements P_m for each $m \in \Pi$

PROOF: By the definition of structural failure models, $\gamma(P_S)$ implements

$$P_\phi = \bigcap_{m \in \Pi} P_m \cap \bigcap_{m \in \Xi} \phi(P_m).$$

As $P_\phi \subseteq P_m$ for each $m \in \Pi$, P_ϕ also implements each $P_m, m \in \Pi$.

$\langle 1 \rangle 5.$ $\alpha(P_S)$ does not implement P_m for any $m \in \Pi$

PROOF: $\alpha(P_S)$ induces an externally visible property that includes an externally visible trace with e_1 as first state. P_m induces an externally visible property that only includes externally visible traces with e_0 as initial state.

$\langle 1 \rangle 6.$ Q.E.D.

PROOF: By $\langle 1 \rangle 4$ and $\langle 1 \rangle 5$, $\alpha(P_S)$ and $\gamma(P_S)$ are not equivalent.

Note that the theorem only holds for *given* component properties. Other component properties may be found whose composition yields an equivalent system property. In this case, applying a channel failure model describes the desired fault assumption. However, we consider such an approach to be of minor interest as a failure model should not put restrictions on how to specify fault-free components.

Furthermore, the component properties to be found would not be valid representations of the real-world components. In contrast, process failure models do not require to find new component properties: given valid component properties, a process failure model can be found to describe any fault assumption.

Example 3.14 (Weak Distributed Commit)
Although the proof of Theorem 3.2 considers a trivial system without practical relevance, the incompleteness of channel failure models is not of mere theoretical interest. For example, consider the *weak distributed commit* problem, a variant of the *distributed commit* problem, which arises in distributed databases when finishing a transaction. Each process *proposes* whether to *commit* or to *abort* the transaction and is supposed to eventually *decide* on the outcome while considering that abort proposals have veto rights: If a (correct) process proposes to abort the transaction, each process is supposed to decide for abortion. Formally, the problem is specified by the following properties:

Termination Every correct process eventually decides on some value.

Agreement No two correct processes decide differently.

Weak Validity (With Veto) If a correct process decides to commit the transaction, then all correct processes proposed to commit. If a correct process decides to abort the transaction, then some correct process proposed to abort or some process is faulty.

In an implementation of this problem, a process can safely decide to abort the transaction if it has initially proposed to abort without considering any message received. Now let us consider a process failure model that allows a process to decide commit if being faulty although it proposed to abort. For example, Byzantine failures allow processes to do so.[2] However, this fault model cannot be given in terms of a channel failure model: As a process may decide without considering a message and as processes and channels only interact via messages, no channel can affect the decision in this case. For the same reason, we conjecture that transmission failure models are not complete.

3.4.3 Hybrid Failure Models

An obvious generalisation of process and channel failure models are *hybrid failure models* that allow to attribute faults to processes and channels. In particular, such models allow valid component specifications in the sense that a fault is attributed to the component that is responsible for the fault in the real-world. For example, Rushby [1994], Siu et al. [1998], Azadmanesh and Kieckhafer [2000], and Schmid et al. [2002] explicitly distinguish process and channel failures. A hybrid failure model defines a fault assumption by weakening both, process and channel properties, of a system.

[2] Despite such faults, the problem remains solvable. For example, a solution to the *weak Byzantine generals* problem as presented by Lamport [1983b] can be transformed to solve weak distributed commit.

Definition 3.6 (Hybrid Failure Model)
A hybrid failure model χ is a fault model that is given in terms of a functional failure model ϕ and a structural failure model σ. It maps P_S to a distributed system property $\psi(P_S)$ with

$$\chi(P) = \sigma\left(\bigcap_{m \in (\Pi \cup \Xi)} \phi(P_m)\right).$$

Example 3.15
We illustrate hybrid failure models by formalising a special case of Siu et al.'s [1998] fault assumption: Their results imply that *Byzantine consensus* (see Chapter 5) can be solved if $3t_p < |\Pi|$ and $3t_p + 2t_c < c$, where t_p is the number of arbitrarily failed processes, c is the minimal number of disjoint paths between any pair of processes, and t_c is the number of arbitrarily failed channels. Using the functional failure model ϕ_B for Byzantine failures from Example 3.2 (p. 43), this failure assumption can be defined by the hybrid failure model χ with

$$\begin{aligned}
\chi(P_S) &= \sigma\left(\bigcap_{m \in (\Pi \cup \Xi)} \phi_B(M_m)\right),\\
\sigma(P) &= P \cap \{\tau \in \Sigma^\infty :\\
&\qquad \wedge 3 \cdot |F(\tau) \cap \Pi| < |\Pi|\\
&\qquad \wedge 3 \cdot |F(\tau) \cap \Pi| + 2 \cdot |F(\tau) \cap \Xi| < c\}.
\end{aligned}$$

Obviously, hybrid failure models generalise process and channel failure models as each process or channel failure model can be trivially formulated as a hybrid failure model. In particular, the completeness result for process failure models also applies to hybrid failure models.

Corollary 3.1 (Completeness of Hybrid Failure Models)
Consider a distributed system property $P_S = \bigcap_{m \in (\Pi \cup \Xi)} P_m$, where P_m is a component property for $m \in (\Pi \cup \Xi)$. For every fault model α, there exists a functional failure model ϕ and a structural failure model σ such that

$$\alpha(P) \equiv \sigma\left(\bigcap_{m \in (\Pi \cup \Xi)} \phi(P_m)\right).$$

PROOF: The corollary immediately follows from Theorem 3.1 and the definitions of process and hybrid failure models with the identity mapping for channel properties as the functional failure model.

We did not put any restrictions on structural failure models so far except for strengthening distributed system properties. Hence, a structural failure model may describe the extent of faults in arbitrary precision and accuracy. However, arbitrary precision and accuracy are not desired in general as they may draw evaluation infeasible. The challenge is to find classes of structural failure models that allow to describe relevant real-world phenomena accurately, but remain tractable. Next, we have a look at tractable structural failure models for dependent faults.

3.5 Set-Based Structural Failure Models

In the literature on fault-tolerant distributed computing, thresholds are the predominant models to describe the extent of faults. Thresholds are attractive for their conceptual simplicity and for being tractable, documented by numerous results obtained with thresholds. However, threshold models do not allow to accurately describe dependent faults as has been observed in the literature [Keidar and Marzullo, 2002, Junqueira and Marzullo, 2003b, Fitzi et al., 1999]. Unfortunately, there is empirical evidence that dependent faults are significant in real-world systems and affect the dependability of distributed systems significantly [Tang and Iyer, 1992, 1993, Long et al., 1995, Amir and Wool, 1996, Weatherspoon et al., 2002, Bakkaloglu et al., 2002, Yalagandula et al., 2004, Warns et al., 2008]. Hence, threshold models do not allow to accurately describe realistic fault assumptions, which possibly leads to invalid evaluation results.

In this section, we focus on structural failure models that are given in terms of sets instead of thresholds. While sets are conceptually not as simple as thresholds, the resulting models are accurate for dependent faults and – as will be illustrated in Chapter 4 and Chapter 5 – are tractable for developing and evaluating fault-tolerant distributed systems. For the sake of simplicity, we only consider process failure models, which is not a restriction per se as process failure models are complete (see Theorem 3.1, p. 53).

For preparation, we define two special properties of sets, *monotonicity* and *symmetry*, and a notation for restricting sets to certain subsets. We will use these definitions to relate set-based structural failure models to dependent faults later on.

Let U be some arbitrary set of elements and $V \subseteq U$ be some subset of U. Furthermore, let $\mathscr{S} \subseteq \mathscr{P}(U)$ be some set of sets with elements in U.

Definition 3.7 (Monotone Set)
The set $\mathscr{S}$ is monotone iff $\forall S_1 \in \mathscr{S}, S_2 \subseteq S_1 : S_2 \in \mathscr{S}$.

We call $\kappa_M(\mathscr{S}) = \{S_1 \subseteq U : \exists S_2 \in \mathscr{S} : S_1 \subseteq S_2\}$ the monotone closure of $\mathscr{S}$. In particular, $\mathscr{S}$ equals $\kappa_M(\mathscr{S})$ iff $\mathscr{S}$ is monotone.

Definition 3.8 (Symmetric Set)
The set $\mathscr{S}$ is symmetric in $V \subseteq U$ iff

1. $\forall S \in \mathscr{S} : S \subseteq V$ and
2. $\forall S_1, S_2 \subseteq V : \quad |S_1| = |S_2| \wedge S_2 \in \mathscr{S} \Rightarrow S_1 \in \mathscr{S}$.

Hence, a set $\mathscr{S}$ that is symmetric in V contains all subsets of V with cardinality k if it contains at least one subset with cardinality k.

For example, consider $U = \{u_1, u_2, u_3\}$. Then the set $\mathscr{S} = \{\{\}, \{u_1\}, \{u_2\}, \{u_1, u_2\}\}$ is symmetric in $V = \{u_1, u_2\}$ and is monotone. However, $\mathscr{S}$ is not symmetric in U, because U has two subsets $\{u_1\}$ and $\{u_3\}$ of the same cardinality, but $\mathscr{S}$ contains only one of them. The set $\{\{\}, \{u_1, u_2\}\}$ is symmetric in V, but is not monotone as it does not contain $\{u_1\} \subseteq \{u_1, u_2\}$. Its monotone closure equals $\mathscr{S}$.

While $\mathscr{S}$ may contain sets with arbitrary elements of U, we may want to restrict the sets in $\mathscr{S}$ to elements of V. We denote such a restriction with the symbol $|$.

Definition 3.9 (Restricted Set)
The set $\mathscr{S}|_V \subseteq \mathscr{P}(U)$ equals $\mathscr{S}$ restricted to elements in V, that is,

$$\mathscr{S}|_V = \{S \cap V : S \in \mathscr{S}\}.$$

For example, if $\mathscr{S} = \mathscr{P}(U)$, then $\mathscr{S}|_{\{u_1, u_2\}} = \{\{\}, \{u_1\}, \{u_2\}, \{u_1, u_2\}\}$.

3.5.1 Dependent Faults

The criticism on threshold models for not being able to describe dependent faults raises the question of what precisely is meant by dependent faults. While definitions for dependence are given by probability theory for events, these definitions cannot immediately be transferred to our system model as the model is not probabilistic. We give an intuitive description of independent faults and formalise this notion in terms of traces and properties. We consider this formalisation reasonable, because it fits to the (informal) notion used in the literature. As it will turn out, threshold models are characterised by independent faults.

Informally, we use the notion of independent faults to describe that faults do not "affect" each other: Processes being faulty may neither enforce nor prevent faults of other processes. We formalise this intuition as follows:

Definition 3.10 (Independent Faults)
Faults are independent in a distributed system property P iff

$$1. \forall \tau_1 \in P, p \in F(\tau_1) : \exists \tau_2 \in P : \quad F(\tau_2) = F(\tau_1) \setminus \{p\} \text{ and}$$
$$2. \forall p_1, p_2 \in F(P), \tau_1 \in P : \quad p_1 \in F(\tau_1) \quad \Rightarrow$$
$$\exists \tau_2 \in P : \quad \{F(\tau_1) \setminus \{p_1\}\} \cup \{p_2\} \subseteq F(\tau_2).$$

If faults are not independent in P, faults are dependent in P.

For example, if the first condition does not hold for some trace $\tau_1 \in P$ and some process $p \in F(\tau_1)$, all processes in $F(\tau_1) \setminus \{p\}$ being faulty enforces that at least one other process – namely p – is faulty. If the second condition does not hold for some processes $p_1, p_2 \in F(P)$ and some trace $\tau_1 \in P$, all processes in $F(\tau_1) \setminus \{p_1\}$ being faulty prevents at least one other process – namely p_2 – from being faulty. In both cases, we do not consider faults to be independent in P.

Consider a distributed system property P that defines a system with three processes, $\Pi = \{p_1, p_2, p_3\}$. If

$$\{F(\tau) \subseteq \Pi : \tau \in P\} = \{\{\}, \{p_1\}, \{p_2\}, \{p_3\}, \{p_1, p_2\}, \{p_1, p_3\}, \{p_2, p_3\}\},$$

faults are independent in P: Faults are neither enforced nor prevented by other faults. If the set of faulty processes per trace equals $\{\{\}, \{p_1\}, \{p_1, p_2\}, \{p_2, p_3\}\}$, faults are not independent, because if p_3 is faulty, p_2 is also faulty, but p_1 is not.

In addition to distinguishing independent from dependent faults, the latter can be further subclassified into *undirected dependent* and *directed dependent faults*. The intuition behind this classification is that, in a distributed system property with directed dependent faults, a process is faulty whenever another process is faulty, but not necessarily vice versa (i.e., there is a directed impact). In a property with undirected dependent faults this is not the case; no fault enforces another fault. For a formalisation of *undirected dependent faults*, we adapt the definition of independent faults by negating its second condition; for directed dependent faults, we negate the first condition and omit the second.

Definition 3.11 (Undirected Dependent Faults)
Faults are undirected dependent in a distributed system property P iff

$$1. \forall \tau_1 \in P, p \in F(\tau_1) : \exists \tau_2 \in P : \quad F(\tau_2) = F(\tau_1) \setminus \{p\}$$
$$2. \exists p_1, p_2 \in F(P), \tau_1 \in P : \quad p_1 \in F(\tau_1) \quad \wedge$$
$$\forall \tau_2 \in P : \quad (F(\tau_1) \setminus \{p_1\}) \cup \{p_2\} \not\subseteq F(\tau_2).$$

Definition 3.12 (Directed Dependent Faults)
Faults are directed dependent in a distributed system property P iff

$$\exists \tau_1 \in P, p \in F(\tau_1) : \forall \tau_2 \in P : \quad F(\tau_2) \neq F(\tau_1) \setminus \{c\}.$$

For example, consider a distributed system property P with three processes p_1, p_2, and p_3. If the set of faulty processes per trace equals $\{\{\},\{p_1\},\{p_2\},\{p_3\},\{p_1,p_2\}\}$, faults are not independent, because p_1 being faulty prevents p_3 from being faulty, but allows p_2 to be faulty. However, the faults are not directed dependent. For example, p_1 being faulty does not enforce that p_2 is faulty. Alternatively, assume that the set of faulty processes per trace equals $\{\{\},\{p_2\},\{p_3\},\{p_1,p_2\}\}$. In this case, p_1 being faulty prevents p_3 from becoming faulty, but enforces that p_2 is faulty. There is a directed impact from p_1 to p_2 as, whenever p_1 is faulty, p_2 is faulty as well.

Structural failure models describe the extent of faults in a distributed system property; they determine whether faults are independent or not. Therefore, we extend the notion of independent and dependent faults from properties to structural failure models: A structural failure model σ describes independent (undirected dependent, directed dependent) faults for a distributed system property P iff faults are independent (undirected dependent, directed dependent) in $\sigma(P)$.

If describing a structural failure model by a threshold does not allow to describe dependent faults, other means of describing such models must be found that cover dependent faults. As the criteria for independent and dependent faults are only given in terms of process sets, we now consider to describe structural failure models in terms of process sets and find that they indeed allow to describe dependent faults.

3.5.2 Set-Based Structural Failure Models

We say that a structural failure model is based on a set $\mathscr{D}$ of process sets if the structural failure model permits all traces whose set of faulty processes is included in $\mathscr{D}$ and only those traces. Note that $\emptyset \in \mathscr{D}$ if a structural failure model is based on $\mathscr{D}$, because any fault assumption must permit that no process is faulty at all. As we show below, the class of set-based structural failure models covers independent, undirected dependent, and directed dependent faults. We call a set-based structural failure model also a *Didep model* (from "directed dependent").

Definition 3.13 (Set-Based Structural Failure Model)
A structural failure model σ is based on a set $\mathscr{D} \subseteq \mathscr{P}(\Pi)$ of process sets iff

$$\sigma(P) \equiv P \cap \{\tau \in \Sigma^\infty : F(\tau) \in \mathscr{D}\}$$

for all distributed system properties P. In this case, we call σ a Didep model.

A Didep model is uniquely defined by the set that it is based on. Therefore, if comparing two Didep models, it suffices to compare their sets. In particular, when considering the expressiveness of two subclasses of set-based models, it suffices to reason about them in terms of process sets. For example, it suffices to look at the process sets to determine whether a class is less expressive than another class.

Theorem 3.3
Let Σ_1 and Σ_2 be two classes of set-based structural failure models. Σ_1 is less expressive than Σ_2 iff, for each structural failure model $\sigma_1 \in \Sigma_1$, there is a structural failure model $\sigma_2 \in \Sigma_2$ such that σ_1 and σ_2 are based on the same set.

PROOF: We prepare the actual proof in the first step and show both directions in the subsequent steps.

$\langle 1 \rangle 1$. Let σ_1 and σ_2 be two set-based structural failure models. σ_1 and σ_2 are based on the same set iff $\sigma_1(P) \equiv \sigma_2(P)$ for all distributed system properties P.

PROOF: If σ_1 and σ_2 are based on the same set $\mathscr{D}$, then

$$\sigma_1(P) \equiv P \cap \{\tau \in \Sigma^\infty : F(\tau) \in \mathscr{D}\} \equiv \sigma_2(P)$$

for all distributed system properties by the definition of set-based models.

We prove the opposite direction by contraposition. Assume that σ_1 and σ_2 are based on different sets $\mathscr{D}_1$ and $\mathscr{D}_2$. Then, $\sigma_1(P) \not\equiv \sigma_2(P)$ for a distributed system property P with $\{F(\tau) : \tau \in P\} = \mathscr{P}(\Pi)$.

$\langle 1 \rangle 2$. If Σ_1 is less expressive than Σ_2, then, for each $\sigma_1 \in \Sigma_1$, there is a $\sigma_2 \in \Sigma_2$ such that both are based on the same set.

PROOF: If Σ_1 is less expressive than Σ_2, then, for each $\sigma_1 \in \Sigma_1$, there is a $\sigma_2 \in \Sigma_2$ such that $\sigma_1(P) \equiv \sigma_2(P)$ for all distributed system properties P. By $\langle 1 \rangle 1$, σ_1 and σ_2 are based on the same set.

$\langle 1 \rangle 3$. If there is a $\sigma_2 \in \Sigma_2$ for each $\sigma_1 \in \Sigma_1$ such that both are based on the same set, then Σ_1 is less expressive than Σ_2.

PROOF: If there is a $\sigma_2 \in \Sigma_2$ for each $\sigma_1 \in \Sigma_1$ such that both are based on the same set, then, by $\langle 1 \rangle 1$, there is a $\sigma_2 \in \Sigma_2$ for each $\sigma_1 \in \Sigma_1$ such that $\sigma_1(P) \equiv \sigma_2(P)$ for each distributed system property P. Then, Σ_1 is less expressive than Σ_2.

$\langle 1 \rangle 4$. Q.E.D.

PROOF: By $\langle 1 \rangle 2$ and $\langle 1 \rangle 3$.

On the one hand, a set of process sets can be used to define a structural failure model. On the other hand, they can also be used to describe a given structural failure model. As sets of process sets offer limited precision, such a description may abstract away some details about the model.

Set-Abstractions Using sets or thresholds to describe structural failure models means to abstract from possibly complex fault assumptions for the sake of obtaining tractable models. Given a class of structural failure models with a certain precision, one is interested in the model of this class that describes the fault assumption for the system currently under investigation most accurately.

If relying on set-based models, one is interested in the set $\mathscr{D} \subseteq \mathscr{P}(\Pi)$ that describes a fault assumption as accurate as possible. In particular, $\mathscr{D}$ should contain the set of faulty processes for each trace, but no other process sets. If this is the case, $\mathscr{D}$ is called *sound* and *complete*. More precisely, we call $\mathscr{D}$ *complete* for a distributed system property P iff it contains the set of faulty processes for each $\tau \in P$ and *sound* iff it does not contain other process sets.

Definition 3.14 (Sound and Complete Sets)
A set $\mathscr{D} \subseteq \mathscr{P}(\Pi)$ of process sets is *sound* for a distributed system property P and a structural failure model σ iff

$$\forall D \in \mathscr{D} : \exists \tau \in \sigma(P) : D = F(\tau).$$

$\mathscr{D}$ is *complete* for P and σ iff

$$\forall \tau \in \sigma(P) : F(\tau) \in \mathscr{D}.$$

In particular, a sound and complete set is unique for a distributed system property and a structural failure model, which immediately follows from its definition.

Corollary 3.2
If $\mathscr{D}_1$ and $\mathscr{D}_2$ are sound and complete sets for a distributed system property P and a structural failure model σ, then $\mathscr{D}_1 = \mathscr{D}_2$.

For a given distributed system property, each structural failure model can be easily abstracted by a sound and complete set by including the set of faulty processes for each trace and no other process set.

Lemma 3.1
For a distributed system property P and a structural failure model σ, the set $\mathscr{D} \subseteq \mathscr{P}(\Pi)$ with

$$\mathscr{D} = \{F(\tau) \subseteq \Pi : \ \tau \in \sigma(P)\},$$

is sound and complete.

Of course, some information may be lost with set-abstractions of a structural failure model. In general, if the set $\mathscr{D}$ is sound and complete for a distributed system property P and a structural failure model σ, $\sigma(P) \not\equiv \sigma_{\mathscr{D}}(P)$, where $\sigma_{\mathscr{D}}$ is the Didep model based on $\mathscr{D}$. However, for verification, $\sigma_{\mathscr{D}}(P)$ is a safe approximation of $\sigma(P)$: As the following theorem shows, it suffices to verify $\sigma_{\mathscr{D}}(P)$ for the verification of $\sigma(P)$.

Theorem 3.4
Let P and Q be distributed system properties and σ be a structural failure model. If $\mathscr{D}$ is sound and complete for P and σ, and $\sigma_{\mathscr{D}}$ is the Didep model that is based on $\mathscr{D}$, then $\sigma(P)$ implements Q if $\sigma_{\mathscr{D}}(P)$ implements Q.

PROOF: The result follows from the following lemma.

Lemma 3.2
If the set $\mathscr{D} \subseteq \mathscr{P}(\Pi)$ is sound and complete for a structural failure model σ and a distributed system property P, then $\sigma(P)$ implements $\sigma_{\mathscr{D}}(P)$ for $\sigma_{\mathscr{D}}$ being the Didep model that is based on $\mathscr{D}$.

PROOF:
$\langle 1 \rangle 1.$ $\sigma(P)$ implements P
PROOF: As σ is a structural failure model.
$\langle 1 \rangle 2.$ $\sigma(P) \subseteq \{\tau \in \Sigma^{\infty} : F(\tau) \in \mathscr{D}\}$
PROOF: By the definition of $\mathscr{D}$.
$\langle 1 \rangle 3.$ $\sigma_{\mathscr{D}}(P) \equiv P \cap \{\tau \in \Sigma^{\infty} : F(\tau) \subset \mathscr{D}\}$
PROOF: By the definition of set-based structural failure models.
$\langle 1 \rangle 4.$ Q.E.D.
PROOF: By $\langle 1 \rangle 1 - \langle 1 \rangle 3$.

While some information may be lost when abstracting structural failure models by sets, Didep models are precise enough to describe dependent faults. We now show that their precision suffices to distinguish whether a model describes independent, undirected dependent, and directed dependent faults.

Didep Models and Dependent Faults We relate independent and dependent faults to Didep models by the following three theorems. In particular, it turns out that monotonicity and symmetry of sound and complete sets characterise whether faults are independent, undirected dependent, or directed dependent. Let $\mathscr{D} \subseteq \mathscr{P}(\Pi)$ be a sound and complete set for a distributed system property P and a structural failure model σ.

Theorem 3.5
σ describes independent faults for P iff $\mathscr{D}$ is monotone and symmetric in $F(\sigma(P))$.

PROOF: Remember that $\mathscr{D} = \{F(\tau) \subseteq \Pi : \tau \in \sigma(P)\}$ is unique. In step 1, we prove that $\mathscr{D}$ is monotone and symmetric in $F(\sigma(P))$ if faults are independent in $\sigma(P)$. In step 2, we prove the opposite direction.
$\langle 1 \rangle 1.$ ASSUME: Faults are independent in $\sigma(P)$.
PROVE: $\mathscr{D}$ is monotone and symmetric in $F(\sigma(P))$.
PROOF: We separately prove that $\mathscr{D}$ is monotone in step 1 and is symmetric in step 2.

$\langle 2 \rangle 1$. $\mathscr{D}$ is monotone.

PROOF: It suffices to prove that if $\tau_0 \in \sigma(P)$ and $D \subseteq F(\tau_0)$, then $D \in \mathscr{D}$. The proof is by induction, with the base case proved in step 1 and the induction step in step 2.

ASSUME: $\tau_0 \in \sigma(P), D \subseteq F(\tau_0)$

PROVE: $D \in \mathscr{D}$

LET:
- $\{p_1, \ldots, p_n\} = F(\tau_0) \setminus D$
- $D_i = F(\tau_0) \setminus \{p_1, \ldots, p_i\}$ for $1 \leq i \leq n$

$\langle 3 \rangle 1$. $D_0 \in \mathscr{D}$

PROOF: By the definition of $\mathscr{D}$ as $D_0 = F(\tau_0)$.

$\langle 3 \rangle 2$. If $D_i \in \mathscr{D}$, then $D_{i+1} \in \mathscr{D}$ for $i < n$.

PROOF: By the definition of $\mathscr{D}$ and Lemma 3.1 (p. 65), $\exists \tau_i \in \sigma(P) : D_i = F(\tau_i)$. By the definition of D_i, $p_{i+1} \in D_i$. By the first condition of independent faults, $\exists \tau_{i+1} \in \sigma(P) : F(\tau_{i+1}) = F(\tau_i) \setminus \{p_{i+1}\}$. As $D_{i+1} = F(\tau_{i+1})$, $D_{i+1} \in \mathscr{D}$ by Lemma 3.1.

$\langle 3 \rangle 3$. Q.E.D.

PROOF: By $\langle 3 \rangle 1$, $\langle 3 \rangle 2$, and mathematical induction, $D_n \in \mathscr{D}$. By the definition of D_i, $D_n = D$.

$\langle 2 \rangle 2$. $\mathscr{D}$ is symmetric in $F(\sigma(P))$.

PROOF: We prove the two conditions of symmetric sets in separate steps.

PROVE:
- $\forall D \in \mathscr{D} : D \subseteq F(\sigma(P))$
- $\forall D_1, D_2 \subseteq F(\sigma(P)) : |D_1| = |D_2| \wedge D_2 \in \mathscr{D} \Rightarrow D_1 \in \mathscr{D}$

$\langle 3 \rangle 1$. $\forall D \in \mathscr{D} : D \subseteq F(\sigma(P))$

PROOF: Immediately from the definition of $F(\sigma(P))$ and $\mathscr{D}$.

$\langle 3 \rangle 2$. $\forall D_1, D_2 \subseteq F(\sigma(P)) : |D_1| = |D_2| \wedge D_2 \in \mathscr{D} \Rightarrow D_1 \in \mathscr{D}$

PROOF: It suffices to prove this for some arbitrary $D_1, D_2 \subseteq F(\sigma(P))$. The proof is by induction, with the base case proved in step 1 and the induction step in step 2.

ASSUME: $D_1, D_2 \subseteq F(\sigma(P)), |D_1| = |D_2|, D_2 \in \mathscr{D}$

PROVE: $D_1 \in \mathscr{D}$

LET:
- $\{p_1, \ldots, p_n\} = D_2 \setminus D_1$
- $\{q_1, \ldots, q_n\} = D_1 \setminus D_2$
- $F_i = D_2 \setminus \{p_1, \ldots, p_i\} \cup \{q_1, \ldots, q_i\}$ for $1 \leq i \leq n$

$\langle 4 \rangle 1$. $F_0 \in \mathscr{D}$

PROOF: By assumption as $F_0 = D_2$.

$\langle 4 \rangle 2$. If $F_i \in \mathscr{D}$, then $F_{i+1} \in \mathscr{D}$ for $i < n$.

PROOF: By Lemma 3.1, $\exists \tau_i \in \sigma(P) : F_i = F(\tau_i)$. As $p_{i+1} \in F_i$ by the definition of F_i and $q_{i+1} \in F(\sigma(P))$, $\exists \tau'_{i+1} \in \sigma(P) : F(\tau_i) \setminus \{p_{i+1}\} \cup \{q_{i+1}\} \subseteq F(\tau'_{i+1})$ by the second condition of independent faults. By the definition of $\mathscr{D}$ and as $\mathscr{D}$ is monotone by $\langle 2 \rangle 1$, $F_{i+1} \in \mathscr{D}$ as $F_{i+1} = F(\tau_i) \setminus \{p_{i+1}\} \cup \{q_{i+1}\}$.

$\langle 4 \rangle 3$. Q.E.D.

PROOF: By $\langle 4 \rangle 1$, $\langle 4 \rangle 2$, and mathematical induction, $F_n \in \mathscr{D}$. By the definition of F_i, $F_n = D_1$.

$\langle 3 \rangle 3$. Q.E.D.

PROOF: $\langle 3 \rangle 1$ and $\langle 3 \rangle 2$

$\langle 2 \rangle 3$. Q.E.D.

PROOF: $\langle 2 \rangle 1$ and $\langle 2 \rangle 2$

$\langle 1 \rangle 2$. ASSUME: $\mathscr{D}$ is monotone and symmetric in $F(\sigma(P))$.

PROVE: Faults are independent in $\sigma(P)$.

PROOF: We prove the two conditions of independent faults in separate steps.

$\langle 2 \rangle 1$. $\forall \tau_1 \in \sigma(P), p \in F(\tau_1) : \exists \tau_2 \in \sigma(P) : \quad F(\tau_2) = F(\tau_1) \setminus \{p\}$

PROOF: It suffices to prove this for some arbitrary $\tau_1 \in \sigma(P)$ and $p \in F(\tau_1)$.

ASSUME: $\tau_1 \in \sigma(P), p \in F(\tau_1)$

PROVE: $\exists \tau_2 \in \sigma(P) : F(\tau_2) = F(\tau_1) \setminus \{p\}$

$\langle 3 \rangle 1$. $\exists D_1 \in \mathscr{D} : D_1 = F(\tau_1)$

PROOF: By the definition of $\mathscr{D}$ and Lemma 3.1.

$\langle 3 \rangle 2$. $\exists D_2 \in \mathscr{D} : D_2 = D_1 \setminus \{p\}$

PROOF: As $\mathscr{D}$ is monotone.

$\langle 3 \rangle 3$. $\exists \tau_2 \in \sigma(P) : F(\tau_2) = D_2$

PROOF: By $\langle 3 \rangle 2$ and Lemma 3.1.

$\langle 3 \rangle 4$. Q.E.D.

PROOF: By $\langle 3 \rangle 1$ – $\langle 3 \rangle 3$.

$\langle 2 \rangle 2$. $\forall p_1, p_2 \in F(\sigma(P)), \tau_1 \in \sigma(P) : p_1 \in F(\tau_1) \Rightarrow \exists \tau_2 \in \sigma(P) : F(\tau_1) \setminus \{p_1\} \cup \{p_2\} \subseteq F(\tau_2)$

PROOF: It suffices to prove this for some arbitrary $\tau_1 \in \sigma(P)$, $p_1 \in F(\tau_1)$, and $p_2 \in F(\sigma(P))$.

ASSUME: $\tau_1 \in \sigma(P), p_1 \in F(\tau_1), p_2 \in F(\sigma(P))$

PROVE: $\exists \tau_2 \in \sigma(P) : F(\tau_1) \setminus \{p_1\} \cup \{p_2\} \subseteq F(\tau_2)$

$\langle 3 \rangle 1$. $\exists D_1 \in \mathscr{D} : D_1 = F(\tau_1)$

PROOF: By the definition of $\mathscr{D}$ and Lemma 3.1.

$\langle 3 \rangle 2$. $\exists D_2 \in \mathscr{D} : D_2 = D_1 \setminus \{p_1\} \cup \{p_2\}$

PROOF: As $\mathscr{D}$ is symmetric in $F(\sigma(P))$ and $p_2 \in F(\sigma(P))$.

$\langle 3 \rangle 3$. $\exists \tau_2 \in \sigma(P) : F(\tau_2) = D_2$

PROOF: By $\langle 3 \rangle 2$ and Lemma 3.1.

$\langle 3 \rangle 4$. Q.E.D.

PROOF: By $\langle 3 \rangle 1$ – $\langle 3 \rangle 3$.

$\langle 2 \rangle 3$. Q.E.D.

PROOF: By $\langle 2 \rangle 1$ and $\langle 2 \rangle 2$.

$\langle 1 \rangle 3$. Q.E.D.
PROOF: By $\langle 1 \rangle 1$ and $\langle 1 \rangle 2$

Theorem 3.6
σ describes undirected dependent faults for P iff $\mathscr{D}$ is monotone but not symmetric in $F(\sigma(P))$.

PROOF: In step 1, we prove that $\mathscr{D}$ is monotone but not symmetric in $F(\sigma(P))$ if faults are undirected dependent in $\sigma(P)$. In step 2, we prove the opposite direction.
$\langle 1 \rangle 1$. ASSUME: Faults are undirected dependent in $\sigma(P)$.
PROVE: $\mathscr{D}$ is monotone but not symmetric in $F(\sigma(P))$.
PROOF: We separately prove that $\mathscr{D}$ is monotone in step 1 and is not symmetric in $F(\sigma(P))$ in step 2.
$\langle 2 \rangle 1$. $\mathscr{D}$ is monotone.
PROOF: The proof is equal to the proof of step $\langle 2 \rangle 1$ below step $\langle 1 \rangle 1$ in Theorem 3.5 except for relying on the first condition of undirected dependent faults.
$\langle 2 \rangle 2$. $\mathscr{D}$ is not symmetric in $F(\sigma(P))$.
PROOF: We need to prove that $\exists D_1, D_2 \subseteq F(\sigma(P)) : |D_1| = |D_2| \wedge D_2 \in \mathscr{D} \wedge D_1 \notin \mathscr{D}$.
$\langle 3 \rangle 1$. $\exists p_1, p_2 \in F(\sigma(P)), \tau_1 \in \sigma(P) : p_1 \in F(\tau_1) \wedge \forall \tau_2 \in \sigma(P) : F(\tau_1) \setminus \{p_1\} \cup \{p_2\} \not\subseteq F(\tau_2)$
PROOF: As faults are undirected dependent in $\sigma(P)$.
$\langle 3 \rangle 2$. $\exists D_2 \in \mathscr{D} : D_2 = F(\tau_1)$
PROOF: By the definition of $\mathscr{D}$ and Lemma 3.1.
$\langle 3 \rangle 3$. Let $D_1 = D_2 \setminus \{p_1\} \cup \{p_2\} \subseteq F(\sigma(P))$.
PROOF: Such an D_1 exists, because, by $\langle 3 \rangle 1$, $p_2 \in F(\sigma(P))$ and $D_2 \subseteq F(\sigma(P))$.
$\langle 3 \rangle 4$. $D_1 \notin \mathscr{D}$
PROOF: By $\langle 3 \rangle 1 - \langle 3 \rangle 3$.
$\langle 3 \rangle 5$. Q.E.D.
PROOF: By $\langle 3 \rangle 2$ and the definition of $\mathscr{D}$, $D_2 \subseteq F(\sigma(P))$ and $D_2 \in \mathscr{D}$. By $\langle 3 \rangle 3$, $D_1 \subseteq F(\sigma(P))$ and $|D_1| = |D_2|$. By $\langle 3 \rangle 4$, $D_1 \notin \mathscr{D}$.
$\langle 2 \rangle 3$. Q.E.D.
PROOF: $\langle 2 \rangle 1$ and $\langle 2 \rangle 2$
$\langle 1 \rangle 2$. ASSUME: $\mathscr{D}$ is monotone and not symmetric in $F(\sigma(P))$.
PROVE: Faults are undirected dependent in $\sigma(P)$.
PROOF: We prove the two conditions of undirected dependent faults in separate steps.
$\langle 2 \rangle 1$. $\forall \tau_1 \in \sigma(P), p \in F(\tau_1) : \exists \tau_2 \in \sigma(P) : \quad F(\tau_2) = F(\tau_1) \setminus \{p\}$

PROOF: The proof is equal to the proof of step ⟨2⟩1 below step ⟨1⟩2 in Theorem 3.5.

⟨2⟩2.

$$\exists p_1, p_2 \in F(\sigma(P)), \tau_1 \in \sigma(P): \wedge\, p_1 \in F(\tau_1) \wedge\, \forall \tau_2 \in \sigma(P): F(\tau_1) \setminus \{p_1\} \cup \{p_2\} \not\subseteq F(\tau_2)$$

PROOF:

⟨3⟩1.

$$\exists D_1, D_2 \subseteq F(\sigma(P)), p_1 \in D_2, p_2 \in D_1: \wedge\, D_1 = (D_2 \setminus \{p_1\}) \cup \{p_2\} \wedge\, D_2 \in \mathscr{D} \wedge\, D_1 \notin \mathscr{D}$$

PROOF: As $\mathscr{D}$ is not symmetric,

$$\exists D_1, D_2 \subseteq F(\sigma(P)): |D_1| = |D_2| \wedge D_2 \in \mathscr{D} \wedge D_1 \notin \mathscr{D}.$$

W.l.o.g., we can choose D_1 and D_2 such that they exactly differ in two processes p_1 and p_2.

⟨3⟩2. $\exists \tau_1 \in \sigma(P): D_2 = F(\tau_1)$

PROOF: By the definition of $\mathscr{D}$ and Lemma 3.1.

⟨3⟩3. $\forall D \in \mathscr{D}: D_1 \not\subseteq D$

PROOF: Otherwise, $\mathscr{D}$ would not be monotone, because $D_1 \notin \mathscr{D}$ by ⟨3⟩1.

⟨3⟩4. $\forall \tau_2 \in \sigma(P): D_1 \not\subseteq F(\tau_2)$

PROOF: By the definition of $\mathscr{D}$, Lemma 3.1, and ⟨3⟩3.

⟨3⟩5. Q.E.D.

PROOF: By ⟨3⟩1, $p_1, p_2 \in F(\sigma(P))$. By ⟨3⟩2, $\tau_1 \in \sigma(P)$. By ⟨3⟩2 and ⟨3⟩1, $p_1 \in F(\tau_1)$. By ⟨3⟩4 and ⟨3⟩1, $F(\tau_1) \setminus \{p_1\} \cup \{p_2\} \not\subseteq F(\tau_2)$ for each $\tau_2 \in \sigma(P)$.

⟨2⟩3. Q.E.D.

PROOF: By ⟨2⟩1 and ⟨2⟩2.

⟨1⟩3. Q.E.D.

PROOF: By ⟨1⟩1 and ⟨1⟩2

Theorem 3.7
σ describes directed dependent faults for P iff $\mathscr{D}$ is not monotone.

PROOF: In step 1, we prove that $\mathscr{D}$ is not monotone if faults are directed dependent in $\sigma(P)$. In step 2, we prove the opposite direction.

⟨1⟩1. ASSUME: Faults are directed dependent in $\sigma(P)$.
PROVE: $\mathscr{D}$ is not monotone.

PROOF:

⟨2⟩1. $\exists D_1 \in \mathscr{D}, p \in D_1: \forall \tau_2 \in \sigma(P): \quad F(\tau_2) \neq D_1 \setminus \{p\}$

PROOF: As faults are directed dependent in $\sigma(P)$ and by the definition of $\mathscr{D}$.

⟨2⟩2. $\exists D_2 \subseteq D_1 : D_2 \notin \mathscr{D}$
PROOF: With $D_2 = D_1 \setminus \{p\}$ by ⟨2⟩1 and the definition of $\mathscr{D}$.
⟨2⟩3. Q.E.D.
PROOF: By ⟨2⟩1 and ⟨2⟩2, $D_1 \in \mathscr{D}$, $D_2 \subseteq D_1$, but $D_2 \notin \mathscr{D}$.
⟨1⟩2. ASSUME: $\mathscr{D}$ is not monotone.
PROVE: Faults are directed dependent in $\sigma(P)$.
PROOF:
⟨2⟩1. $\exists \tau_1 \in \sigma(P), D_2 \subseteq F(\tau_1), p \in F(\tau_1) : D_2 = F(\tau_1) \setminus \{p\} \wedge D_2 \notin \mathscr{D}$
PROOF: As $\mathscr{D}$ is not monotone, $\exists \tau_1 \in \sigma(P), D_2 \subseteq F(\tau_1) : D_2 \notin \mathscr{D}$. W.l.o.g., we can choose τ_1 and D_2 such that D_2 equals $F(\tau_1)$ except for a process p.
⟨2⟩2. $\forall \tau_2 \in \sigma(P) : F(\tau_2) \neq D_2$
PROOF: Otherwise, by the definition of $\mathscr{D}$, $D_2 \in \mathscr{D}$, which would contradict ⟨2⟩1.
⟨2⟩3. Q.E.D.
PROOF: By ⟨2⟩1 and ⟨2⟩2.
⟨1⟩3. Q.E.D.
PROOF: By ⟨1⟩1 and ⟨1⟩2

Induced Dependences As the latter theorem asserts, Didep models allow to describe directed dependent faults, which, for example, occur in the case when a process is faulty whenever another process is faulty. More generally, each Didep model $\mathscr{D}$ induces a set of processes U such that there is a process $q \in U$ for each $p \in \Pi$ with p being faulty whenever q is faulty. As we will see later, the processes in U play an important role for the redundancy that a system requires for being fault-tolerant. While such an induced set is not unique for a Didep model, we assume that $\mu(\mathscr{D})$ denotes a unique set obtained by choosing an induced set with minimal cardinality and minimal rank (based on an arbitrary but fixed total order for process sets with equal cardinality). In particular, $\mu(\mathscr{D})$ satisfies

- $\forall p \in \Pi : \exists q \in \mu(\mathscr{D}) : \forall D \in \mathscr{D} : q \in D \Rightarrow p \in D$ and
- (minimality) $\forall U \subset \mu(\mathscr{D}) : \exists p \in \Pi : \forall q \in U : \exists D \in \mathscr{D} : q \in D \wedge p \notin D$

Example 3.16
For example, consider a set of processes $\Pi = \{p_1, \ldots, p_4\}$ and a structural failure model based on

$$\mathscr{D} = \{\emptyset, \{p_1\}, \{p_2\}, \{p_3\}, \{p_1, p_2\}, \{p_3, p_4\}\}.$$

Then, $\mu(\mathscr{D})$ equals $\{p_1, p_2, p_3\}$ (uniquely in this case). The process p_4 is faulty whenever p_3 is faulty and can, therefore, be omitted from $\mu(\mathscr{D})$. Any other processes p cannot be omitted, because $\{p\} \in \mathscr{D}$.

Note that $\mu(\mathscr{D})$ equals Π if $\mathscr{D}$ only describes undirected dependent or independent faults, but is a proper subset of Π in case of directed dependent faults.

3.5.3 Threshold Assumptions and Dependent Faults

The Theorems 3.5 – 3.7 allow to easily evaluate whether a structural failure model describes dependent faults for a distributed system property. If a sound and complete Didep set is is monotone and symmetric, the Didep model describes independent faults and, otherwise, dependent faults. We now abstract threshold assumptions by Didep models and find that threshold assumptions indeed only describe independent faults. More precisely, we refine the criticism found in the literature and show that thresholds only cover independent faults if they describe a structural failure model accurately. If a threshold is not sound and complete, it may also describe dependent faults.

Let us first revisit our definition of threshold assumptions from Example 3.5 (p. 48). Intuitively, a threshold model is a structural failure model that is based on a natural number.

Definition 3.15 (Threshold Model)
A structural failure model σ is based on a threshold $t \in \mathbb{N}$ iff

$$\sigma(P) \equiv P \cap \{\tau \in \Sigma^{\infty} : |F(\tau)| \leq t\}$$

for all distributed system properties P. In this case, we call σ a threshold model.

Analogously to process sets, a threshold may not be an accurate abstraction of a fault assumption. For example, assume a distributed system property P and a structural failure model σ that is based on a threshold t. If P does not have a trace with t failed processes, the property $\sigma(P)$ also does not. Applying σ only ensures that no trace has more than t failed processes, but gives no guarantees that there is a trace with t or less than t faulty processes (except for a trace with no faulty process).

Definition 3.16 (Sound and Complete Thresholds)
A threshold $t \in \mathbb{N}$ is *sound* for a distributed system property P and a structural failure model σ iff

$$\forall M \subseteq F(\sigma(P)) : |M| \leq t \Rightarrow \exists \tau \in \sigma(P) : M = F(\tau).$$

The threshold t is *complete* for P and σ iff

$$\forall \tau \in \sigma(P) : |F(\tau)| \leq t.$$

Hence, if a threshold t is sound, then any combination of less than or equal to t (of possibly faulty) processes are faulty in some trace. If t is complete, no other combination is possible.

The relation between sound and complete thresholds and sound and complete sets can be exploited to show that sound and complete thresholds only describe independent faults.

Lemma 3.3
A threshold $t \in \mathbb{N}$ is sound and complete for a distributed system property P and a structural failure model σ iff the set

$$\mathscr{D} = \{D \subseteq F(\sigma(P)) : |D| \leq t\}$$

is sound and complete for P and σ.

PROOF: We observe that

$$\forall D \in \mathscr{D} : D \subseteq F(\sigma(P)) \wedge |D| \leq t$$

and

$$\forall D \subseteq F(\sigma(P)) : |D| \leq t \Rightarrow D \in \mathscr{D}$$

follow from the definition of $\mathscr{D}$. With these observations, the rest of the proof follows straightforward from the definitions of sound and complete thresholds and sets.

Theorem 3.8
A structural failure model σ describes independent faults for a distributed system property P iff there exists a threshold $t \in \mathbb{N}$ that is sound and complete for P and σ.

PROOF: Assume that P is a distributed system property and σ is a structural failure model.

$\langle 1 \rangle 1$. If there exists a $t \in \mathbb{N}$ that is sound and complete for P and σ, then σ describes independent faults for P.

PROOF: By Lemma 3.3, the set $\mathscr{D} = \{D \subseteq F(\sigma(P)) : |D| \leq t\}$ is sound and complete for P and σ. $\mathscr{D}$ is monotone and symmetric in $F(\sigma(P))$. By Theorem 3.5, σ describes independent faults for P.

$\langle 1 \rangle 2$. If σ describes independent faults for P, then there exists a $t \in \mathbb{N}$ that is sound and complete for P and σ.

PROOF:
By Lemma 3.1, the set $\mathscr{D} = \{F(\tau) \subseteq \Pi : \tau \in \sigma(P)\}$ is sound and complete for P and σ. By Theorem 3.5, $\mathscr{D}$ is monotone and symmetric in $F(\sigma(P))$. There exists a $t \in \mathbb{N}$ such that $\mathscr{D} = \{D \subseteq F(\sigma(P)) : |D| \leq t\}$. By Lemma 3.3, t is sound and complete for P and σ.

$\langle 1 \rangle 3$. Q.E.D.

PROOF: By $\langle 1 \rangle 1$ and $\langle 1 \rangle 2$.

This result confirms previous (informal) criticism on threshold-based fault models for only covering independent faults [Keidar and Marzullo, 2002]. However, the result refines the criticism: only fault models with sound and complete thresholds are affected. Previous criticism implicitly assumed that thresholds are sound and complete if used to describe a failure model. Let us illustrate by an example that inaccurate thresholds may describe dependent faults as well.

Example 3.17
Consider a distributed system property P for two processes p_1 and p_2 and a set of sets of faulty processes

$$\{F(\tau) \subseteq \Pi : \tau \in P\} = \{\emptyset, \{p_1\}, \{p_1, p_2\}\}.$$

In this case, faults are directed dependent in P, because p_2 may be faulty, but not on its own. Let σ be the structural failure model that is based on the threshold $t = 2$. The threshold t is not sound for P and σ as, for $M = \{p_2\}$, $M \subseteq F(\sigma(P))$, $|M| \leq t$, but $\forall \tau \in \sigma(P) : M \neq F(\tau)$. The sound and complete set for P and σ is $\{\emptyset, \{p_1\}, \{p_1, p_2\}\}$, which is neither monotone nor symmetric. Hence, σ describes directed dependent faults for P although σ is a threshold model. The underlying reason for this is that faults are already directed dependent in P.

Set-based models are strictly more expressive than threshold models as they are able to describe dependent faults. This advantage is gained by more complex means of describing a failure model, namely sets instead of thresholds. We now have a look at previously known subclasses of fault models that are given in terms of process sets. As it will turn out, all of these classes are strictly less expressive than the class of Didep models.

3.5.4 Classes of Set-Based Structural Failure Models

The idea to describe fault models in terms of process sets is not new. Different approaches have formalised the extent of faults by sets of processes: Hirt and Maurer [1997] have proposed *adversary structures*, Junqueira and Marzullo [2003b] *core* and *survivor sets*, Malkhi and Reiter [1997] *fail-prone systems*, and Junqueira et al. [2005], Junqueira and Marzullo [2005a] *multi-site models* to specify possibly faulty processes by sets. We give a brief overview of these approaches and classify them with respect to their expressiveness. It will turn out that the class of Didep models is strictly more expressive than each of these classes. Therefore, Didep models allow to model some fault assumptions more accurately.

Adversary Structures Hirt and Maurer [1997] have introduced the notion of *adversary structures* for the domain of secure multi-party computation (i.e., computations that tolerate faulty processes while keeping the input of correct processes private). An adversary structure is defined as the monotone set of all subsets of processes (also called "players") that are possibly faulty in a trace. For example, the adversary structure

$$\mathscr{A} = \{\emptyset, \{p_1\}, \{p_2\}, \{p_3\}, \{p_1, p_2\}\} \tag{3.1}$$

for a set of processes $\Pi = \{p_1, p_2, p_3\}$ denotes that either no process is faulty, exactly one process is faulty, or only p_1 and p_2 are faulty.

Adversary structures are inspired by the notion of *access structures* for sharing secrets. For sharing a secret, the secret is split into *shares* that are distributed to different processes. A subset of the shares is necessary to reconstruct the secret. An access structure is the set of all subsets of processes whose shares are qualified to reconstruct the secret [Ito et al., 1987, Benaloh and Leichter, 1988]. Access structures generalise previously used thresholds for reconstructing secrets ("reconstructing the secret requires to access at least t processes"). Hirt and Maurer [1997] have adapted this notion by describing possibly faulty processes with sets and applied this model to secure multi-party computations under the assumption that a faulty process may behave arbitrarily. They present an implementation for such computations that tolerates an adversary structure iff no three sets in the structure add up to the whole process set. This strictly generalises threshold-based results, which state that less than $n/3$ faulty processes can be tolerated [Ben-Or et al., 1988].

The implementation of Hirt and Maurer [1997] also solves some fault-tolerant distributed computing problems (e.g., agreement and broadcast) as these are special cases of secure multi-party computations. However, the implementation is not efficient in this case: the computation and message complexity is exponential in the number of processes in general. Problems of fault tolerance can be solved more efficiently by dedicated solutions. For example, Fitzi and Maurer [1998] have presented a solution with polynomial computation and message complexity to the problem of Byzantine consensus. Subsequently, adversary structures have been used to develop various solutions to fault tolerance problems. For example, Cachin [2001] has presented an architecture for secure and fault-tolerant service replication in the context of the MAFTIA project[3] that investigated how to tolerate malicious and accidental faults in Internet applications.

So far, adversary structures have only been used in the context of process failure models; channels are assumed to be correct. While adversary structures as used by Hirt and Maurer [1997] and Fitzi and Maurer [1998] are defined for single process failure modes (e.g., Byzantine failures), Fitzi et al. [1999] extended adversary structures to multiple modes: they define a *hybrid adversary structure* as a set of pairs of sets of processes. The first element of such a pair denotes the processes that fail arbitrarily, the second element denotes the processes that eavesdrop. For example, the hybrid adversary structure

$$\{(\emptyset,\emptyset),(\{p_1\},\emptyset),(\{p_2\},\emptyset),(\{p_3\},\emptyset),(\emptyset,\{p_3\}),(\{p_1\},\{p_3\})\}$$

[3]`http://www.maftia.org/`

for a set of processes $\Pi = \{p_1, p_2, p_3\}$ denotes that either exactly one process fails arbitrarily, only p_3 eavesdrop on other processes, or p_1 fails arbitrarily and p_3 eavesdrop on other processes.

Adversary structures are not bound to a particular failure mode. They can be used with different failure modes such as crash or crash-recovery failures. In particular, eavesdropping – being of minor importance for traditional fault tolerance – can be substituted for another failure mode when using hybrid adversary structures. For example, Kursawe and Freiling [2005] have used hybrid adversary structures to combine Byzantine and crash failures.

We focus on adversary structures for single failure modes. Hirt and Maurer [1997] define an adversary structure as the monotone set of all subsets of processes that are possibly faulty in a trace. Hence, an adversary structure immediately describes a set-based structural failure model.

Definition 3.17 (Adversary Structure Model)
An adversary structure is a monotone set $\mathscr{A} \subseteq \mathscr{P}(\Pi)$ of process sets. We call a set-based structural failure σ an adversary structure model iff σ is based on an adversary structure.

The advantage of adversary structures over thresholds lies in being more expressive; sound and complete adversary structures may describe independent as well as dependent faults. For example, consider the adversary structure $\mathscr{A}$ given in Equation 3.1. The structural failure model based on $\mathscr{A}$ cannot be accurately described by a threshold as such a threshold must be greater than or equal to 2 to allow p_1 and p_2 to be faulty in a trace. However, such a threshold permits p_2 and p_3 to be faulty in a trace, which is not allowed by $\mathscr{A}$. Indeed, the class of threshold models is strictly less expressive than the class of adversary structures. We will look into the relationships between different classes of structural failure models in more detail below.

While adversary structures can describe dependent faults, they are not able to describe all kinds of dependent faults. In particular, they can describe undirected dependent faults but not directed dependent faults.

Corollary 3.3
If an adversary structure $\mathscr{A}$ is sound and complete for a distributed system property P and a structural failure model σ, σ describes independent faults for P if $\mathscr{A}$ is symmetric in $F(\sigma(P))$ and, otherwise, undirected dependent faults.

PROOF: Immediately from the Theorems 3.5–3.7 as an adversary structure is monotone by definition.

Next, we consider the class of fail-prone systems that were developed independently to adversary structures. They also describe structural failure models by process sets and, as we will see, are equivalent to adversary structures. The difference between both kinds of models is purely syntactical; fail-prone systems omit redundant nonmaximal process sets that are included in adversary structures. Hence, a fail-prone system requires less sets than an adversary structures to describe the same structural failure model.

Fail-Prone Systems Malkhi and Reiter [1997, 1998] have introduced the notion of *fail-prone systems* while studying *Byzantine quorums*. Quorums are sets of processes that are accessed before performing a critical operation that requires coordination or agreement. They are widely used means to implement coordination in fault-tolerant distributed systems. We will address quorums in more detail in Chapter 4. Whereas traditionally being used to tolerate "benign" (e.g., crash or crash-recovery) faults, Malkhi and Reiter [1997] were the first to study requirements and constructions of quorums for arbitrary faults. Subsequently, fail-prone systems have been adopted by others [Bazzi, 2000, Martin et al., 2002] for further quorum constructions.

Malkhi and Reiter [1997] define a fail-prone system $\mathscr{B}$ as a set of maximal subsets of processes (called "servers"). For each set B in $\mathscr{B}$, there is a trace that has some subset of B as faulty processes. A set B in $\mathscr{B}$ is maximal in the sense that no proper superset of B is in $\mathscr{B}$. For example, the fail-prone system

$$\mathscr{B} = \{\{p_3\}, \{p_1, p_2\}\}$$

for a set of processes $\Pi = \{p_1, p_2, p_3\}$ denotes that, for a trace, either

- no process is faulty as the empty set is a subset of $\{p_3\}$ and of $\{p_1, p_2\}$,
- exactly one process is faulty as $\{p_1\}$ and $\{p_2\}$ are subsets of $\{p_1, p_2\}$ and $\{p_3\}$ is a subset of $\{p_3\}$, or
- only p_1 and p_2 are faulty as $\{p_1, p_2\}$ is a subset of $\{p_1, p_2\}$.

While an adversary structure immediately describes a set-based structural failure model, the subsets of the sets in a fail-prone system describe a set-based structural failure model. In other words, the monotone closure of a fail-prone system describes the structural failure model.

Definition 3.18 (Fail-Prone System Model)
A fail-prone system is a set $\mathscr{B} \subseteq \mathscr{P}(\Pi)$ of process sets with

$$\forall B_1, B_2 \in \mathscr{B} : B_1 \not\subset B_2.$$

We call a set-based structural failure model σ a fail-prone system model iff σ is based on the monotone closure $\kappa_M(\mathscr{B})$ of a fail-prone system $\mathscr{B}$.

As the monotone closure of a set is monotone, faults are at most undirected dependent if accurately described by a fail-prone system. Analogously to adversary structures, they cannot accurately describe any directed dependent faults.

Corollary 3.4
If the monotone closure $\kappa_M(\mathscr{B})$ of a fail-prone system $\mathscr{B}$ is sound and complete for a distributed system property P and a structural failure model σ, σ describes independent faults for P if $\mathscr{B}$ is symmetric in $F(\sigma(P))$ and, otherwise, undirected dependent faults for P.

PROOF: The monotone closure $\kappa_M(\mathscr{B})$ of a fail-prone system $\mathscr{B}$ is monotone. By Theorem 3.5 and 3.6, σ either describes independent or undirected dependent faults then. $\mathscr{B}$ is symmetric in $F(\sigma(P))$ iff $\kappa_M(\mathscr{B})$ is as well. If $\kappa_M(\mathscr{B})$ is symmetric in $F(\sigma(P))$, then, by Theorem 3.5, σ describes independent faults for P. Otherwise, by Theorem 3.6, σ describes undirected dependent faults for P.

When comparing the examples for fail-prone systems and for adversary structures above, the close relationship between fail-prone systems and adversary structures is obvious. By definition, all sets in a fail-prone system $\mathscr{B}$ are maximal, that is, no set is a superset of another set in $\mathscr{B}$. Semantically, $\mathscr{B}$ allows all subsets of each set in $\mathscr{B}$ (and only these subsets) to be faulty. Each adversary structure also contains some maximal sets and, in particular, is uniquely defined by its maximal sets: the monotone closure of the maximal sets of an adversary structure equals the adversary structure itself. As each adversary structure $\mathscr{A}$ is monotone, it allows all subsets of each maximal set in $\mathscr{A}$ (and only these subsets) to be faulty. Hence, the sets in fail-prone systems correspond to the maximal sets in adversary structures. In fact, fail-prone systems describe the same class of structural failure models as adversary structures. The only difference lies in syntactically omitting the nonmaximal sets. These sets are redundant, because they are in the monotone closure of the maximal sets.

Similarly to adversary structures, fail-prone systems only have been used for process failure models so far; channels are assumed to be correct. In contrast to adversary structures, no hybrid extension to support multiple failure modes has been proposed so far. However, an extension analogously to the extension for adversary structures would be straightforward.

While the close relationship between adversary structures and fail-prone systems is easy to see, the relationship between adversary structures and the class of core and survivor set models is less obvious, although the latter are expressed in terms of process sets as well.

Cores / Survivor Sets Junqueira and Marzullo [2001] have introduced the notion of *cores* and *survivor sets* to model dependent faults. They define a core as a minimal subset of processes. For each trace, at least one process in the core is not faulty. A core is minimal in the sense that no proper subset of a core forms a core (for the same system property). A survivor set is a minimal subset of processes such that, for some trace, all of the processes are nonfaulty. Analogously to cores, a survivor set is minimal in the sense that no proper subset of a survivor set forms a survivor. Junqueira [2006] has shown that cores and survivor sets are equivalent ways of describing faults and give a mapping between both representations: Given a set of cores, the corresponding set of survivor sets is the set of all minimal subsets of processes that intersect every core. Given a set of survivor sets, the corresponding set of cores is the set of all minimal subsets of processes that intersect every survivor set.

For example, consider a system that consists of three processes $\Pi = \{p_1, p_2, p_3\}$. The set of cores $\{\{p_1, p_3\}, \{p_2, p_3\}\}$ denotes that, for each trace, at least one of $\{p_1, p_3\}$ and at least one of $\{p_2, p_3\}$ is not faulty. Hence, either

- no process is faulty,
- exactly one process is faulty as, in this case, either p_3 is not faulty or p_1 and p_2 are not faulty, or
- only p_1 and p_2 are faulty as, in this case, p_3 is not faulty.

A corresponding set of survivor sets is $\{\{p_3\}, \{p_1, p_2\}\}$ as

- p_3 is not faulty if p_1 and p_2 are jointly faulty and
- p_1 and p_2 are not faulty if p_3 is faulty.

Both sets correspond to an adversary structure $\{\emptyset, \{p_1\}, \{p_2\}, \{p_3\}, \{p_1, p_2\}\}$.

Cores and survivor sets have been used to study different problems of fault-tolerant distributed computing. In particular, reaching consensus was addressed in detail. Junqueira and Marzullo [2001] have considered the synchronous timing model with crash failures and studied necessary and sufficient conditions to solve consensus in terms of cores and survivor sets. Their results generalise results previously obtained with threshold models. Subsequently, they have extended their studies of consensus to Byzantine failures and the asynchronous timing model with failure detectors [Junqueira and Marzullo, 2002b,a, 2003b, Junqueira, 2006]. Besides consensus, cores and survivor sets were used to study the problem of "weak leader election" [Junqueira and Marzullo, 2005d] and to design a distributed backup system [Junqueira et al., 2003, 2005].

While adversary structures and fail-prone systems have been used to design and evaluate fault-tolerant implementations, the question how to construct such models has largely been neglected. Junqueira and Marzullo [2001], Junqueira [2006] have shown how to derive cores and survivor sets, for example, from probabilistic fault assumptions and assumptions that explicitly model causes for failures. We will further discuss such mappings in Section 3.7. In contrast to adversary structures, no hybrid extension of cores and survivor sets has been proposed yet.

As Junqueira and Marzullo [2001] have shown that cores and survivor sets are equivalent means to describe a fault assumption, it suffices to focus on survivor sets. A survivor set S denotes that there is at least one trace such that the processes in the set are not faulty. It permits all traces whose set of faulty processes is a subset of its complement $\Pi \setminus S$. A set of survivor sets permits all traces, whose set of faulty processes is a subset of the complement of a survivor. In other words, it describes a structural failure model that is based on the monotone closure of the complements of each survivor set.

Definition 3.19 (Survivor Sets Model)
A set of survivor sets is a set $\mathscr{S} \subseteq \mathscr{P}(\Pi)$ of process sets with

$$\forall S_1, S_2 \in \mathscr{S} : S_1 \not\subset S_2.$$

We call a set-based structural failure model σ a survivor sets model iff σ is based on the monotone closure $\kappa_M(\{\Pi \setminus S : S \in \mathscr{S}\})$ for a set of survivor sets $\mathscr{S}$.

When comparing the definitions of survivor sets and fail-prone systems, it becomes obvious that both are complementary. A survivor set permits that all subsets of its complement are faulty, while a set B in a fail-prone system permits all subsets of B are faulty; that is, a set of survivor sets and a corresponding fail-prone system are elementwise complementary.

Lemma 3.4
If $\mathscr{S}$ is a set of survivor sets, then $\mathscr{B} = \{\Pi \setminus S : S \in \mathscr{S}\}$ is a fail-prone system.

PROOF: We prove this by contraposition.
ASSUME: $\mathscr{B}$ is not a fail-prone system.
PROVE: $\mathscr{S}$ is not a set of survivor sets.

$\langle 1 \rangle 1.$ $\exists B_1, B_2 \in \mathscr{B} : B_1 \subset B_2$
PROOF: As $\mathscr{B}$ is a set of process sets, but not a fail-prone system.

$\langle 1 \rangle 2.$ $\exists S_1, S_1 \in \mathscr{S} : (\Pi \setminus S_1) = B_1 \quad \wedge \quad (\Pi \setminus S_2) = B_2$
PROOF: By the construction of $\mathscr{B}$ and $\langle 1 \rangle 1$.

$\langle 1 \rangle 3.$ $S_2 \subset S_1$
PROOF: By $\langle 1 \rangle 1$, $\langle 1 \rangle 2$, and simple set theory.

$\langle 1 \rangle 4.$ Q.E.D.
PROOF: By $\langle 1 \rangle 2$ and $\langle 1 \rangle 3$, we have a set in $\mathscr{S}$ that is a proper subset of another set in $\mathscr{S}$. Hence, at least one set in $\mathscr{S}$ is not minimal violating the definition of survivor sets.

As we will see below, the classes of fail-prone systems and survivor sets are equivalent and, therefore, cores and survivor sets only describe independent or undirected dependent faults. In analogy to fail-prone systems, a survivor sets model based on $\mathscr{S}$ describes independent faults for a distributed system property P if $\mathscr{S}$ is symmetric in $F(\sigma(P))$.

Corollary 3.5
If $\mathscr{S}$ is a set of survivor sets and $\kappa_M(\{\Pi \setminus S : S \in \mathscr{S}\})$ is sound and complete for a distributed system property P and a structural failure model σ, σ describes independent faults for P if $\mathscr{S}$ is symmetric in $F(\sigma(P))$ and σ describes undirected dependent faults for P otherwise.

PROOF: Given a set $\mathscr{S}$ of survivor sets, the set $\mathscr{B} = \{\Pi \setminus S : S \in \mathscr{S}\}$ is a fail-prone system by Lemma 3.4. In particular, $\mathscr{S}$ is symmetric in $F(\sigma(P))$ iff $\mathscr{B}$ is symmetric in $F(\sigma(P))$. As $\kappa_M(\{\Pi \setminus S : S \in \mathscr{S}\}) = \kappa_M(\mathscr{B})$, the corollary follows from Corollary 3.4.

All models presented so far are based on subsets of Π. For large-scale systems with many processes, such approaches result in a large number of sets, which may be inconvenient. In addition to cores and survivor sets, Junqueira and Marzullo have also given further fault models that are dedicated to multi-site systems, whose processes are partitioned into sites. These fault models generally require less sets for describing a fault assumption, while allowing to describe dependent faults.

Multi-Site Models A large-scale distributed system is often a *multi-site system* that consists of a set of sites, each containing a set of processes. Junqueira and Marzullo [2005c,a] have empirically evaluated different multi-site systems and found that complete sites frequently become unavailable. Possible reasons are power outages, failures of shared resources, and network problems. Motivated by this observation, they introduced different fault models, namely *multi-site threshold models*, *multi-site hierarchical models*, and *multi-site bimodal models*, which explicitly consider such site faults. A multi-site failure model describes that – in addition to single processes – complete sites may be faulty. If a site is faulty, all its processes are faulty, which models, for example, the loss of a critical resource such as power.

Junqueira and Marzullo [2005a,c] use multi-site models to construct quorum sets that are more available and have smaller sizes than quorum sets that are constructed from threshold models. They demonstrate the benefits of such a construction by running an implementation of Paxos [Lamport, 1998] (a variant of the consensus problem) in a multi-site system. The implementation shows better availability and response times than previous ones due to the quorum construction.

For a multi-site system, the set of sites is assumed to be a partition of the set of processes. Let $\mathscr{Z} \subseteq \mathscr{P}(\Pi)$ be a partition of the set of processes Π, that is,

- $\mathscr{Z} = \{Z_1, \dots, Z_m\}$,
- $Z_i \subseteq \Pi, Z_i \neq \emptyset$ for $1 \leq i \leq m$,
- $\bigcup_{1 \leq i \leq m} Z_i = \Pi$, and
- $\forall Z_i, Z_j \in \mathscr{Z} : Z_i \neq Z_j \Rightarrow Z_i \cap Z_j = \emptyset$.

A *multi-site threshold model* describes faults by two kinds of thresholds: The threshold $t_{\mathscr{Z}}$ describes how many sites are faulty at most; the threshold t_i describes how many processes of site $Z_i \in \mathscr{Z}$ are faulty at most if Z_i is not faulty.

Definition 3.20 (Multi-Site Threshold Model)
A structural failure model σ is based on a threshold $t_{\mathscr{Z}} \in \mathbb{N}$ and thresholds $t_i \in \mathbb{N}$ for each $Z_i \in \mathscr{Z}$ iff

$$\begin{aligned}\sigma(P) \equiv P \cap \{\tau \in \Sigma^\infty : \\ &\wedge \forall Z_i \in \mathscr{Z} : Z_i \subseteq F(\tau) \vee |Z_i \cap F(\tau)| \leq t_i \\ &\wedge |\{Z \in \mathscr{Z} : Z \subseteq F(\tau)\}| \leq t_{\mathscr{Z}}\}\end{aligned}$$

for all distributed system properties P. In this case, we call σ a multi-site threshold model.

Multi-site threshold models describe independent process faults within a site and independent faults for complete sites. Nevertheless, the resulting fault model includes some dependent faults: Consider a multi-site threshold model with at most one faulty site and a site $Z_i \in \mathscr{Z}$ with 3 processes and $t_i = 1$. As an arbitrary site may be faulty, Z_i may be faulty in a trace. Hence, all 3 processes in Z_i can be faulty. However, the model does not permit any trace in which only two processes of Z_i are faulty. Hence, two processes of Z_i being faulty enforce that the third process is faulty as well.

Subsequently, Junqueira and Marzullo [2005a] have extended multi-site threshold models to *multi-site hierarchical models*, which additionally cover dependent process faults within a site and dependent site faults. In particular, the thresholds are replaced by fail-prone systems: Instead of a threshold for site faults, the set $\mathscr{B}_{\mathscr{Z}} \subseteq \mathscr{P}(\mathscr{Z})$ gives a "site fail-prone system"; that is, the set of maximal subsets of sites that are possibly faulty in the same trace. Instead of thresholds for the respective sites, there is a set $\mathscr{B}_i$ for each site Z_i that gives a fail-prone system for Z_i if Z_i is not faulty.

Definition 3.21 (Multi-Site Hierarchical Model)
A multi-site hierarchical model is based on a tuple of sets $\mathscr{B}_{\mathscr{Z}} \subseteq \mathscr{P}(\mathscr{Z})$ and $\mathscr{B}_i \subseteq \mathscr{P}(\Pi)$ for each $Z_i \in \mathscr{Z}$ with

$$\forall B_{\mathscr{Z}_i}, B_{\mathscr{Z}_j} \in \mathscr{B}_{\mathscr{Z}} : B_{\mathscr{Z}_i} \not\subseteq B_{\mathscr{Z}_j} \quad \text{and} \quad \forall Z_k \in \mathscr{Z} : \forall B_i, B_j \in \mathscr{B}_k : B_i \not\subseteq B_j.$$

A set-based structural failure model σ is based on $\mathscr{B}_{\mathscr{Z}} \subseteq \mathscr{P}(\mathscr{Z})$ and $\mathscr{B}_i \subseteq \mathscr{P}(\Pi), Z_i \in \mathscr{Z}$ iff σ is based on

$$\{D \subseteq \Pi : \wedge \exists B_{\mathscr{Z}} \in \mathscr{B}_{\mathscr{Z}} : \{Z \in \mathscr{Z} : Z \subseteq D\} \subseteq B_{\mathscr{Z}} \\ \wedge \forall Z_i \in \mathscr{Z} : Z_i \not\subseteq D \Rightarrow \exists B \in \mathscr{B}_i : Z_i \cap D \subseteq B\}.$$

The set of faulty sites $\{Z \in \mathscr{Z} : Z \subseteq D\}$ must be permitted by $\mathscr{B}_{\mathscr{Z}}$. The set of faulty processes $Z_i \cap D$ in a nonfaulty site Z_i must be permitted by $\mathscr{B}_i$. In this case, we call σ a multi-site hierarchical model.

Junqueira and Marzullo [2005a] have presented a construction of highly available quorum sets from multi-site hierarchical models: Survivor sets are constructed from a multi-site hierarchical model and directly used as quorums if the sets pairwise intersect. If this is not the case, some survivor sets need to be removed, which they show to be an NP-hard problem. Additionally, they have introduced a variant of multi-site hierarchical models, the *multi-site bimodal models*, that allow to efficiently determine which survivor sets need to be removed when necessary.

Essentially, a multi-site bimodal model is given in the same terms – $\mathscr{B}_{\mathscr{Z}}$ and $\mathscr{B}_i$ for each $Z_i \in \mathscr{Z}$ – as a multi-site hierarchical model. Additionally, a bimodal model distinguishes a site $Z \in \mathscr{Z}$ that must not be included in any $B_{\mathscr{Z}} \in \mathscr{B}_{\mathscr{Z}}$. Moreover, a bimodal model permits that all sites except one arbitrary site are faulty. If a site is the only nonfaulty one, all processes in this site are assumed to be nonfaulty. Note that Z is faulty iff all other sites except for one are faulty as well. Hence, if faults are modelled by a multi-site bimodal model, a system may operate in one of two modes: Faults follow a given multi-site hierarchical model or the processes of a single site and only these processes are faulty.

Definition 3.22 (Multi-Site Bimodal Model)
A multi-site bimodal model is described by a tuple of sets $\mathscr{B}_{\mathscr{Z}} \subseteq \mathscr{P}(\mathscr{Z})$ and $\mathscr{B}_i \subseteq \mathscr{P}(\Pi)$ for each $Z_i \in \mathscr{Z}$ with

- $\forall B_{\mathscr{Z}_i}, B_{\mathscr{Z}_j} \in \mathscr{B}_{\mathscr{Z}} : B_{\mathscr{Z}_i} \not\subseteq B_{\mathscr{Z}_j}$,
- $\forall Z_k \in \mathscr{Z} : \forall B_i, B_j \in \mathscr{B}_k : B_i \not\subseteq B_j$, and
- $\exists Z \in \mathscr{Z} : \forall B_{\mathscr{Z}} \in \mathscr{B}_{\mathscr{Z}} : Z \notin B_{\mathscr{Z}}$.

A set-based structural failure model σ is a multi-site bimodal model iff σ is based on

$$\begin{aligned}&\{D \subseteq \Pi : \wedge \exists B_{\mathscr{Z}} \in \mathscr{B}_{\mathscr{Z}} : \{Z \in \mathscr{Z} : Z \subseteq D\} \subseteq B_{\mathscr{Z}} \\ &\qquad \wedge \forall Z_i \in \mathscr{Z} : Z_i \not\subseteq D \Rightarrow \exists B \in \mathscr{B}_i : (Z_i \cap D) \subseteq B\} \\ &\cup \{D \subseteq \Pi : \exists Z \in \mathscr{Z} : D = \Pi \setminus Z\}.\end{aligned}$$

Compared to multi-site hierarchical models, bimodal models impose additional restrictions to allow for a simple construction of quorum systems. In particular, no bimodal model permits that all processes become faulty. This restriction is handy for comparing bimodal models to other classes of structural failure models. As most classes allow to model that all processes become faulty, these classes are not less expressive than the class of bimodal models.

Lemma 3.5
If a multi-site bimodal model is based on $\mathscr{D} \subseteq \mathscr{P}(\Pi)$, then $\Pi \notin \mathscr{D}$.

PROOF: For each $D \in \mathscr{D}$, there is a site such that the site is not a subset of D from the definition of bimodal models. As the site is a subset of Π, Π is not in $\mathscr{D}$.

Bimodal models have some properties of theoretical interest. Besides allowing simple quorum constructions [Junqueira and Marzullo, 2005a], they allow to describe some directed dependent faults although they are not able to describe all kinds of independent faults. For example, a threshold model can describe that all processes may be faulty. This cannot be described by a bimodal model although faults are "only" independent. We now look into the relationships among the presented classes of structural failure models in more detail.

Relationships among Classes In general, a more expressive class of structural failure models allows to find more resilient and more efficient solutions to a given problem while being less tractable. As a special case, a problem may be solvable under an expressive class, while being impossible to solve under a less expressive class. Let us now have a look at the relationships among the classes presented so far.

Figure 3.2 summarises the resulting relationships. All presented classes are strictly less expressive than the class of Didep models. The class of threshold models is strictly less expressive than all other classes except for the class of bimodal models. The class of bimodal models is orthogonal to all other classes: It is neither less expressive than any other class (except for the Didep class) nor is any other class less expressive than the class of bimodal models. The classes based on adversary structures, core / survivor sets, and fail-prone systems are equivalent and

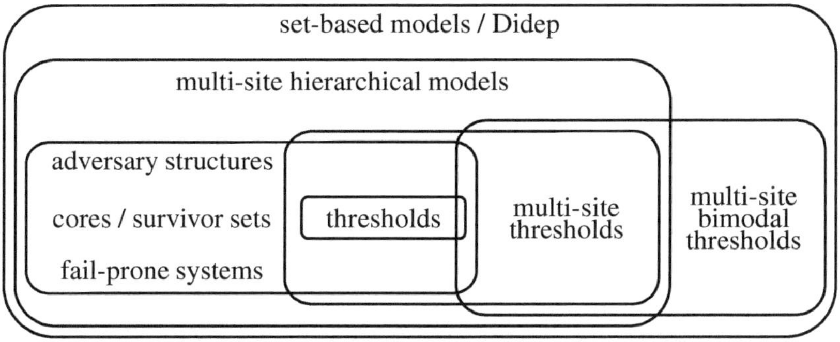

Figure 3.2: Hierarchy of structural failure model classes. Class A is a proper subset of class B iff A is strictly less expressive than B. Class A equals class B iff A is equivalent to B. A and B are not equal but have a nonempty intersection iff A is not less expressive than B and B is not less expressive than A.

strictly less expressive than the class of multi-site hierarchical models. The class of multi-site threshold models is neither less expressive than the class of adversary structures nor vice versa, but strictly less expressive than the class of multi-site hierarchical models. We prove the relationships shown in Fig. 3.2 in the following theorem. We only prove the necessary relationships, others follow from the transitivity of the less-expressive-than relation.

Theorem 3.9
The classes of structural failure models are related to each other as shown in Fig. 3.2.

PROOF: We prove each relationship separately. To prove that a class C_1 is strictly less expressive than a class C_2, we need to show that C_1 is less expressive than C_2, but not vice versa. To prove that C_1 is equivalent to C_2, we need to show that C_1 is less expressive than C_2 and vice versa.

$\langle 1 \rangle$1. The class of threshold models is strictly less expressive than the class of multi-site threshold models.

PROOF: Each threshold model is based on a number $t \in \mathbb{N}$. Such a model equals a multi-site threshold model with $\mathscr{Z} = \{\Pi\}$, $t_{\mathscr{Z}} = 0$ and $t_i = t$ for each site $Z_i \in \mathscr{Z}$.

The multi-site threshold model with $t_{\mathscr{Z}} = 1$ and $t_i = 1$ for each $Z_i \in \mathscr{Z}$ cannot be based on a simple threshold: Consider a distributed system with $\Pi = \{p_1, p_2, p_3\}$, where all processes are in a single site. The multi-site model is based on $\{\emptyset, \{p_1\}, \{p_2\}, \{p_3\}, \Pi\}$. This cannot be described by a threshold model.

⟨1⟩2. The class of threshold models is strictly less expressive than the class of adversary structure models.

PROOF: Each threshold model σ is based on a number $t \in \mathbb{N}$ and, therefore, based on $\mathscr{D} = \{D \subseteq F(\sigma(P)) : |D| \leq t\}$ for a distributed system property P. As this set is monotone, it is an adversary structure. Hence, σ is also an adversary structure model.

The adversary structure model that is based on $\{\emptyset, \{p_1\}, \{p_2\}, \{p_3\}, \{p_1, p_2\}\}$ cannot be described by a threshold.

⟨1⟩3. Neither is the class of threshold models less expressive than the class of multi-site bimodal models, nor vice versa.

PROOF: Consider a distributed system with $|\Pi| = n$. The threshold model based on $t = n$ permits that all processes are faulty. By Lemmna 3.5, this cannot be described by a multi-site bimodal model.

A multi-site bimodal model permits that all processes in a site are faulty, but not necessarily all subsets of processes in a site. Such a model cannot be described by a threshold as threshold models are based on monotone sets.

⟨1⟩4. The classes of adversary structure models and of core / survivor sets are equivalent.

PROOF: Each survivor sets model is based on $\kappa_M(\{\Pi \setminus S : S \in \mathscr{S}\}) \subseteq \mathscr{P}(\Pi)$ for some set of survivor sets $\mathscr{S}$. As $\kappa_M(\{\Pi \setminus S : S \in \mathscr{S}\})$ is monotone and, therefore, an adversary structure, the survivor sets model itself is an adversary structure model.

Every adversary structure model is described by some adversary structure $\mathscr{A}$. In particular, $\mathscr{A} = \kappa_M(\mathscr{A}|_{\max})$, where $\mathscr{A}|_{\max}$ is the set of all sets in $\mathscr{A}$ that do not have a proper superset in $\mathscr{A}$. $\mathscr{S} = \{\Pi \setminus A : A \in \mathscr{A}|_{\max}\}$ is a set of survivor sets by set theory and, therefore, the adversary structure model itself is a survivor sets model.

⟨1⟩5. The classes of adversary structure models and of fail-prone system models are equivalent.

PROOF: Each fail-prone system model is based on $\kappa_M(\mathscr{B}) \subseteq \mathscr{P}(\Pi)$ for some fail-prone system $\mathscr{B}$. As $\kappa_M(\mathscr{B})$ is monotone and, therefore, an adversary structure, the fail-prone system model itself is an adversary structure model.

Every adversary structure model is based on some adversary structure $\mathscr{A}$. In particular, $\mathscr{A} = \kappa_M(\mathscr{A}|_{\max})$, where $\mathscr{A}|_{\max}$ is the set of all sets in $\mathscr{A}$ that do not have a proper superset in $\mathscr{A}$. As $\mathscr{A}|_{\max}$ only contains maximal sets and, therefore, is also a fail-prone system, the adversary structure model itself is a fail-prone system model.

$\langle 1\rangle 6$. Neither is the class of adversary structure models less expressive than the class of multi-site threshold models, nor vice versa.

PROOF: Let the processes be partitioned to a single site; that is, $\mathscr{Z} = \{\Pi\}$. The multi-site threshold model based on $t_{\mathscr{Z}} = 1$ and $t_i = 1$ for $Z_i = \Pi$ permits that either at most one or all processes are faulty. This cannot be described by any adversary structure as adversary structures are monotone.

Consider a distributed system with $\Pi = \{p_1, p_2, p_3\}$. The structural failure model based on the adversary structure $\mathscr{A} = \{\emptyset, \{p_1\}, \{p_2\}, \{p_3\}, \{p_1, p_2\}, \{p_1, p_3\}\}$ cannot be described by any multi-site threshold model for any partitioning of Π.

$\langle 1\rangle 7$. The class of adversary structure models is strictly less expressive than the class of multi-site hierarchical models.

PROOF: Each adversary structure model is equivalent to a fail-prone system model by $\langle 1\rangle 5$. As a fail-prone system model is a special case of a multi-site hierarchical model, each adversary structure model is also a multi-site hierarchical model.

Consider a distributed system with $\Pi = \{p_1, p_2\}$ and $\mathscr{Z} = \{\Pi\}$. The multi-site hierarchical model based on $\mathscr{B}_{\mathscr{Z}} = \{\{\Pi\}\}$ and $\mathscr{B}_i = \{\{p_1\}\}$ for $Z_i = \Pi$ is based on $\{\emptyset, \{p_1\}, \{p_1, p_2\}\}$. As the set is not monotone, no adversary structure model can be based on this set.

$\langle 1\rangle 8$. Neither is the class of adversary structure models less expressive than the class of multi-site bimodal models, nor vice versa.

PROOF: Consider a distributed system with a set of processes $\Pi = \{p_1, p_2, p_3\}$. The adversary structure model based on $\mathscr{P}(\Pi)$ allows all processes to be faulty. This cannot be described by any bimodal model by Lemma 3.5.

Assume that a distributed system has two sites $Z_1 = \{p_1, p_2\}$ and $Z_2 = \{p_3\}$. The multi-site bimodal model based on $\mathscr{B}_{\mathscr{Z}} = \{\{Z_1\}\}$, $\mathscr{B}_1 = \{\{p_1\}\}$, $\mathscr{B}_2 = \{\emptyset\}$ is based on $\{\emptyset, \{p_1\}, \{p_3\}, \{p_1, p_2\}\}$. As this set is not monotone, the model cannot be described by an adversary structure.

$\langle 1\rangle 9$. Neither is the class of multi-site bimodal models less expressive than the class of multi-site hierarchical models, nor vice versa.

PROOF: Consider a distributed system with a set of processes $\Pi = \{p_1, p_2, p_3\}$ and $\mathscr{Z} = \{\{p_1\}, \{p_2\}, \{p_3\}\}$. The multi-site bimodal model based on $\mathscr{B}_{\mathscr{Z}} = \{\emptyset\}$, $\mathscr{B}_i = \{\emptyset\}$ for $Z_i \in \mathscr{Z}$, and $Z_N = \{p_1\}$ is based on $\{\emptyset, \{p_1, p_2\}, \{p_1, p_3\}, \{p_2, p_3\}\}$. This model cannot be based on any multi-site hierarchical model for any partition of Π.

Assume that $\mathscr{Z} = \{\Pi\}$. The multi-site hierarchical model based on $\mathscr{B}_{\mathscr{Z}} = \{\{\Pi\}\}$ and $\mathscr{B}_i = \{\{p_1\}, \{p_2\}, \{p_3\}\}$ permits that all processes become faulty in a trace. This cannot be modelled by any bimodal model.

$\langle 1 \rangle 10$. The class of multi-site threshold models is strictly less expressive than the class of multi-site hierarchical models.

PROOF: Consider a multi-site threshold model based on $t_{\mathscr{Z}}$ and t_i for each $Z_i \in \mathscr{Z}$. This model equals the multi-site hierarchical model based on $\mathscr{B}_{\mathscr{Z}} = \{Z \subseteq \mathscr{Z} : |Z| = t\}$ and $\mathscr{B}_i = \{D \subseteq Z_i : |D| = t_i\}$ for each Z_i.
Assume that $\mathscr{Z} = \{Z_1, Z_2\}$ with $Z_1 = \{p_1, p_2\}$ and $Z_2 = \{p_3\}$. The multi-hierarchical model based on $\mathscr{B}_{\mathscr{Z}} = \{\{Z_1\}, \{Z_2\}\}$, $\mathscr{B}_1 = \{\{p_1\}\}$, and $\mathscr{B}_2 = \{\emptyset\}$ is described by $\{\emptyset, \{p_1\}, \{p_3\}, \{p_1, p_2\}, \{p_1, p_3\}\}$. This cannot be modelled by any multi-site threshold model for any partition of Π.

$\langle 1 \rangle 11$. Neither is the class of multi-site threshold models less expressive than the class of multi-site bimodal models, nor vice versa.

PROOF: Consider a distributed system with $\Pi = \{p_1, p_2, p_3\}$ and $\mathscr{Z} = \{\Pi\}$. The multi-site threshold model based on $t_{\mathscr{Z}} = 1$ and $t_i = 3$ for $Z_i = \Pi$ permits that all processes become faulty in a trace. This cannot be modelled by a bimodal model.
By $\langle 1 \rangle 9$, there is a bimodal model that cannot be based on multi-site hierarchical model. As multi-site threshold models are strictly less expressive than multi-site hierarchical models, there is a bimodal model that cannot be based on a multi-site threshold model.

$\langle 1 \rangle 12$. The class of multi-site bimodal models is strictly less expressive than the class of Didep models.

PROOF: As each bimodal model is a set-based model, it is also a Didep model. Consider a Didep model based on a set that includes Π. Such a model cannot be described by a bimodal model.

$\langle 1 \rangle 13$. The class of multi-site hierarchical models is strictly less expressive than the class of Didep models.

PROOF: As each multi-site hierarchical model is a set-based structural failure model, it is also a Didep model.
Consider a distributed system with $|\Pi| = \{p_1, p_2\}$. The Didep model based on $\{\emptyset, \{p_1\}, \{p_1, p_2\}\}$ cannot be based on any multi-site hierarchical model for any partitioning of Π.

$\langle 1 \rangle 14$. Q.E.D.

PROOF: By $\langle 1 \rangle 1 - \langle 1 \rangle 13$.

While Didep models are the most expressive class in Fig. 3.2, it limits the precision of structural failure models significantly. While they allow to describe dependent faults, they, for example, cannot accurately model fault propagation among components. We now look into a class of structural failure models that describes fault assumptions by sequences of components instead of component sets. This class is strictly more expressive than Didep models as it covers dependent faults as well as fault propagation.

3.6 Sequence-Based Structural Failure Models

Dependent faults are often caused by the loss of a resource that is critical for more than one component. For example, a power outage at a site may cause all processes at this site to fail. Empirical studies have shown that large-scale outages in power transmission systems are typically caused by fault cascades: A critical component fails and the impact of this failure propagates through large parts of the system causing other components to fail as well [Dobson et al., 2004, 2005]. As power outages affect distributed systems, a propagation of power outages is likely to cause propagating (and dependent) faults in distributed systems.

Analogously to dependent faults, the consideration of propagating faults raises the question of what we understand by propagating faults. Intuitively, we consider a fault as propagating from process p_i to process p_j if p_i becomes faulty first whenever both processes are faulty. We formalise this intuition by sequences of processes that describe which processes are faulty in a trace and in which order they become faulty, which requires to define the point in time, when a process becomes faulty. Remember that being faulty is defined as a predicate on traces and not on states. As we intend to have a consistent definition for different variants of faults (e.g., crash, crash-recovery, and arbitrary), we define this point in time by the first state in a trace, where the process is failed. Formally, we define $T_p(\langle s_0, s_1, \ldots \rangle) = i$ for a process $p \in \Pi$ if p is faulty in the trace $\langle s_0, s_1, \ldots \rangle \in \Sigma^\infty$ and s_i is the first state in τ with $\mathit{failed}_p(s_i)$ being true. An alternative definition of T_p could have been based on the point in time when p fails for the last time. However, by our definition, $T_p(\tau)$ is well-defined for a process p and a trace τ even if p is faulty due to being infinitely often nonfailed.

Let Π^* denote the set of all finite sequences over Π. Analogously to the definition of $F(\tau)$, we define $F_S(\tau) \in \Pi^*$ as the sequence of all processes that are faulty in τ ordered with respect to $T_p(\tau)$. Formally,

$$F_S(\tau) = \langle p_1, \ldots, p_k \rangle$$

for a trace τ iff

$$F(\tau) = \{p_1, \ldots, p_k\}$$

and

$$\forall i,j \in \{1,\ldots,k\} : i < j \Rightarrow T_{p_i}(\tau) < T_{p_j}(\tau).$$

As propagating faults are given by sequences of processes, we also describe a structural failure model for propagating faults by process sequences.

Definition 3.23 (Sequence-Based Structural Failure Model)
A structural failure model σ is based on a set $\mathscr{S} \subseteq \Pi^*$ of process sequences iff

$$\sigma(P) \quad \equiv \quad P \cap \{\tau \in \Sigma^\infty : \exists S \in \mathscr{S} : S = F_S(\tau)\}$$

for all distributed system properties P. In this case, we call σ a sequence-based structural failure model.

The results that were obtained for Didep models in Section 3.5 can be transferred to sequence-based models. We only summarise these results and omit their proofs due to the similarity to the results and proofs for set-based models.

- It suffices to consider the sets of process sequences when comparing two classes of sequence-based structural failure models (cf. Theorem 3.3).
- If relying on sets of process sequences to describe fault models, a structural failure model is most accurately described by a *sound* and *complete* set of process sequences. A set $\mathscr{S} \subseteq \Pi^*$ of process sequences is *sound* for a distributed system property P and a structural failure model σ iff $\forall S \in \mathscr{S} : \exists \tau \in \sigma(P) : S = F_S(\tau)$. $\mathscr{S}$ is *complete* for P and σ iff $\forall \tau \in \sigma(P) : F_S(\tau) \in \mathscr{S}$ (cf. Definition 3.14).
- A sound and complete set of process sequences is unique for a distributed system property and a structural failure model (cf. Corollary 3.2).
- For a distributed system property P and a structural failure model σ, the set $\mathscr{S} \subseteq \Pi^*$ with $\mathscr{S} = \{F_S(\tau) \in \Pi^* : \tau \in \sigma(P)\}$ is sound and complete (cf. Lemma 3.1).
- While accuracy is reduced when using sequence-based models, sequence-based models impose safe over-approximation (cf. Theorem 3.4).

Just as Didep models achieve better expressiveness than threshold models by relying on sets instead of a number, sequence-based models achieve better expressiveness than Didep models by relying on sequences instead of sets. The following example illustrates the increased expressiveness.

Example 3.18 (Sequence-Based Structural Failure Model)
Consider a distributed system with three processes p_1, p_2, and p_3 and a structural failure model σ based on

$$\mathscr{S} = \{\langle\rangle, \langle p_2\rangle, \langle p_3\rangle, \langle p_2, p_3\rangle, \langle p_1, p_3\rangle, \langle p_3, p_1\rangle\}.$$

σ allows that either no process is faulty, only p_2 or p_3 are faulty, first p_2 becomes faulty and then p_3, or p_1 and p_3 are jointly faulty in an arbitrary order. Hence, there is a propagation from p_2 to p_3 if both are faulty. Despite the propagation, the faults are not directed dependent; both processes may be faulty on their own. While the faults of p_1 and p_3 are directed dependent, the dependence is not caused by a propagation; both processes may become faulty in an arbitrary order. This example illustrates that dependence and propagation are orthogonal concepts. Some faults may be dependent but not propagating; others may be propagating but not dependent.

If relying on process sets, $\mathscr{S}$ is best approximated by the Didep model based on

$$\mathscr{D} = \{\{\}, \{p_2\}, \{p_3\}, \{p_2, p_3\}, \{p_1, p_3\}\},$$

which describes the directed dependent faults of p_1 and p_3, but does not cover the fault propagation from p_2 to p_3.

Theorem 3.10
The class of Didep models is strictly less expressive than the class of sequence-based structural failure models.

PROOF:
$\langle 1 \rangle 1$. The class of Didep models is less expressive than the class of sequence-based models.
PROOF: Consider an arbitrary Didep model $\mathscr{D} = \{S_1, \ldots, S_m\}$ and the set of process sequences
$$\mathscr{S} = \{\langle p_1, \ldots, p_i \rangle : \{p_1, \ldots, p_i\} \in \mathscr{D}\}.$$
From the definitions of set- and sequence-based models, it follows that the structural failure model based on $\mathscr{D}$ equals the structural failure model based on $\mathscr{S}$.
$\langle 1 \rangle 2$. The class of sequence-based models is not less expressive than the class of Didep models.
PROOF: We prove this by contradiction. Consider a distributed system property P with $\Pi = \{p_1, p_2\}$ and $F_S(P) = \{\langle\rangle, \langle p_1 \rangle, \langle p_2 \rangle, \langle p_1, p_2 \rangle, \langle p_2, p_1 \rangle\}$. Let $\sigma_{\mathscr{S}}$ be a structural failure model that is based on $\mathscr{S} = \{\langle\rangle, \langle p_1 \rangle, \langle p_2 \rangle, \langle p_1, p_2 \rangle\}$ and $\sigma_{\mathscr{D}}$ a Didep model based on an arbitrary set $\mathscr{D} \subseteq \mathscr{P}(\Pi)$.
Assume that $\sigma_{\mathscr{D}}(P) \equiv \sigma_{\mathscr{S}}(P)$.
By the definition of $\sigma_{\mathscr{S}}$, $F_S(\sigma_{\mathscr{S}}(P)) = \mathscr{S}$ such that $F(\sigma_{\mathscr{S}}(P)) = \mathscr{P}(\Pi)$. As $\{p_1, p_2\} \in F(\sigma_{\mathscr{S}}(P))$, $\mathscr{D}$ must have $\{p_1, p_2\} \in \mathscr{D}$. By the definition of set-based models, $\langle p_2, p_1 \rangle \in F_S(\sigma_{\mathscr{D}}(P))$ then. This implies that $\sigma_{\mathscr{D}}(P) \not\equiv \sigma_{\mathscr{S}}(P)$ as $\langle p_2, p_1 \rangle \notin F_S(\sigma_{\mathscr{S}}(P))$, a contradiction.
$\langle 1 \rangle 3$. Q.E.D.
PROOF: By $\langle 1 \rangle 1$ and $\langle 1 \rangle 2$.

3.7 Stochastics, Sets, and Sequences

Many approaches for evaluating fault-tolerant distributed systems rely on stochastic fault models, that is, models based on probability theory. For tractability, most of these models rely on simplifying assumptions. Prominent examples are the assumptions that component failures are stochastically independent and identically distributed. For example, replication schemes are often evaluated under such assumptions [Barbara and Garcia-Molina, 1987, Agrawal and Abbadi, 1992, Cheung et al., 1992, Amir and Wool, 1998, Theel and Pagnia, 1998].

Empirical evidence for dependent and propagating faults raised the interest for more accurate stochastic fault models. In this section, we present an approach for abstracting stochastic models by nonprobabilistic Didep and sequence-based structural failure models. In particular, the approach relies on the concept of *assumption coverage*, the probability that an assumption holds for a given system. Exemplarily, we apply our approach to some stochastic models for dependent and propagating faults.

Abstracting Stochastic Fault Models In stochastic fault models, probability distributions govern the occurrence of component failures in a system. In general, stochastic fault models permit that arbitrary processes become faulty in an arbitrary order. However, many cases are unlikely to occur due to the probability distributions. For example, if the fault probability is below 0.5 for each process and faults are independent, then cases with more faulty processes are less likely than cases with less faulty processes. The most likely case is that no process is faulty; the most unlikely case is that all processes are faulty.

We abstract a stochastic model using the concept of *assumption coverage* (cf. Powell [1992]). The assumption coverage of an assumption A is the probability $Prob(A)$ that A is valid, that is, A indeed holds in practice. Applied to Didep models, the assumption coverage $Prob(\mathscr{D})$ of a Didep model based on $\mathscr{D} \subseteq \mathscr{P}(\Pi)$ is the probability that the exact set of faulty processes is in $\mathscr{D}$.

For this section, we assume that a stochastic fault model allows to associate a "probability of occurrence" to every set / sequence of processes that describes the extent of faults. A probability $Prob(D)$ that is associated to a process set D gives the probability that, if the system runs, then exactly the processes in D are faulty. A probability $Prob(S)$ that is associated to a process sequence S gives the probability that, if the system runs, then the processes in S indeed become faulty in the order as given by S. If not stated otherwise, we focus on Didep models in the rest of this section. However, the same ideas apply to sequence-based models as well.

We abstract a stochastic fault model by constructing a Didep model from the process sets with the highest associated "probabilities of occurrence" but omit process sets with low probabilities. Assume that all process sets are ordered by their associated probability in decreasing order. The sets with low ranks (i.e., high associated probabilities) most likely describe the actual occurrence of component failures. The sets with high ranks are unlikely to describe the actual occurrence of faults.

Consider a stochastic fault model that is to be abstracted by a Didep model. The stochastic model associates a "probability of occurrence" to every process set $D \subseteq \Pi$. Assume that $\langle D_1, \ldots, D_{2^n} \rangle$ is the sequence of such process sets ordered by their associated probability in decreasing order. Then, the Didep model given by $\mathscr{D} = \{D_1, \ldots, D_k\}$ abstracts the stochastic model with an assumption coverage

$$Prob(\mathscr{D}) = \sum_{i=1}^{k} Prob(D_i).$$

That is, the probability mass of covered cases equals the assumption coverage: The actual set of faulty processes is in $\mathscr{D}$ with a probability of $Prob(\mathscr{D})$. With a probability of

$$1 - Prob(\mathscr{D}) = 1 - \sum_{i=k+1}^{2^n} Prob(D_i)$$

the exact set of faulty processes is not covered by $\mathscr{D}$.

For example, consider a distributed system that consists of three processes p_1, p_2, and p_3 and permanent component failures. Assume that the failure probability is 10^{-2} for each process and that failures of different processes are stochastically independent. This stochastic model can be abstracted by a (symmetric) Didep model based on

$$\mathscr{D} = \{\{\}, \{p_1\}, \{p_2\}, \{p_3\}, \{p_1, p_2\}, \{p_1, p_3\}, \{p_2, p_3\}\},$$

if the assumption coverage shall be at least $1 - 10^{-5}$: The probability that all three processes jointly fail is less than 10^{-5} and the probability of each other fault scenario is greater than 10^{-5}. Hence, only the case that all processes are faulty can be omitted.

The Didep set may not be symmetric, for example, in case of dependent faults. Consider that p_2 and p_3 jointly fail with high probability if p_1 fails, but only with very low probability if p_1 does not fail. This may result in a Didep model based on

$$\mathscr{D} = \{\{\}, \{p_2\}, \{p_3\}, \{p_1, p_2, p_3\}\}.$$

Stochastic Models for Dependent and Propagating Faults Various approaches for stochastic models of dependent and propagating faults have been proposed in the literature. For example, Lee et al. [1991], Tang and Iyer [1992, 1993] have proposed to model dependences by *conditional probabilities* or by *failure correlation coefficients*. Bakkaloglu et al. [2002] have modelled dependent faults by a special probability distribution, namely the *beta-binomial distribution*. Limbourg et al. [2007] trace dependent component failures back to the spatial arrangement of components. They have modelled dependent faults by so-called *copulas*. A copula is a multi-variate distribution function that allows to describe measures of dependence in terms of marginal distributions.

Dobson et al. [2004, 2005] have introduced the *CASCADE models* for propagating faults. Exemplarily, we describe CASCADE in more detail and show how to abstract a CASCADE model by a sequence-based structural failure model. While the model was developed to describe cascading (i.e., propagating) faults of electrical power transmission systems, the model is suitable for other distributed systems as well. Failures within an execution of a system are modelled as follows. CASCADE associates a real-valued *load* to each component of a system. The loads of the components are initialised following a given probability distribution. Additionally, they are initially increased by a constant disturbance. Failures occur in "rounds": Being initially nonfailed, a component fails in a round when its load exceeds a threshold. Whenever a component fails, a constant amount of load is added to the load of every component for the next round. Due to this additional load, further components may fail, that is, faults propagate in the system. In particular, with an increasing number of failures, the system gets more loaded and further failures become more likely.

In principle, a CASCADE model allows that arbitrary processes fail in an arbitrary order. However, different cases have different probabilities of occurrence. These probabilities depend on the probability distribution of the initial loads. A CASCADE model can be abstracted by a sequence-based model as described above: The most likely cases must be covered by the sequence-based model; less likely cases can be omitted. A CASCADE model defines a partial order on process failures for an execution of a system. To obtain a sequence-based model, all process sequences that satisfy the partial order must be considered.

3.8 Summary

Fault-tolerant distributed systems bear a considerable complexity. Models as means of abstraction are crucial for the design and evaluation of such systems. The decision which abstractions are appropriate is critical as, if an abstraction neglects important aspects of the real world, the resulting model is unlikely to yield realistic results. For example, the popular threshold models abstract from dependent faults. However, there is empirical evidence that dependent faults are significant in real-world systems.

This chapter addressed the issue of fault models and their expressiveness. While considering a fault model as a weakening of specifications, we introduced functional and structural failure models as a formal foundation for component failure models. In particular, this formalisation allowed to show that, in principle, component failure models do not bear any disadvantages with respect to expressiveness: any fault model can be expressed by a process failure model. This result contrasts previous claims that component failure models, for example, cannot handle dynamic and transient faults [Santoro and Widmayer, 1989, Charron-Bost and Schiper, 2007].

Motivated by previous criticism on threshold models, we have formalised the notion of dependent faults and subsequently refined the criticism on thresholds: thresholds cannot handle dependent faults iff they are sound and complete. We have classified previous fault models for dependent faults. As previous models do not cover dependent faults, we have introduced the class of Didep models that is strictly more expressive than previous classes. A better accuracy can be achieved when using Didep models. While Didep models suffice to express dependent faults, they cannot accurately describe propagation of faults within a system. We have addressed this concern by an additional class that models faults by process sequences.

The chapter leaves several directions for future work. In particular, the relation between stochastic and nonprobabilistic fault models deserves further attention. For example, different stochastic models incorporate different notions of dependence. The relationships between these notions and our notion of dependence is an open issue. Of course, such relationships depend on the way a stochastic model is abstracted. We have presented one possible approach that considers the most likely scenarios but abstracts away unlikely one. Other approaches may additionally consider the "severity" of a scenario and, therefore, keep and abstract away different scenarios.

A decision for a fault model leaves the question how to actually solve a given problem using the model. We will address this question in the next chapter and, in particular, show that solving problems does not become more complex when using Didep models.

4 Constructing Coteries

A distributed system generally requires some coordination and agreement among the participating processes. For example, in the case of a distributed database, it is essential that the processes agree on whether to commit or abort the distributed transactions. In a distributed operating system, processes need to coordinate their usage of shared resources. Such challenges are rather easy to solve in fault-free systems, for example, by introducing a central coordinator process that is accessed by each process before performing a critical operation. In systems with faulty components however, coordination and agreement become hard or even impossible to solve. A central coordinator does not suffice as this coordinator may crash and prevent other processes from making progress.

Lamport [1978a] has presented a fundamental approach to coordination and agreement in fault-tolerant distributed systems that relies on pre-defined *majority graphs*, which are a special case of the more general concept of *quorums*. A quorum is a set of processes that is accessed before performing a critical operation that requires coordination or agreement. If every quorum shares a process with every other quorum, no two critical operations are performed without accessing at least one common process, which can coordinate both operations. Hence, there is no pre-determined central coordinator as a single-point-of-failure. A set of quorums that intersect pairwise and in which no quorum is a subset of another quorum is called a *coterie*. In contrast to systems with a central coordinator, a system that relies on a coterie can tolerate crashed processes as long as there remains a quorum of noncrashed processes.

As a fundamental approach for coordination and agreement, quorums became widely used means for realising fault-tolerant distributed systems in theory and in practice. The range of applications include protocols for concurrency control [Bernstein et al., 1987], mutual exclusion [Maekawa, 1985], consensus [Mostéfaoui and Raynal, 1999], and committing transactions [Skeen, 1982]. For example, the *OpenVMS*[1] operating system relies on quorums for preventing data corruptions in high availability clusters: The connection manager of OpenVMS enforces that modifications on shared resources require the permission from a quorum.

Of course, no coterie allows to tolerate arbitrary severe faults. In particular, the redundancy provided by *static coteries* is exhausted if no quorum of noncrashed

[1] `http://h71000.www7.hp.com/`

processes remains. Such a situation may occur early as the quorums of a static coterie are fixed at design time: A static coterie cannot adapt to failures. A possible resort are *dynamic coteries* that allow to adapt the set of quorums during runtime. For example, upon the detection of a crashed process, another process may discard the current set of quorums and install a new one that does not contain the crashed processes. Although such a transition requires some agreement and coordination in itself, a dynamic coterie allows to achieve a quality being impossible to achieve with a static coterie.

Different applications usually have different nonfunctional requirements. While performance may have top priority in one system, availability may be of top priority in another system. Choosing a set of quorums implies a trade-off among different qualities such as *load*, *capacity*, *availability*, and *probe complexity*. Due to this trade-off, no single set of quorums can match the requirements of all applications. In this chapter, we focus on coteries with high availability and low probe complexity, which are of particular importance for fault-tolerant systems. Intuitively, the availability of a set of quorums measures how well the quorums allow to cope with faults. A coterie is *highly available* iff it allows to tolerate all assumed faults. The probe complexity gives the minimal number of probes required to either find a quorum of noncrashed processes or to detect that no such quorum exists in the worst case.

Contribution The question of how to construct a coterie for given requirements has stimulated a significant amount of research. We contribute to this line of research by a constructive characterisation of highly available coteries in terms of structural failure models. More precisely, we show that, in the presence of crash failures, the conditions of k*-well-formedness* and k*-reachable-well-formedness* are necessary and sufficient conditions for the existence of highly available static and dynamic coteries, respectively.

The characterisation is constructive in the sense that we describe how to derive a highly available coterie from 2-well-formed Didep models. Exploiting the expressiveness of Didep models, we give a construction for highly available coteries that dominate coteries obtained from previous constructions based on dependent fault models. We extend the results to Byzantine failures and show that a 4-well-formed Didep model is necessary and sufficient for the existence of a highly available static coterie. Additionally, we show that, surprisingly, using dynamic coteries does not yield advantages for high availability in case of Byzantine failures.

Besides high availability, we address the quality of probe complexity. We refine the notion of probe complexity by considering sequence-based structural failure models. In contrast to the original notion, the refined probe complexity gives a tight bound for a distributed system and is significantly smaller than the original probe complexity under many fault models. Additionally, we present a probe strategy that only requires a number of probes equal to the refined probe complexity in the worst case due to exploiting the knowledge provided by the current fault model. The strategy is universal in the sense that it is defined for all sets of quorums. In particular, while previous strategies meet the probe complexity only for "nondominated" coteries, our strategy meets the refined probe complexity for all quorum sets.

Overview This chapter is organised as follows. We distinguish related work from our contributions in Section 4.1 and give a brief introduction to quorums in Section 4.2. Section 4.3 presents constructive characterisations of highly available static coteries in terms of Didep models. Section 4.4 gives a constructive characterisation of highly available dynamic coteries for crash failures and, for Byzantine failures, shows that a highly available static coterie exists if a highly available dynamic coterie exists. In Section 4.5, we refine the notion of probe complexity and give a new probe strategy, before we conclude this chapter in Section 4.6.

4.1 Related Work

Different approaches have been proposed in the literature on how to construct coteries with good availability characteristics. In principle, each approach falls into one of three categories depending on what kind of fault model the approach is based upon: no explicit fault model at all, a probabilistic fault model, or a nonprobabilistic fault model.

Our approach falls into the last category: we construct highly available coteries from given nonprobabilistic fault models based on Didep models. Closely related to our results, Junqueira and Marzullo [2005a,c] have shown how to derive coteries from core / survivor set and multi-site models. Malkhi and Reiter [1998] have given related constructions of highly available quorums from fail-prone systems. In contrast to both approaches, we use Didep models that are more expressive and, thereby, obtain coteries that *dominate* coteries obtained from such previous constructions. Peleg and Wool [1995] have shown that, if a coterie dominates another coterie, the former has better availability characteristics. Additionally, we address the question of how to construct highly available *dynamic* coteries from nonprobabilistic fault models, which – as far as we are aware – has not been addressed in the literature yet. As a related result, Alvisi et al. [2000] have shown how to construct dynamic coteries despite Byzantine failures for better performance. However, we show that dynamic coteries do not bear advantages over static coteries for high availability in the presence of Byzantine failures.

With approaches based on probabilistic fault models, probability distributions govern the occurrence of failures. Often, such models assign some probabilities to each process. For example, they assign an availability value to each process, that is, a probability that the process is nonfailed if accessed by another process. Constructions based on such models exploit the information about faults to derive coteries with good availability characteristics. The results obtained under probabilistic fault models can be summarised as follows. If all processes have an availability < 0.5, then the coterie with the highest availability is given by a single quorum with a single process, namely a process with the highest availability [Barbara and Garcia-Molina, 1987, Amir and Wool, 1998]. If all processes have an availability > 0.5, the construction of Tong and Kain [1991] yields a coterie with optimal availability. As a special case, if all processes have the same availability > 0.5, the coterie with the highest availability is given by simple process majorities [Barbara and Garcia-Molina, 1987]. Amir and Wool [1998] have shown how to construct a coterie with optimal availability if the processes have different availabilities, some below 0.5 and some above 0.5. As a major shortcoming, all of these results have been obtained under the assumption of independent faults (for the sake of a tractable probabilistic fault model). Using the abstraction from probabilistic models to Didep models as given in Section 3.7, our approach allows to reproduce these results. Moreover, our approach is more general in the sense that it also covers dependent faults. Tang and Iyer [1993] have shown that covering dependent faults is of major importance as even small fault correlations have a significant impact on the overall availability of a distributed system.

Approaches that do not rely on an explicit fault model usually derive coteries from logical structures such as grids [Cheung et al., 1992], trees [Agrawal and Abbadi, 1992], or finite projective planes [Maekawa, 1985]. For example, Cheung et al. [1992] have proposed to logically organise the processes as a grid and construct quorums from rows and columns of the grid. They compare the availability of grid quorums to the availability obtained with coteries obtained from voting schemes and find that grids allow to obtain the same level of availability with better performance. While such constructions are interesting for their trade-offs among different qualities, they do not yield highly available coteries in general, because they do not take fault assumptions into account or are based on implicit and possibly invalid fault assumptions. In contrast, we do not care about the logical structure underlying a coterie, but derive highly available coteries from given Didep models.

Peleg and Wool [2002] have introduced the probe complexity as another quality of coteries that is of major importance for fault tolerance. Their notion of probe complexity assumes crash failures, but is independent of a particular assumption on the extension of faults and, therefore, gives the number of probes required under the worst possible structural assumption. In contrast, we define another variant of probe complexity – called *refined probe complexity* – that explicitly considers a given sequence-based structural failure model. Under a sequence-based worst-case model both values are equal for a given coterie, but for less severe models the refined probe complexity is lower than the original one. Our approach has the advantage that the refined probe complexity is tight for a distributed system property.

Besides defining probe complexity, Peleg and Wool [2002] have additionally given a universal probe strategy and have shown that, for nondominated coteries, the strategy needs a number of probes equal to the probe complexity in the worst case. In contrast, we present a universal probe strategy that needs a number of probes equal to the refined probe complexity in the worst case. As the refined probe complexity is below the original one in general, the strategy is more efficient than the original one. Closely related, Neilsen [1997] has presented a probe strategy for probabilistic fault models. While his strategy reduces the average case probe complexity, it does not reduce the worst-case probe complexity. Furthermore, his strategy relies on an assumption of independent faults, while our strategies also covers dependent and propagating faults.

4.2 Introduction to Quorums

A quorum is a set of processes. The construction of quorums depends on the number and types of operations that must be coordinated. In particular, competitive operations are distinguished from noncompetitive ones.

Competitive and Noncompetitive Operations If quorums are used for a single type of operation, we can safely assume that the operations require coordination and/or agreement. Otherwise, there would be no need for using quorums. Barbara and Garcia-Molina [1986] call such a type of operation *competitive* as the processes compete in performing their operations. For example, entering a critical section for *mutual exclusion* is a competitive type of operation. Another example is updating a replicated database: Ideally, a replicated database should behave equivalently to a nonreplicated one; that is, *one-copy equivalence* [Bernstein et al., 1987] should be preserved. If all operations on the database are competitive, one-copy equivalence can be guaranteed.

Although relying on a single type of operation allows to achieve coordination and agreement, this approach may be overly pessimistic. For example, a replicated database may distinguish read from write operations as two operations are only in conflict (possibly violating one-copy equivalence) if at least one write operation is involved. Two read operations are never in conflict; they can proceed concurrently without coordination and agreement. Barbara and Garcia-Molina [1986] call such a type of operation *noncompetitive*.

Barbara and Garcia-Molina [1986] have shown that – with respect to quorums – it suffices to consider three different scenarios:

1. There is only one competitive type of operation.
2. There are two types of operations; one is competitive, the other is not.
3. There are two types of operations; both are noncompetitive.

Other scenarios are combinations of these scenarios or can be reduced to one of them.

Static Coteries Competitive operations must rely on quorums that share processes. We use the term *static coterie* for a set of such quorums that is fixed and does not change over the life-time of a distributed system. Besides sharing processes, we additionally require that each quorum is minimal in a coterie; that is, no subset of a quorum is in the coterie. Otherwise, critical operations could be performed by accessing a proper superset of a quorum, which requires more messages without any advantages. This notion of coteries is common in the literature [Garcia-Molina and Barbara, 1985, Ahamad et al., 1991, Cheung et al., 1992] and, sometimes, also denoted by the term *quorum system* [Naor and Wool, 1998, Malkhi and Reiter, 1998, Peleg and Wool, 2002]. More formally,

Definition 4.1 (Static Coterie)
A set $\mathscr{Q} \subseteq \mathscr{P}(\Pi)$ of process sets is a *static coterie* iff

1. $\forall Q \in \mathscr{Q}: \ Q \neq \emptyset$,
2. (intersection) $\forall Q_i, Q_j \in \mathscr{Q}: \ Q_i \cap Q_j \neq \emptyset$, and
3. (minimality) $\forall Q_i, Q_j \in \mathscr{Q}: \ Q_i \not\subset Q_j$.

Example 4.1 (Static Coterie)
Consider a distributed system with a set of processes $\Pi = \{p_1, \dots, p_4\}$. Then, the set $\mathscr{Q}$ with

$$\mathscr{Q} = \{\{p_1, p_2, p_3\}, \{p_1, p_2, p_4\}, \{p_1, p_3, p_4\}, \{p_2, p_3, p_4\}\}$$

is a static coterie that is formed from majorities of processes in Π. If process p_2 wants to perform a competitive operation, it may decide to access p_1, p_2, and p_3. If p_4 wants to concurrently perform a competitive operation, it may decide to access p_1, p_2, and p_4. Both processes access p_1 and p_2, which are able to coordinate the concurrent operations.

Static Quorum Sets If a competitive type of operation is combined with a noncompetitive one (e.g., writing with reading), the competitive operations must rely on quorums of a coterie, whereas the noncompetitive ones may rely on quorums that do not share any process (although they must share a process with each quorum for the competitive type, respectively). Hence, noncompetitive operations may rely on a set of quorums that does not have the intersection condition of coteries. We call such sets *quorum sets*.

Definition 4.2 (Static Quorum Set)
A set $\mathcal{Q} \subseteq \mathcal{P}(\Pi)$ of process sets is a *static quorum set* iff

1. $\forall Q \in \mathcal{Q}: \; Q \neq \emptyset$ and
2. (minimality) $\forall Q_i, Q_j \in \mathcal{Q}: \; Q_i \not\subset Q_j$.

Example 4.2 (Static Quorum Set)
Consider a distributed system with a set of processes $\Pi = \{p_1, \ldots, p_4\}$. Then, the set $\mathcal{Q}^{-1}$ with

$$\mathcal{Q}^{-1} = \{\{p_1, p_2\}, \{p_1, p_3\}, \{p_1, p_4\}, \{p_2, p_3\}, \{p_2, p_4\}, \{p_3, p_4\}\}$$

is a static quorum set, but not a coterie as $\{p_1, p_2\}$ and $\{p_3, p_4\}$ do not share a process. $\mathcal{Q}^{-1}$ and $\mathcal{Q}$ from Example 4.1 above allow to realise coordination for a competitive type and a noncompetitive type of operation. If process p_1 intends to perform a noncompetitive operation, it may decide to access $Q_1 = \{p_1, p_2\} \in \mathcal{Q}^{-1}$. If p_2 intends to concurrently perform a noncompetitive operation, it may decide to access $Q_2 = \{p_3, p_4\} \in \mathcal{Q}^{-1}$. Process p_1 is not affected by the operation of p_2 and vice versa. If p_3 wants to concurrently perform a competitive operation, it may decide to access $Q_3 = \{p_1, p_2, p_4\} \in \mathcal{Q}$. As Q_3 shares processes with both, Q_1 and Q_2, the competitive operation is coordinated with both noncompetitive ones.

Quality of Quorum Sets Different metrics have been proposed to measure the quality of a quorum set. For example, Naor and Wool [1998] have proposed the metrics *availability*, *load*, and *capacity* for coteries. Intuitively, the load measures how frequently a process is accessed as a part of a quorum and, therefore, cannot perform other work. The capacity measures how many quorum accesses a coterie can handle per time unit.

As our primary concern is fault tolerance, we focus on the metrics *availability* and *probe complexity* that are of particular importance for fault-tolerant systems. Intuitively, the availability of a quorum set measures how well the set allows to cope with faults; the more faults a quorum set allows to tolerate, the more available the quorum set is. In particular, we are interested in *highly available* coteries that allow to tolerate all assumed faults. For example, consider a distributed system with three processes and the fault assumption that at most one process may fail by crashing. The coterie that has each pair of processes as a quorum is highly available, because, in each trace, a process may access a quorum of correct processes. We will address the question how to construct highly available coteries from fault models in the next section.

Probing a process means to determine whether the process is crashed, for example, by sending him a message and waiting for a response. If the system is synchronous, the probed processes can be considered as crashed if it does not respond within a certain period of time. The *probe complexity* as introduced by Peleg and Wool [2002] measures the worst-case number of probes that are necessary to either find a quorum of noncrashed processes or to detect that no such quorum exists.

Probing processes allows a fault-tolerant system that relies on a quorum set to find out whether the redundancy required for fault tolerance is exhausted: If probing reveals that no quorum of noncrashed processes remains, further operations cannot be performed. Otherwise, if probing finds a quorum of noncrashed processes, this quorum can be accessed for performing an operation.

Note that, while we are mainly interested in high availability and low probe complexity, our constructions improve other qualities compared to previous constructions for highly available coteries. In particular, our constructions yield coteries that *dominate* coteries from previous constructions. Naor and Wool [1998] have shown that dominating coteries are "better" with respect to the qualities of load and capacity.

Domination While different coteries generally impose different quality tradeoffs, some coteries are superior to other coteries in general. For example, consider a set of processes $\Pi = \{p_1, \ldots, p_4\}$ and the coteries

$$\mathcal{Q}_1 = \{\{p_1, p_2\}, \{p_1, p_3\}, \{p_1, p_4\}, \{p_2, p_3, p_4\}\}$$
$$\mathcal{Q}_2 = \{\{p_1, p_2, p_3\}, \{p_1, p_2, p_4\}, \{p_1, p_3, p_4\}, \{p_2, p_3, p_4\}\}.$$

Clearly, $\mathcal{Q}_1$ is superior to $\mathcal{Q}_2$, because all sets of processes that may grant permission under $\mathcal{Q}_2$ may also grant permission under $\mathcal{Q}_1$ but not vice versa. For example, p_1 and p_2 may grant permission under $\mathcal{Q}_1$, but not under $\mathcal{Q}_2$. Furthermore, $\mathcal{Q}_1$ has smaller quorums, which results in a lower message complexity. Garcia-Molina and Barbara [1985] have introduced the term $\mathcal{Q}_1$ *dominates* $\mathcal{Q}_2$ to denote that $\mathcal{Q}_1$ is superior to $\mathcal{Q}_2$ in this sense.

Definition 4.3 (Domination for Static Coteries)
Let $\mathcal{Q}_i, \mathcal{Q}_j$ be static coteries. $\mathcal{Q}_i$ *dominates* $\mathcal{Q}_j$ iff

1. $\mathcal{Q}_i \neq \mathcal{Q}_j$ and
2. $\forall Q_j \in \mathcal{Q}_j : \exists Q_i \in \mathcal{Q}_i : Q_i \subseteq Q_j$.

The coterie $\mathcal{Q}_2$ – formed from proper majorities – is dominated by another coterie and, therefore, called a dominated coterie.

Definition 4.4 (Dominated and Nondominated Static Coteries)
A coterie $\mathcal{Q}$ is *dominated* iff there is a coterie that dominates $\mathcal{Q}$. If there is no such coterie, $\mathcal{Q}$ is *nondominated*.

Domination and (Non)competitive Operations If quorums are used for a single (competitive) type of operation, a dominated coterie $\mathcal{Q}$ should be avoided and be replaced by a nondominated coterie that dominates $\mathcal{Q}$. While the actual complexity class is still unknown, constructing such a nondominated coterie from a dominated coterie is suspected to be NP-hard [Garcia-Molina and Barbara, 1985, Bioch and Ibaraki, 1995, Harada and Yamashita, 2005]. Additionally, a nondominated coterie is not unique for a coterie in general. For example, $\mathcal{Q}_2$ from the example above is dominated by the nondominated $\mathcal{Q}_1$, but is also dominated by the nondominated coteries

$$\begin{aligned}
\mathcal{Q}_3 &= \{\{p_1,p_2\},\{p_2,p_3\},\{p_2,p_4\},\{p_1,p_3,p_4\}\},\\
\mathcal{Q}_4 &= \{\{p_1,p_3\},\{p_2,p_3\},\{p_3,p_4\},\{p_1,p_2,p_4\}\}, \text{ and}\\
\mathcal{Q}_5 &= \{\{p_1,p_4\},\{p_2,p_4\},\{p_3,p_4\},\{p_1,p_2,p_3\}\}.
\end{aligned}$$

The choice of a nondominated coterie depends on the actual system requirements and the characteristics of the individual processes.

While a dominated coterie $\mathcal{Q}$ is inferior to a coterie that dominates $\mathcal{Q}$, combining competitive and noncompetitive types of operation requires to use dominated coteries as discussed by Barbara and Garcia-Molina [1986]. The reduction in quality (e.g., in performance) for the competitive operations due to using a dominated coterie is the price to pay for having an improved quality for the noncompetitive operations. For example, consider the *Read One Write All* strategy, which corresponds to using the whole process set as the only write quorum and single processes as read quorums. The write coterie clearly is dominated and results, for example, in bad write performance: Each process must be accessed for writing. Read operations exhibit optimal performance as only a single process needs to be accessed.

Garcia-Molina and Barbara [1985] have shown how to construct the best quorum set for a noncompetitive type of operation given a coterie for a competitive type from *minimal transversals*. A transversal Q^{-1} of a coterie $\mathcal{Q}$ is a process set that shares a process with each quorum of $\mathcal{Q}$. Q^{-1} is minimal iff no proper subset of Q^{-1} is a transversal. The set $\mathcal{Q}^{-1}$ of all minimal transversals of $\mathcal{Q}$ is a quorum set, whose quorums share a process with each quorum of $\mathcal{Q}$, but not necessarily among each other. With domination for quorum sets analogously defined to domination for coteries, $\mathcal{Q}^{-1}$ dominates any quorum set, whose processes share a process with each quorum of $\mathcal{Q}$, and, therefore, is the best choice for the noncompetitive operations. As the optimal quorum set for noncompetitive operations can be easily constructed from the coterie for the competitive operations, we do not further consider the construction of quorum sets explicitly. However, let us emphasise that nondominated coteries are not optimal for every application: In case of noncompetitive operations, a *dominated* coterie for the competitive operations is optimal: They allow to use a quorum set that is not a coterie for the noncompetitive operations, which results in better performance for the noncompetitive operations. Consequently, probe strategies should be defined and optimised not only for nondominated coteries, but also for dominated coteries and quorum sets.

Coterie Constructions from Logical Structures A choice of certain quorums for a distributed system implies a trade-off among different qualities. Different constructions for quorums have been proposed that focus on different qualities. Many of these constructions do not explicitly consider a fault model, but impose a logical structure on the processes, which is exploited to derive quorums.

An obvious construction for a coterie is to form the quorums from proper majorities of the processes. However, such coteries are not nondominated in general as has been illustrated above and, therefore, are not optimal if a single type of operation must be supported. Another disadvantage of this approach is that the cardinality of the quorums is in $O(n)$, where n denotes the number of processes in a system. Other constructions allow to achieve better quorum cardinalities being in $O(\sqrt{n})$.

Different constructions based on different logical structures have been proposed in the literature. For example, such logical structures include votes [Thomas, 1979, Gifford, 1979], grids [Cheung et al., 1992], trees [Agrawal and Abbadi, 1992], or finite projective planes [Maekawa, 1985]. Let us illustrate such constructions by two examples, trees and grids, which support combinations of competitive and noncompetitive operations.

Example 4.3 (Coterie Construction from a Grid)
Cheung et al. [1992] have proposed to logically organise the processes of a distributed system as a grid. The competitive type of operations relies on a coterie whose quorums are formed by all processes of one column and single processes from each column, respectively. The noncompetitive type of operation relies on a quorum set whose quorums are formed by single processes from each column. Figure 4.1 illustrates the grid construction for twelve processes arranged in a 3×4 grid. The coterie for the competitive type of operation contains the quorum $\{p_1, p_4, p_5, p_6, p_9, p_{11}\}$ as shown in Fig. 4.1a, because the subset $\{p_1, p_5, p_9\}$ forms a column of the grid and the subset $\{p_1, p_4, p_6, p_{11}\}$ contains a single

process from each column. The quorum set for the noncompetitive type contains the quorum $\{p_1, p_7, p_{10}, p_{12}\}$ as shown in Fig. 4.1b, because this set contains a single process from each column. These two quorums share a single process, p_1. Note that the cardinality of quorums for both, competitive and noncompetitive operations, is in $O(\sqrt{n})$.

Example 4.4 (Coterie Construction from a Tree)
Agrawal and Abbadi [1992] have presented different constructions that logically arrange the processes in a tree. In a simple variant, the competitive type of operation relies on a coterie whose quorums are formed from majorities of processes on each level of the tree. For example, consider the tree shown in Fig. 4.2. The thirteen processes are arranged in a tree such that each inner node has three children. The coterie for the competitive type of operation contains the quorum $\{p_1, p_3, p_4, p_5, p_6, p_7, p_9, p_{13}\}$ as shown in Fig. 4.2a, because $\{p_1\}, \{p_3, p_4\}$, and $\{p_5, p_6, p_7, p_9, p_{13}\}$ form majorities on levels 1, 2, and 3 of the tree, respectively. The noncompetitive type of operation relies on a quorum set whose quorums are formed by a majority of processes on a single level of the tree. For the example, this quorum set contains the quorum $\{p_2, p_3\}$ as illustrated in Fig. 4.2b, because this set forms a majority on the second level of the tree.

Dynamic Coteries The quality of static coteries is lower than possible, because such coteries are fixed and cannot adapt to changing system conditions such as process failures. In contrast, a *dynamic coterie* allows to adapt to changing system conditions and, therefore, allows to achieve a higher quality than possible with static coteries. The adaptation of a dynamic coterie is realised by switching among different static coteries using an appropriate one for the current conditions. For example, if some processes suffer from high load or cause long delays due to high network latency, a dynamic coterie may switch over to a new static coterie excluding these processes from the quorums to reduce their workload and decrease overall latency. Analogously to static coteries, different constructions have been proposed for dynamic coteries.

Example 4.5 (Dynamic Grid)
Rabinovich and Lazowska [1992] have proposed a dynamic variant of the grid construction, which allows to exclude crashed processes from quorums. Consider a distributed system with twelve processes $p_1, \ldots, p_{12}$. The dynamic grid protocol may initially arrange the processes in a 3×4-grid (equal to the static variant) as illustrated in Fig. 4.1. If process p_7 crashes (and the crash is detected), the protocol allows to exclude p_7 and switch to a new static coterie with $p_i, i > 7$, taking the position of p_{i-1} in the grid as shown in Fig. 4.3a. The protocol also allows to completely reshape the grid as illustrated in Fig. 4.3b: If, additionally, p_9 and p_{12} fail, the grid may be reshaped to a 3×3 grid.

Epoch Changes An adaptation of the currently used static coterie requires some agreement and coordination itself to ensure agreement and coordination of the

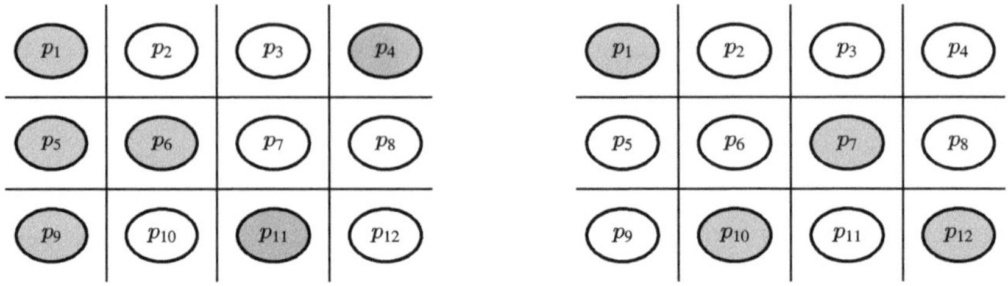

(a) A quorum for a competitive operation (b) A quorum for a noncompetitive operation

Figure 4.1: Example of the grid construction. Twelve processes are arranged in a 3×4-grid. Each column together with a process from each column forms a quorum for a competitive operation. A quorum for a noncompetitive operation is formed by a process from each column. Example quorums are highlighted by gray background colour.

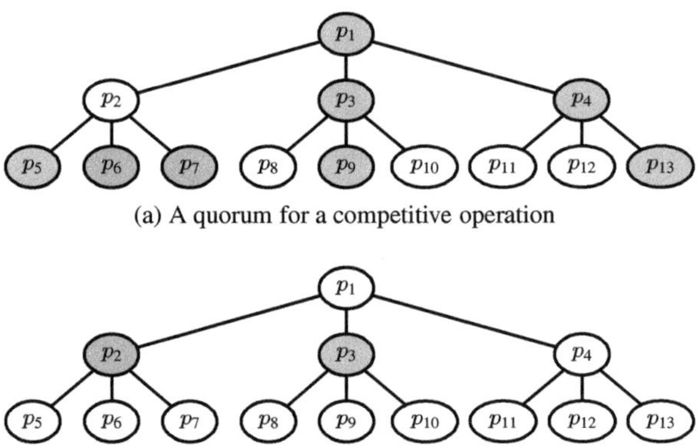

(a) A quorum for a competitive operation

(b) A quorum for a noncompetitive operation

Figure 4.2: Example of the simple tree construction. Thirteen processes are arranged in a tree such that each inner node has three children. A majority of processes on each level of the tree forms a quorum for a competitive operation. A majority on a single level forms a quorum for a noncompetitive operation. Example quorums are highlighted by gray background colour.

actual operations: As an adaptation may cause a transition between two static coteries with disjoint quorums, every process needs to know the current static coterie when accessing a quorum. Otherwise, two processes may concurrently access disjoint quorums for competitive operations. Hence, a transition from a static coterie

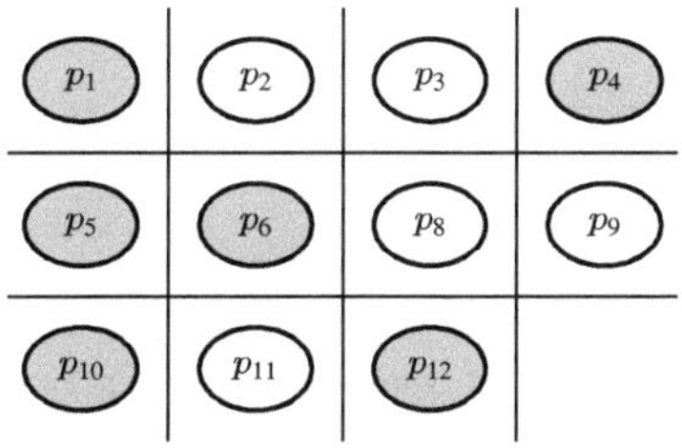

(a) The grid when p_7 is failed. The process has been excluded from the grid such that new quorums are formed.

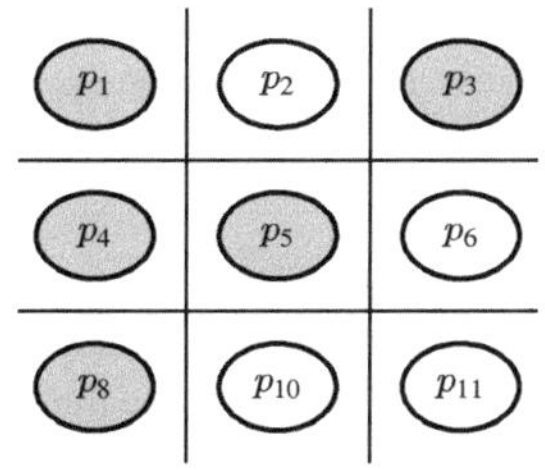

(b) The grid when, additionally, p_9 and p_{12} are failed. Both are excluded from the grid, which has been reshaped to 3×3.

Figure 4.3: Example of the dynamic grid construction and twelve processes. Initially, the grid equals the 3×4-grid of Fig. 4.1. Example quorums for competitive operations are highlighted by gray background colour.

to a subsequent one must be coordinated, which is called *epoch change* by Rabinovich and Lazowska [1992].

Gifford [1979] and Rabinovich and Lazowska [1992] have described how to realise coordinated transitions in principle: A quorum for a competitive operation from the current static coterie and one from the subsequent static coterie must be informed about the transition. If a process tries to access a quorum of an outdated static coterie, it accesses at least one process that knows about the subsequent coterie. Learning about the subsequent coterie, the process then tries to access a subsequent quorum. The intersection condition of quorums for competitive operations ensures that two concurrent transitions to new static coteries are coordinated.

With these preliminaries, we are now ready to consider constructions of highly available static coteries from Didep models.

4.3 Highly Available Static Coteries

High Availability Intuitively, the availability of a coterie measures the extent to which the coterie allows a system to cope with faults. In particular, we are interested in *highly available* coteries that allow to tolerate all assumed faults. For example, if a highly available coterie is used to coordinate the operations in a replicated database, a nonfaulty process is able to perform operations no matter which faults – within the limits of all assumed faults – do occur. Of course, being highly available or not depends on the functional and on the structural failure model that are used. For example, a coterie that is highly available in the presence of crash failures may not be highly available in the presence of Byzantine failures. We now discuss how to construct a highly available coterie in the presence of either crash or Byzantine failures from Didep models.

Crash Failures Assume that processes only fail by crashing. If a process tries to access a quorum, a failed process disturbs the coordination by not responding. Furthermore, assume that processes have some means of detecting that a process does not respond. For example, such means are provided by failure detectors or by using time-outs in synchronous systems. For tolerating all assumed faults, it suffices that the static coterie contains a quorum of nonfaulty processes for each trace.

Definition 4.5 (Highly Available Static Coteries despite Crash Failures)
A static coterie $\mathcal{Q}$ is *highly available* for a distributed system property P despite crash failures iff

$$\forall \tau \in P : \exists Q \in \mathcal{Q} : \ Q \cap F(\tau) = \emptyset.$$

When modelling faults with Didep models, a highly available static coterie does exist iff the union of every pair of sets in the Didep model does not cover the set of all processes. Formally, we capture this condition by "well-formedness."

Definition 4.6 (k-Well-Formedness)
A set $\mathcal{D} \subseteq \mathcal{P}(\Pi)$ of process sets is *k-well-formed* iff

$$\forall D_{i_1}, \ldots, D_{i_k} \in \mathcal{D} : \ D_{i_1} \cup \ldots \cup D_{i_k} \neq \Pi.$$

A 2-well-formed sound and complete Didep model characterises the existence of a highly available coterie despite crash failures.

Theorem 4.1
There exists a highly available static coterie for a distributed system property P despite crash failures iff the Didep model $\mathcal{D} = \{F(\tau) \subseteq \Pi : \tau \in P\}$ is 2-well-formed.

PROOF: We prove this theorem by the following two lemmas.

Lemma 4.1
If a static coterie is highly available for a distributed system property P despite crash failures, the Didep model $\mathcal{D} = \{F(\tau) \subseteq \Pi : \tau \in P\}$ is 2-well-formed.

PROOF: We assume that a highly available static coterie does exist and that $\mathcal{D}$ is not 2-well-formed and obtain a contradiction.
In summary, if a Didep model is not 2-well-formed, it contains two process sets whose union covers the set of all processes. As a highly available static coterie must contain quorums tolerating all assumed faults, at least two quorums are disjoint in this case. This violates the intersection condition of static coteries.

ASSUME: $\mathscr{Q}$ is a static coterie that is highly available for P and $\mathscr{D}$ is not 2-well-formed.

PROVE: FALSE

$\langle 1\rangle 1.$ $\exists \tau_i, \tau_j \in P: F(\tau_i) \cup F(\tau_j) = \Pi$

PROOF: As $\mathscr{D}$ is not 2-well-formed.

$\langle 1\rangle 2.$ $\Pi \setminus F(\tau_j) \subseteq F(\tau_i)$

PROOF: By $\langle 1\rangle 1$.

$\langle 1\rangle 3.$ $\exists Q_i, Q_j \in \mathscr{Q}: (Q_i \cap F(\tau_i) = \emptyset) \wedge (Q_j \cap F(\tau_j) = \emptyset)$

PROOF: As $\mathscr{Q}$ is highly available for P.

$\langle 1\rangle 4.$ $Q_j \subseteq \Pi \setminus F(\tau_j)$

PROOF: By $\langle 1\rangle 3$.

$\langle 1\rangle 5.$ $Q_i \cap (\Pi \setminus F(\tau_j)) = \emptyset$

PROOF: By $\langle 1\rangle 3$ and $\langle 1\rangle 2$.

$\langle 1\rangle 6.$ $Q_i \cap Q_j = \emptyset$

PROOF: By $\langle 1\rangle 4$ and $\langle 1\rangle 5$.

$\langle 1\rangle 7.$ Q.E.D.

PROOF: By $\langle 1\rangle 3$ and $\langle 1\rangle 6$, $\mathscr{Q}$ is not a static coterie as the intersection condition of static coteries is violated.

A given coterie implicitly describes a Didep model, namely the set of all process sets whose faults can be tolerated by the coterie. If the coterie is highly available for a property, it implicitly describes a 2-well-formed Didep model. We complement this duality by constructively showing that a 2-well-formed sound and complete Didep model is not only necessary, but also sufficient for the existence of a highly available static coterie.

Intuitively, each set D in a Didep model describes a possible fault scenario that a coterie needs to be prepared for. If the Didep model also includes a superset of D, it suffices that the coterie is prepared for the superset as it can also cope with D then. Furthermore, remember that, if $\mathscr{D}$ is a sound and complete Didep model, the processes that are not in $\mu(\mathscr{D})$ (see p. 71) are faulty whenever other processes are faulty. Hence, the processes that are not in $\mu(\mathscr{D})$ do not contribute to the redundancy required for being fault-tolerant and, therefore, may be neglected. In other words, it suffices to consider $\mathscr{D}|_{\mu(\mathscr{D})}$ for the construction of a coterie.

We derive a static coterie that is highly available for a distributed system property P by taking the set of all complements of all maximal sets in $\mathscr{D}|_{\mu(\mathscr{D})}$ for a 2-well-formed Didep model $\mathscr{D}$ that is sound and complete for P.

Lemma 4.2
If the Didep model $\mathscr{D} = \{F(\tau) \subseteq \Pi : \tau \in P\}$ for a distributed system property P, the set

$$\mathscr{Q} = \left\{ Q \subseteq \Pi :\ \exists D_i \in \mathscr{D}|_{\mu(\mathscr{D})} : (Q = \mu(\mathscr{D}) \setminus D_i) \wedge \left(\forall D_j \in \mathscr{D}|_{\mu(\mathscr{D})} :\ D_i \not\subset D_j \right) \right\}$$

is a static coterie and is highly available for P despite crash failures.

PROOF: As a prerequisite, we first show that $\mathscr{D}|_{\mu(\mathscr{D})}$ has similar properties as $\mathscr{D}$ itself in the sense that the worst-case set $\mu(\mathscr{D})$ is not in $\mathscr{D}|_{\mu(\mathscr{D})}$ and that no two subsets of $\mathscr{D}|_{\mu(\mathscr{D})}$ cover $\mu(\mathscr{D})$. Then, we proof that $\mathscr{Q}$ is a static coterie and indeed is highly available for P.

$\langle 1 \rangle 1.$ $\forall D_i, D_j \in \mathscr{D}|_{\mu(\mathscr{D})} : D_i \neq \mu(\mathscr{D}) \wedge D_i \cup D_j \neq \mu(\mathscr{D})$

PROOF: If $\mu(\mathscr{D}) \in \mathscr{D}|_{\mu(\mathscr{D})}$, then $\Pi \in \mathscr{D}$ as each process is faulty when all processes in $\mu(\mathscr{D})$ are faulty. This contradicts the assumption that $\mathscr{D}$ is 2-well-formed. Hence, $D_i \neq \mu(\mathscr{D})$.

Analogously, if there are two sets in $\mathscr{D}|_{\mu(\mathscr{D})}$, whose union covers $\mu(\mathscr{D})$, there are two sets in $\mathscr{D}$ covering Π, which contradicts that $\mathscr{D}$ is 2-well-formed.

$\langle 1 \rangle 2.$ $\mathscr{Q}$ is a static coterie. That is, for all $Q_i, Q_j \in \mathscr{Q}$,

1. $Q \neq \emptyset$,
2. $Q_i \cap Q_j \neq \emptyset$, and
3. $Q_i \not\subset Q_j$.

PROOF: It suffices to prove the conditions for some arbitrary $Q_i, Q_j \in \mathscr{Q}$. Before proving each condition separately, we relate them to sets in $\mathscr{D}|_{\mu(\mathscr{D})}$.

$\langle 2 \rangle 1.$ $\exists D_i, D_j \in \mathscr{D}|_{\mu(\mathscr{D})} : (D_i = \mu(\mathscr{D}) \setminus Q_i) \wedge (D_j = \mu(\mathscr{D}) \setminus Q_j) \wedge (D_j \not\subset D_i)$

PROOF: By the construction of $\mathscr{Q}$.

$\langle 2 \rangle 2.$ $Q_i \neq \emptyset$

PROOF: By $\langle 2 \rangle 1$, if Q_i would equal the empty set, then D_i would equal $\mu(\mathscr{D})$, which violates $\langle 1 \rangle 1$. Hence, $Q_i \neq \emptyset$.

$\langle 2 \rangle 3.$ $Q_i \cap Q_j \neq \emptyset$

PROOF: By $\langle 2 \rangle 1$, if $Q_i \cap Q_j$ would equal the empty set, then $D_i \cup D_j$ would equal $\mu(\mathscr{D})$ violating $\langle 1 \rangle 1$.

$\langle 2 \rangle 4.$ $Q_i \not\subset Q_j$

PROOF: By $\langle 2 \rangle 1$, if $Q_i \subset Q_j$, then $D_j \subset D_i$, which contradicts $\langle 2 \rangle 1$.

$\langle 2 \rangle 5.$ Q.E.D.

PROOF: By $\langle 2 \rangle 2 - \langle 2 \rangle 4$.

$\langle 1 \rangle 3.$ $\forall \tau \in P : \exists Q \in \mathscr{Q} :\ Q \cap F(\tau) = \emptyset$

PROOF: It suffices to show this for an arbitrary trace $\tau \in P$. By the definition of sound and complete Didep models, there exists an $D_j \in \mathscr{D}|_{\mu(\mathscr{D})}$ with $D_j = F(\tau)|_{\mu(\mathscr{D})}$. By the construction of $\mathscr{Q}$, there exists an $D_i \in \mathscr{D}|_{\mu(\mathscr{D})}$ with a $Q = \mu(\mathscr{D}) \setminus D_i$ and $D_j \subseteq D_i$. By set reasoning, $Q \cap F(\tau)|_{\mu(\mathscr{D})} = \emptyset$. As $Q \subseteq \mu(\mathscr{D})$ and $\left(F(\tau) \setminus F(\tau)|_{\mu(\mathscr{D})}\right) \cap \mu(\mathscr{D}) = \emptyset$, $Q \cap F(\tau) = \emptyset$.

⟨1⟩4. Q.E.D.
PROOF: By ⟨1⟩2, $\mathscr{Q}$ is a static coterie and, by ⟨1⟩3, $\mathscr{Q}$ is highly available for P.

This lemma completes the characterisation of highly available coteries despite crash failures. The following example illustrates the advantages of the construction over previous constructions.

Example: Highly Available Coteries despite Crash Failures For a distributed system with four processes, $\Pi = \{p_1, \ldots, p_4\}$, the well-known constructions of Majority Consensus Voting [Thomas, 1979] and of the Grid Protocol [Cheung et al., 1992] yield the same static coterie

$$\mathscr{Q}_1 = \{\{p_1, p_2, p_3\}, \{p_1, p_2, p_4\}, \{p_1, p_3, p_4\}, \{p_2, p_3, p_4\}\}$$

independent of the fault assumption. This coterie is highly available if at most one process crashes as expressed by the Didep model

$$\mathscr{D}_1 = \{\emptyset, \{p_1\}, \{p_2\}, \{p_3\}, \{p_4\}\}.$$

Yet it is not highly available if additionally p_1 and p_2 crash in the same trace and the Didep failure model becomes

$$\mathscr{D}_2 = \mathscr{D}_1 \cup \{\{p_1, p_2\}\}.$$

In this case, the static coterie derived with Majority Consensus Voting or the Grid Protocol cannot tolerate all assumed faults. However, $\mathscr{D}_2$ is 2-well-formed and our construction yields a highly available coterie

$$\mathscr{Q}_2 = \{\{p_1, p_2, p_3\}, \{p_1, p_2, p_4\}, \{p_3, p_4\}\}$$

that can tolerate all assumed faults. As a side note, this illustrates that the mere number of quorums of a coterie is no indicator for high availability: Although $\mathscr{Q}_2$ offers less options for choosing a quorum than $\mathscr{Q}_1$, it allows to tolerate more fault scenarios.

Advantages over Previous Constructions Some results that are closely related to Theorem 4.1 have been previously obtained for other classes of set-based structural failure models [Junqueira, 2006, Fitzi and Maurer, 1998]. As these classes are strictly less expressive than Didep models, our theorem generalises such results. In particular, our construction yields coteries that dominate coteries obtained with previous constructions: Intuitively, our construction yields smaller quorums in the presence of directed dependent faults (i.e., $\mu(\mathscr{D}) \subset \Pi$), because it only considers processes in $\mu(\mathscr{D})$ for quorums. Previous constructions consider all processes in Π.

For example, consider a distributed system property P with a sound and complete Didep model

$$\mathscr{D} = \{\emptyset, \{p_2\}, \{p_3\}, \{p_4\}, \{p_1, p_2\}\}.$$

As p_2 is faulty whenever p_1 is faulty and no other dependent faults occur, $\mu(\mathscr{D}) = \{p_1, p_3, p_4\}$. Our construction yields the highly available coterie

$$\mathscr{Q}_1 = \{\{p_1, p_3\}, \{p_1, p_4\}, \{p_3, p_4\}\}.$$

If relying on adversary structures, the fault model of P cannot be described accurately. Hence, the fault assumption must be (over-)approximated by

$$\mathscr{A} = \{\emptyset, \{p_1\}, \{p_2\}, \{p_3\}, \{p_4\}, \{p_1, p_2\}\}.$$

Hence, the information about directed dependent faults is lost. A construction based on adversary structures would yield the highly available coterie

$$\mathscr{Q}_2 = \{\{p_3, p_4\}, \{p_1, p_2, p_3\}, \{p_1, p_2, p_4\}\},$$

which is dominated by $\mathscr{Q}_1$.

Note that our construction may yield coteries with less and with larger quorums than constructions that are based on logical structures. While coteries based on such structures allow to achieve low message complexity, they are not highly available in general, because the logical structures do not take the fault model into account. In contrast, our construction yields a highly available coterie that is dominated in general. We do not consider this a disadvantage for two reasons:

1. In case of the noncompetitive type of operation, dominated coteries are better suited than nondominated coteries.

2. If required, a nondominated coterie can be constructed from a dominated one.

Although our construction yields dominated coteries in general, no quorum in such a system is redundant. That is, no quorum can be simply removed from a coterie without sacrificing high availability as we show next.

Corollary 4.1
If $\mathscr{Q}$ is a highly available static coterie for a distributed system property P derived as described in Lemma 4.2, no quorum can be removed from $\mathscr{Q}$ without sacrificing high availability.

PROOF: It suffices to prove that $\mathscr{Q}' = \mathscr{Q} \setminus \{Q\}$ for an arbitrary $Q \in \mathscr{Q}$ is not a highly available static coterie for P. Let $\mathscr{D}$ be the sound and complete Didep model for P.

$\langle 1 \rangle 1.$ $\forall Q' \in \mathscr{Q}' : \; Q' \not\subseteq Q$
  PROOF: By the definition of static coteries.
$\langle 1 \rangle 2.$ $\exists S \in \mu(\mathscr{D}) : \; Q = \mu(\mathscr{D}) \setminus S$
  PROOF: By the construction of $\mathscr{Q}$.
$\langle 1 \rangle 3.$ $\forall Q' \in \mathscr{Q}' : \; Q' \cap S \neq \emptyset$
  PROOF: By $\langle 1 \rangle 1$, $\langle 1 \rangle 2$, and the construction of $\mathscr{Q}$.
$\langle 1 \rangle 4.$ $\exists \tau \in P : \; S \subseteq F(\tau)$
  PROOF: As $\mathscr{D}$ is sound and complete for P and by the definition of μ.
$\langle 1 \rangle 5.$ Q.E.D.
  PROOF: By $\langle 1 \rangle 4$ and $\langle 1 \rangle 3$, $\mathscr{Q}'$ is not highly available.

Additionally, it can be shown that no quorum has a redundant process: Omitting a process from a quorum in $\mathscr{Q}$ sacrifices high availability. However, removing processes and/or quorums while adding new ones allows to construct coteries that dominate $\mathscr{Q}$.

Whether a coterie is highly available or not depends on the functional failure model that is used. In particular, the previous results hold for crash failures, but not in the presence of Byzantine failures. We will address Byzantine failures next.

Byzantine Failures Traditionally, coteries have only been used to tolerate "benign" failures such as crash or crash-recovery failures. With such fault assumptions, components may omit messages, but do not alter them or invent new ones. Malkhi and Reiter [1998] were the first to study requirements and constructions of highly available coteries despite Byzantine failures, where components are not "benign", but "malicious." For example, such processes may alter messages, duplicate them, or invent new ones.

For a highly available coterie despite crashes, it suffices that the coterie contains a quorum of nonfaulty processes. However, this does not suffice for Byzantine failures [Malkhi and Reiter, 1998]: Consider a distributed system with a single, competitive type of operation. If some processes p_i and p_j intend to concurrently perform operations in a trace τ, they access the quorums Q_i and Q_j, respectively. The process p_j receives

- relevant answers from each process in $(Q_i \cap Q_j) \setminus F(\tau)$, as these processes are correct and know about both operations,
- irrelevant answers from processes in $Q_j \setminus (Q_i \cup F(\tau))$ as these processes do not know that p_i wants to perform an operation, and
- arbitrary answers from $Q_j \cap F(\tau)$ as these processes are faulty.

From these answers, p_j must come to the decision, whether to perform the operation or not. For a correct decision, the relevant answers must outweigh the arbitrary ones, which requires that each pair of quorums intersects in sufficiently many nonfaulty processes [Malkhi and Reiter, 1998, Alvisi et al., 2000].

Definition 4.7 (Highly Available Static Coteries despite Byzantine Failures)
A static coterie $\mathcal{Q}$ is *highly available* for a distributed system property P despite Byzantine failures iff

$$\forall Q_i, Q_j \in \mathcal{Q} : \forall \tau_i, \tau_j \in P : \left(Q_i \cap Q_j\right) \not\subseteq F(\tau_i) \cup F\left(\tau_j\right) \text{ (consistency).}$$

Intuitively, the consistency condition ensures that, if two processes access a quorum, respectively, both quorums share enough nonfaulty processes to outnumber the common faulty ones. Note that this definition is adopted from Alvisi et al. [2000], which differs from the definition of Malkhi and Reiter [1998]. Malkhi and Reiter [1998] additionally require that each highly available coterie has a quorum of correct processes. However, this condition is not required to perform operations correctly despite Byzantine failures. It suffices that a quorum has enough correct processes.

When modelling faults with Didep models, a highly available static coterie does exist iff the union of every four sets of faulty processes does not cover the set of all processes. Formally, we capture this condition by 4-well-formedness.

Theorem 4.2
There exists a highly available static coterie for a distributed system property P despite Byzantine failures iff the Didep model $\mathcal{D} = \{F(\tau) \subseteq \Pi : \tau \in P\}$ is 4-well-formed.

PROOF: The proof is omitted here as it is closely related to the proof of Theorem 4.1 and to the proof of Corollary 4.4 of Malkhi and Reiter [1998]. In particular, the same construction rule as used in Lemma 4.2 yields highly available coteries for Byzantine failures if $\mathcal{D}$ is 4-well-formed.

Malkhi and Reiter [1998] found closely related results for fail-prone systems. Analogously to the results for crash failures, our results are generalisations of previous results, because we consider the most expressive class of set-based structural failure models.

Example 4.6 (Highly Available Static Coteries despite Byzantine Failures)
Consider a distributed system with a set of processes $\Pi = \{p_1, \ldots, p_7\}$ and a Didep model

$$\mathscr{D} = \{\emptyset, \{p_2\}, \{p_3\}, \{p_4\}, \{p_5\}, \{p_6\}, \{p_7\}, \{p_1, p_2\}, \{p_3, p_4\}\}.$$

The Didep model describes directed dependent faults as p_2 is faulty whenever p_1 is faulty. It also describes undirected dependent faults for p_3 and p_4. As $\mathscr{D}$ is 4-well-formed, our construction yields a highly available static coterie $\mathscr{Q}$ for Byzantine failures with

$$\mathscr{Q}_1 = \{\{p_1, p_5, p_6, p_7\}, \{p_1, p_3, p_4, p_5, p_6\}, \{p_1, p_3, p_4, p_5, p_7\}, \{p_1, p_3, p_4, p_6, p_7\}, \{p_3, p_4, p_5, p_6, p_7\}\}.$$

For example, process p_1 may decide to access the quorum $\{p_1, p_3, p_4, p_5, p_6\}$ before performing a competitive operation in a trace τ. Process p_2 may try to concurrently perform a competitive operation by accessing $\{p_1, p_3, p_4, p_6, p_7\}$. Even if the set of faulty processes $F(\tau)$ equals $\{p_3, p_4\}$, p_1 and p_2 receive relevant answers from p_1 and p_6. As p_1 and p_6 cannot be faulty in the same trace, p_1 and p_2 come to a correct decision on how to proceed.

If $\mathscr{D}$ is (over-)approximated by a fail-prone system, the construction of Malkhi and Reiter [1998] yields the highly available static coterie $\mathscr{Q}_2$ for Byzantine failures with

$$\mathscr{Q}_2 = \{\{p_1, p_2, p_5, p_6, p_7\}, \{p_1, p_2, p_3, p_4, p_5, p_6\}, \{p_1, p_2, p_3, p_4, p_5, p_7\}, \{p_1, p_2, p_3, p_4, p_6, p_7\}, \{p_3, p_4, p_5, p_6, p_7\}\},$$

which is dominated by $\mathscr{Q}_1$.

Note that every coterie that is highly available for Byzantine failures is dominated (except for trivial cases). Hence, nondominated coteries cannot tolerate all assumed Byzantine failures. Nevertheless, coteries can be found that dominate a coterie yielded by our construction, but are still highly available. However, constructions of such coteries and the notion of domination for Byzantine failures in general remain topics for future work.

Theorem 4.1 and Theorem 4.2 illustrate that more expressive classes of structural failure models allow to achieve better resilience: Both theorems strictly generalise results that have been obtained under threshold models. Nevertheless, while the class of Didep models is more expressive than classes of previous set-based structural failure models (e.g., adversary structures, fail-prone systems, and core / survivor sets), the characterisation of highly available coteries is closely related to previous characterisations in terms of adversary structures, fail-prone systems, and core / survivor sets. However, Didep models allow to construct "better" coteries with respect to domination: Our construction yields coteries that dominate coteries derived from less expressive set-based models.

4.4 Highly Available Dynamic Coteries

As shown above, the availability of static coteries has severe limitations: Even relatively mild fault models prohibit the existence of highly available static coteries. The underlying reason for this limitation is that static coteries cannot adapt to the changing conditions of a distributed system, but are fixed at design time to work for *any possible* condition. More precisely, static coteries do not only allow to tolerate the faults in the current trace, but the faults that may occur in any trace.

Neglecting the knowledge of the current conditions in a distributed system possibly leads to less efficient and less resilient systems. For example, if a process has crashed, all quorums that contain this process become useless for performing an operation. These quorums could be omitted from the static coterie during runtime to improve the efficiency of the system (e.g., by reducing the probe complexity). If – over time – enough processes fail (and remain failed), the redundancy provided by a static coterie is exhausted: No further operation can be performed. In general, omitting failed processes from a coterie at runtime delays the point of exhaustion and, therefore, improves the overall availability.

Dynamic Coteries We call coteries that allow to adapt to the current conditions *dynamic coteries*. Essentially, a dynamic coterie allows to switch from one static coterie to another one during runtime to adapt to the current conditions. While dynamic coteries allow to decide for different quality trade-offs at runtime, we focus on systems that adapt to process failures and switch between static coteries for being as resilient as possible.

We model a dynamic coterie $\mathcal{Q}_D$ by a set of pairs. Each pair $\langle C, \mathcal{Q} \rangle$ consists of a set of processes C and a static coterie $\mathcal{Q}$. A distributed system is supposed to switch to $\mathcal{Q}$ if C describes the set of currently crashed processes. For example, if

$$\langle C_0, \mathcal{Q}_0 \rangle = \langle \{\}, \{\{p_1, p_2, p_3\}, \{p_1, p_3, p_4\}, \{p_1, p_2, p_4\}, \{p_2, p_3, p_4\}\} \rangle$$

and

$$\langle C_1, \mathcal{Q}_1 \rangle = \langle \{p_1\}, \{\{p_2, p_3\}, \{p_2, p_4\}, \{p_3, p_4\}\} \rangle$$

are in $\mathcal{Q}_D$, a distributed system is supposed to use $\mathcal{Q}_0$ as the static coterie as long as no process has crashed. If p_1 crashes, the distributed system is supposed to switch over to $\mathcal{Q}_1$, which does not contain a quorum with p_1. Note that $\mathcal{Q}_0$ corresponds to a grid construction based on Π and $\mathcal{Q}_1$ corresponds to a majority construction based on $\Pi \setminus \{p_1\}$. While $\mathcal{Q}_0$ allows to tolerate one failed process, $\mathcal{Q}_1$ allows to tolerate that p_1 and one other process are failed.

Definition 4.8 (Dynamic Coterie)
A set $\mathscr{Q}_D \subseteq \mathscr{P}(\Pi) \times \mathscr{P}(\mathscr{P}(\Pi))$ is a *dynamic coterie* iff

1. $\forall \langle C, \mathscr{Q} \rangle \in \mathscr{Q}_D : \mathscr{Q}$ is a static coterie,
2. $\forall \langle C_i, \mathscr{Q}_i \rangle \in \mathscr{Q}_D, C \subseteq C_i : \exists \langle C_j, \mathscr{Q}_j \rangle \in \mathscr{Q}_D : C = C_j$, and
3. $\forall \langle C_i, \mathscr{Q}_i \rangle, \langle C_j, \mathscr{Q}_j \rangle \in \mathscr{Q}_D : C_i \neq C_j$.

The first condition asserts that a dynamic coterie only allows to switch between static coteries. The second condition asserts that, if the dynamic coterie is prepared for a certain set of crashed processes, it is also prepared for all sets of crashed processes that may occur beforehand. For example, if $\mathscr{Q}_D$ contains $\langle \{p_1, p_2\}, \mathscr{Q}_2 \rangle$, it must also contain some pair $\langle \{p_1\}, \mathscr{Q}_1 \rangle$, because p_1 may crash before p_2. The third condition asserts that the dynamic coterie uniquely defines a static coterie for a set of crashed processes.

Example 4.7 (Dynamic Coterie)
Consider a dynamic coterie $\mathscr{Q}_D$ constructed by the dynamic grid protocol for 12 processes, $\Pi = \{p_1, \ldots, p_{12}\}$. The dynamic grid protocol could initially arrange the processes in a 3×4 grid as illustrated in Fig. 4.1a on page 108. For example, $\mathscr{Q}_D$ then contains

$$\langle \emptyset, \{\{p_1, p_4, p_5, p_6, p_9, p_{11}\}, \ldots\} \rangle$$

meaning that the processes that are highlighted in Fig. 4.1a form a quorum. If process p_7 has crashed, a new grid without p_7 is formed to adapt to the crash. As illustrated in Fig. 4.3a on page 109, $\mathscr{Q}_D$ contains

$$\langle \{p_7\}, \{\{p_1, p_4, p_5, p_6, p_{10}, p_{12}\}, \ldots\} \rangle$$

if each process $p_i, i > 7$, takes the position of p_{i-1} in the grid. Analogously, $\mathscr{Q}_D$ contains

$$\langle \{p_7, p_9, p_{12}\}, \{\{p_1, p_3, p_4, p_5, p_8\}, \ldots\} \rangle$$

if, additionally, the processes p_9 and p_{12} crash as shown in Fig. 4.3b on page 109.

k-Failure Reachability Set Switching the static coterie allows to improve the availability of a distributed system even under harsh fault assumptions (such as "all processes except one may crash"). Remember that a transition to a new static coterie requires some coordination itself, for example, by *epoch changes* (see p. 107). To benefit from dynamic coteries, processes need to be reasonably fast to suspect failed processes and perform epoch changes. Otherwise, successive failures may lead to a situation in which no current quorum contains only noncrashed processes. This would prevent further epoch changes as epoch changes require to access a current quorum. To allow useful dynamic coteries, we assume that at most k processes may crash before the next epoch change occurs[2].

More formally, if C denotes the set of currently failed processes, we assume that C may grow by up to k processes between two epoch changes. Note that C may not grow by k arbitrary processes due to the structural failure model. For convenience, we define a *k-failure reachability set* $\text{Reach}_k(C)$ that describes how C may grow by up to k processes. This reachability set must satisfy the following conditions: In case of permanent faults, the set of currently failed processes grows monotonically in a trace. Hence, C_i must be a subset of all sets in $\text{Reach}_k(C_i)$. Moreover, as we limit the number of additionally failed processes to k, each $C_j \in \text{Reach}_k(C_i)$ has at most k more elements than C_i. Due to a structural failure model, C_j may not contain k arbitrary additional processes, but there must be a trace such that C_j is the set of currently failed processes after C_i was the set of currently failed processes. More formally:

Definition 4.9 (k-Failure Reachability Set)
The set $\text{Reach}_k(C_i) \subseteq \mathscr{P}(\Pi)$ is called the *k-failure reachability set* for a set of processes $C_i \subseteq \Pi$ and a distributed system property P iff

$$\begin{aligned}\text{Reach}_k(C_i) = \{C_j \subseteq \Pi : & \wedge C_i \subseteq C_j \\ & \wedge \left|C_j \setminus C_i\right| \leq k \\ & \wedge \exists \langle s_0, s_1, \ldots \rangle \in P : \\ & \quad \wedge \exists i \geq 0 : C_i = \left\{p \in \Pi : \mathit{failed}_p(s_i) = \text{TRUE}\right\} \\ & \quad \wedge \exists j > i : C_j = \left\{p \in \Pi : \mathit{failed}_p(s_j) = \text{TRUE}\right\}\}.\end{aligned}$$

Example 4.8 (k-Failure Reachability Set)
Consider a distributed system property P with four processes, $\Pi = p_1, \ldots, p_4$, where processes may fail by crashing, and a sound and complete Didep model

$$\mathscr{D} = \{\emptyset, \{p_1, p_2, p_3\}\} \cup \left\{\{p_i, p_j\} : p_i \in \Pi \wedge p_j \in \Pi\right\}.$$

The 1-failure reachability set $\text{Reach}_k(\{p_1\})$ for P is

$$\{\{p_1\}, \{p_1, p_2\}, \{p_1, p_3\}, \{p_1, p_4\}\},$$

because another arbitrary process in Π may fail. The 2-failure reachability set $\text{Reach}_k(\{p_1\})$ for P is

$$\{\{p_1\}, \{p_1, p_2\}, \{p_1, p_3\}, \{p_1, p_4\}, \{p_1, p_2, p_3\}\},$$

because another arbitrary process in Π may fail and the only option for two further failures is that p_2 and p_3 fail.

[2] This notion generalises previous approaches relying on *frequent updates* [Jajodia and Mutchler, 1990] that allow to detect a failure and perform an epoch change before any subsequent failure occurs.

We are now ready to characterise the existence of highly available dynamic coteries. We do this first for crash failures and then for Byzantine failures.

Crash Failures Assume that processes only fail by crashing such that a failed process disturbs coordination by not responding. To be highly available, the current static coterie must provide a quorum of noncrashed processes. Obviously, this condition requires that the dynamic coterie contains a static coterie $\mathscr{Q}$ for each set of processes C that are crashed at any point in time. Hence, $\mathscr{Q}$ contains a quorum of noncrashed processes. More strictly, it requires that $\mathscr{Q}$ contains a quorum of noncrashed processes even if another k processes crash as, otherwise, further epoch changes become impossible.

Definition 4.10 (k-Highly-Available Dynamic Coterie despite Crash Failures)
A dynamic coterie $\mathscr{Q}_D$ is *k-highly-available* for a distributed system property P despite crash failures iff

$$\forall \tau \in P, C_i \subseteq F(\tau) : \exists \langle C_i, \mathscr{Q} \rangle \in \mathscr{Q}_D : \forall C_j \in \text{Reach}_k(C_i) : \exists Q \in \mathscr{Q} : Q \cap C_j = \emptyset.$$

Intuitively, for each $\langle C, \{Q\} \rangle \in \mathscr{Q}_D$, $\mathscr{Q}$ is a highly available static coterie if the reachability set $\text{Reach}_k(C)$ is interpreted as a "local" Didep model for the period between two epoch changes. Hence, an epoch change can install a static coterie that preserves availability if the corresponding reachability set is 2-well-formed. Leveraging this "local" condition to the actual Didep model, we will show that a highly available dynamic coterie exists iff the sound and complete Didep model is *k-reachable-well-formed*.

Definition 4.11 (k-Reachable-Well-Formedness)
The Didep model $\{F(\tau) \subseteq \Pi : \tau \in P\}$ is *k-reachable-well-formed* for a distributed system property P iff for all $F(\tau) \in \mathscr{D}$ and for all $C \subseteq F(\tau)$ the k-failure-reachability set $\text{Reach}_k(C)$ is 2-well-formed.

Theorem 4.3
There exists a k-highly-available dynamic coterie for a distributed system property P despite crash failures iff the Didep model $\mathscr{D} = \{F(\tau) \subseteq \Pi : \tau \in P\}$ is k-reachable-well-formed.

PROOF: We prove the theorem by the following two lemmas.

Lemma 4.3
If a dynamic coterie is k-highly-available for a distributed system property P despite crash failures, the Didep model $\mathscr{D} = \{F(\tau) \subseteq \Pi : \tau \in P\}$ is k-reachable-well-formed for P.

PROOF: We assume that a k-highly-available dynamic coterie does exist and that the $\mathscr{D}$ is not k-reachable-well-formed, and obtain a contradiction.

Intuitively, if a Didep model is not k-reachable-well-formed, there are two ways how up to k additional processes can fail between epoch changes. Thus, the union of both resulting sets of failed processes cover the whole process set. As a k-highly available dynamic coterie must contain a static coterie with quorums that tolerate each way, at least two quorums are disjoint, which violates the intersection condition of static coteries.

ASSUME: $\mathcal{Q}_D$ is a k-highly available dynamic coterie for P and the Didep model $\mathscr{D}$ is not k-reachable-well-formed.

PROVE: FALSE

$\langle 1 \rangle 1$. $\exists D \in \mathscr{D}, C \subseteq D:$ $\text{Reach}_k(C)$ is not 2-well-formed

PROOF: As $\mathscr{D}$ is not k-reachable-formed.

$\langle 1 \rangle 2$. $\exists \tau \in P: \; C \subseteq F(\tau)$

PROOF: By the definition of $\mathscr{D}$ and by $\langle 1 \rangle 1$.

$\langle 1 \rangle 3$. $\exists \langle C, \mathcal{Q} \rangle \in \mathcal{Q}_D:$ $\mathcal{Q}$ is a static coterie

PROOF: By $\langle 1 \rangle 2$ and as $\mathcal{Q}_D$ is a k-highly-available dynamic coterie.

$\langle 1 \rangle 4$. $\exists C_i, C_j \in \text{Reach}_k(C): \; C_i \cup C_j = \Pi$

PROOF: As $\text{Reach}_k(C)$ is not 2-well-formed by $\langle 1 \rangle 1$.

$\langle 1 \rangle 5$. $\exists Q_i, Q_j \in \mathcal{Q}: \; Q_i \cap C_i = \emptyset \wedge Q_j \cap F_j = \emptyset$

PROOF: By $\langle 1 \rangle 4$, $\langle 1 \rangle 3$, and as $\mathcal{Q}_D$ is a k-highly-available dynamic coterie.

$\langle 1 \rangle 6$. Q.E.D.

PROOF: By $\langle 1 \rangle 4$, $\langle 1 \rangle 5$, and set reasoning, $Q_i \cap Q_j = \emptyset$. Hence, $\mathcal{Q}$ is not a static coterie contradicting $\langle 1 \rangle 3$.

Analogously to Lemma 4.2, we constructively show that a k-highly-available dynamic coterie exists for a k-reachable-well-formed Didep model.

Lemma 4.4

If the Didep model $\mathscr{D} = \{F(\tau) \subseteq \Pi : \tau \in \Pi\}$ is k-reachable-well-formed for a distributed system property P, the set

$$\begin{aligned}
\mathcal{Q}_D = \{\langle C, \mathcal{Q} \rangle \; : \exists D \in \mathscr{D} : \wedge\, & C \subseteq D \\
& \wedge\, \mathcal{Q} = \{Q \subseteq \Pi : \; \exists C_i \in \text{Reach}_k(C)|_{\mu(\mathscr{D})} : \\
& \quad \wedge\, Q = \mu(\mathscr{D}) \setminus C_i \\
& \quad \wedge\, \forall C_j \in \text{Reach}_k(C)|_{\mu(\mathscr{D})} : \; C_i \not\subset C_j\}\}
\end{aligned}$$

is a k-highly-available dynamic coterie for P despite crash failures.

PROOF:

ASSUME: P is a distributed system property and $\mathscr{D}$ is a k-reachable-well-formed Didep model for P.

PROVE: $\mathcal{Q}_D$ is a k-highly-available dynamic coterie for P despite crash failures.

$\langle 1\rangle 1$. For all $\langle C, \mathscr{Q}\rangle \in \mathscr{Q}_D$, if $\text{Reach}_k(C)$ is 2-well-formed, then

$$\forall C_i, C_j \in \text{Reach}_k(C)|_{\mu(\mathscr{D})}: \; C_i \cup C_j \neq \mu(\mathscr{D}).$$

PROOF: Otherwise, there would be two sets in $\text{Reach}_k(C)$ that cover the whole process set. This would contradict the assumption that $\mathscr{D}$ is k-reachable-well-formed.

$\langle 1\rangle 2$. $\forall \tau \in P, C \subseteq F(\tau) : \exists \mathscr{Q} \subseteq \mathscr{P}(\Pi) : \langle C, \mathscr{Q}\rangle \in \mathscr{Q}_D$

PROOF: By the definition of $\mathscr{D}$, $\forall \tau \in P : \exists D \in \mathscr{D} : F(\tau) = D$. By the construction of $\mathscr{Q}_D$, there exists a tuple $\langle C, \mathscr{Q}\rangle$ in $\mathscr{Q}_D$ for each $C \subseteq D$.

$\langle 1\rangle 3$. $\forall \langle C, \mathscr{Q}\rangle \in \mathscr{Q}_D : \forall Q_i, Q_j \in \mathscr{Q}: \; Q_i \neq \emptyset \wedge Q_i \cap Q_j \neq \emptyset \wedge Q_i \not\subset Q_j$

PROOF: It suffices to prove this for some arbitrary $\langle C, \mathscr{Q}\rangle \in \mathscr{Q}_D$ and some arbitrary $Q_i, Q_j \in \mathscr{Q}$. By the construction of $\mathscr{Q}$, there are $C_i, C_j \in \text{Reach}_k(C)|_{\mu(\mathscr{D})}$ with $C_i = \mu(\mathscr{D}) \setminus Q_i$, $C_j = \mu(\mathscr{D}) \setminus Q_j$, and $C_j \not\subset C_i$. By $\langle 1\rangle 1$, no two sets in $\text{Reach}_k(C)|_{\mu(\mathscr{D})}$ cover $\mu(\mathscr{D})$. By set reasoning, $C_i \neq \emptyset$, $Q_i \cap Q_j \neq \emptyset$, and $Q_i \not\subset Q_j$.

$\langle 1\rangle 4$. $\forall \langle C, \mathscr{Q}\rangle \in \mathscr{Q}_D, C_i \in \text{Reach}_k(C) : \exists Q \in \mathscr{Q}: \; Q \cap C_i = \emptyset$

PROOF: It suffices to prove this for some arbitrary $\langle C, \mathscr{Q}\rangle \in \mathscr{Q}_D$ and some arbitrary $C_i \in \text{Reach}_k(C)$. By the construction of $\mathscr{Q}_D$, there exists a set $C_j \in \text{Reach}_k(C)|_{\mu(\mathscr{D})}$ and a $Q \in \mathscr{Q}$ with $C_i|_{\mu(\mathscr{D})} \subseteq C_j$ and $Q = \mu(\mathscr{D}) \setminus C_j$. As $Q \subseteq \mu(\mathscr{D})$ and $\left(C_i \setminus C_i|_{\mu(\mathscr{D})}\right) \cap \mu(\mathscr{D}) = \emptyset$, $Q \cap C_i = \emptyset$.

$\langle 1\rangle 5$. Q.E.D.

PROOF: By $\langle 1\rangle 2$, $\langle 1\rangle 3$, and $\langle 1\rangle 4$, $\mathscr{Q}_D$ is a k-highly-available dynamic coterie for P.

Note that a Didep model is 2-well-formed iff it is n-reachable-well-formed with $n = |\Pi|$; that is, there are no two fault scenarios whose union equals the set of all processes. Hence, there exists a highly available static coterie despite crash failures iff there exists an n-highly-available dynamic coterie despite crash failures. However, a Didep model may be k-reachable-well-formed with $k < n$, but not 2-well-formed. Thus, using a dynamic coterie may allow to achieve high availability when being impossible with a static coterie.

As our construction of the static coteries that form a dynamic coterie is closely related to the construction for purely static coteries, the construction yields quorums with the same advantages as described on page 113.

Example 4.9 (k-Highly-Available Dynamic Coterie despite Crash Failures)
Obviously, constructions of dynamic coteries do not yield highly available quorums in general. For example, consider the Dynamic Grid Protocol for a distributed system with twelve processes as illustrated in Fig. 4.3a on page 109. This dynamic coterie can tolerate up to two arbitrary failures between two epoch changes, but not three, because three failures may affect a complete column of the grid. In this case, no quorum of nonfailed processes remains. However, for example, the structural failure model expressing that at most 5 processes fail is 3-reachable-well-formed and even 4-reachable-well-formed. Hence, our construction

yields a 4-highly-available dynamic coterie that can tolerate up to four (instead of only two) failures between two epoch changes.

Byzantine Failures A distributed system that relies on dynamic coteries must provide some means of detecting failures and identifying outdated coteries. Failure detection is necessary to know when to switch the static coterie and to know to which conditions to adapt. Identifying outdated coteries is necessary to ensure that only current quorums are used for performing operations. In the presence of Byzantine failures, these tasks become particularly challenging. While crash failures are rather easy to detect by heartbeat techniques given the system is synchronous [Chandra and Toueg, 1996, Chen et al., 2002], Byzantine failures are significantly harder to detect [Alvisi et al., 2001, Doudou et al., 2002, Kihlstrom et al., 2003]. For example, such failures permit a failed process to always respond correctly in time when being diagnosed but otherwise responding arbitrarily when accessed.

A process must be able to identify an outdated coterie, becausc it does not learn about a transition to a new static coterie when it is not part of a quorum of the epoch change. If such a process subsequently tries to perform a competitive operation, it first accesses an outdated quorum and must learn about a subsequent coterie from some processes of the outdated quorum. In case of crash failures, it suffices that the process is informed by a single process. In case of Byzantine failures, this process may be failed and lie about the subsequent coterie. In particular, it may conceal that a subsequent coterie has been installed.

Due to these issues, the consistency condition for dynamic coteries is subtle: To mask erroneous information about the current coterie, a static coterie must ensure that the intersection of any two of its quorums allows to correctly determine the information about being outdated. Unfortunately, more than k failures may occur before a process tries to perform an operation. Hence, a current coterie must ensure consistency for *all* possible future failures.

We define k-highly-available dynamic coteries despite Byzantine failures as follows.

Definition 4.12 (k-Highly-Available Dynamic Coterie despite Byzantine Failures) A dynamic coterie $\mathcal{Q}_D$ is *k-highly-available* for a distributed system property P despite Byzantine failures iff

$$\begin{aligned} &\forall \langle C, \mathcal{Q} \rangle \in \mathcal{Q}_D : \forall \tau_i, \tau_j \in P : \\ &\quad \left(C \subseteq F(\tau_i) \wedge C \subseteq F(\tau_j)\right) \Rightarrow \forall Q_i, Q_j \in \mathcal{Q} : Q_i \cap Q_j \not\subseteq F(\tau_i) \cup F(\tau_j). \end{aligned}$$

The challenges posed by Byzantine failures are so severe that dynamic coteries do not bear any advantages over static coteries with respect to high availability.

More precisely, whenever a dynamic coterie exists that is k-highly available despite Byzantine failures, a highly-available *static* coterie also does exist.

Theorem 4.4
If $\mathcal{Q}_D$ is a k-highly-available dynamic coterie for a distributed system property P despite Byzantine failures, then there exists a static coterie $\mathcal{Q}$ that is highly-available for P despite Byzantine failures.

PROOF: We show that the conditions for k-highly-available dynamic coteries are sufficient for the existence of a highly available static coterie. In particular, the static coterie $\mathcal{Q}$ with $\langle \emptyset, \mathcal{Q} \rangle \in \mathcal{Q}_D$ is highly available.
$\langle 1 \rangle 1.$ $\exists \mathcal{Q} \subseteq \mathcal{P}(\Pi) : \langle \emptyset, \mathcal{Q} \rangle \in \mathcal{Q}_D$
PROOF: By the definition of dynamic coteries and as $\emptyset \subseteq F(\tau)$ for each $\tau \in P$.
$\langle 1 \rangle 2.$ $\mathcal{Q}$ is a static coterie.
PROOF: As $\mathcal{Q}_D$ is a dynamic coterie.
$\langle 1 \rangle 3.$ $\forall Q_i, Q_j \in \mathcal{Q} : \forall \tau_i, \tau_j \in P : \ (Q_i \cap Q_j) \not\subseteq F(\tau_i) \cup F(\tau_j)$
PROOF: By $\langle 1 \rangle 1$, $\langle \emptyset, \mathcal{Q} \rangle \in \mathcal{Q}_D$. As $\mathcal{Q}_D$ is k-highly-available for P despite Byzantine failures, $\emptyset \subseteq F(\tau)$, and $\forall \tau \in P : \emptyset \subseteq F(\tau)$.
$\langle 1 \rangle 4.$ Q.E.D.
PROOF: By $\langle 1 \rangle 2$ and $\langle 1 \rangle 3$, $\mathcal{Q}$ is highly available despite Byzantine failures.

Example 4.10
Consider a set of processes $\Pi = \{p_1, \ldots, p_7\}$ and the dynamic coterie $\mathcal{Q}_D$ with

$$\begin{aligned}\mathcal{Q}_D = &\{\langle \emptyset, \{Q \subseteq \Pi : |Q| = 6\} \rangle\} \\ &\cup \{\langle \{p\}, \mathcal{Q} \rangle : p \in \Pi \wedge \mathcal{Q} = \{Q \subseteq \Pi : |Q| = 5 \wedge p \notin Q\}\} \\ &\cup \{\langle \{p_i, p_j\}, \mathcal{Q} \rangle : p_i, p_j \in \Pi \wedge \mathcal{Q} = \{Q \subseteq \Pi : |Q| = 4 \wedge p_i, p_j \notin Q\}\}.\end{aligned}$$

This dynamic coterie is 1-highly-available despite Byzantine failures and a distributed system property P with

$$\{F(\tau) \subseteq \Pi : \tau \in P\} = \{\emptyset\} \cup \{\{p\} : p \in \Pi\} \cup \{\{p_1, p\} : p \in \Pi\}.$$

That is, $\mathcal{Q}_D$ tolerates an arbitrary Byzantine failure and, additionally, the Byzantine failures of p_1 and another process. Note that $\{F(\tau) \subseteq \Pi : \tau \in P\}$ is 4-well-formed. Hence, a *static* coterie can be found that is highly available despite Byzantine failures for P. For example, the static coterie $\mathcal{Q}$ with

$$\mathcal{Q} = \{Q \subseteq \Pi : p_1 \notin Q \wedge |Q| = 5\}$$

is such a coterie. Hence, being dynamic does not bring advantages for high availability. In particular, for any property P, for which $\mathcal{Q}_D$ is k-highly-available despite Byzantine failures, a static coterie can be found that is also highly available despite Byzantine failures.

So far, we have focused on the quality of high availability. We have shown how to check whether a highly available coterie exists and, if so, how to construct one. We continue with the quality of probe complexity and show how to exploit fault models for reducing the probe complexity.

4.5 Reducing Probe Complexity

Probing a quorum set allows a process to find a quorum of noncrashed processes or to reveal that no such quorum exists. If a quorum of noncrashed processes is found, this quorum may be accessed for performing a competitive operation. If no such quorum exists, the redundancy required for fault tolerance is exhausted.

For this section, let us assume that channels are reliable, processes fail by crashing, and crashes can be detected. Furthermore, let us assume that no failures occur while probing a quorum set. These assumptions are identical to the assumptions made in previous work on probe complexity [Peleg and Wool, 1996, Neilsen, 1997, Peleg and Wool, 2002]. If we deal with a specific sequence-based structural failure model, we assume that this model is sound and complete for the distributed system property currently under investigation.

Probe Strategies and their Complexity We adopt the notion of an *adaptive probe strategy* from Peleg and Wool [2002] that allows a process to decide which process to probe next based on the results of all previous probes. Peleg and Wool model a probe strategy by a labelled binary tree as illustrated in Fig. 4.4. Finding a quorum of noncrashed processes or revealing that no such quorum exists means to follow a path from the root to a leaf of the tree. An inner node with a label p represents probing the process $p \in \Pi$. The edges to the node's children represent the possible results of probing the process: The left edge represents that p is noncrashed and the right one that it is crashed. Each leaf node of the tree is coloured black or white and represents a stopping condition: If a black leaf node is reached, no quorum of noncrashed processes remains; if a white leaf node is reached, a quorum of noncrashed processes has been found. The label of a white leaf node denotes the quorum that has been found.

Peleg and Wool [2002] define the *probe complexity* of a static quorum set $\mathcal{Q}$ by

$$\mathrm{PC}(\mathcal{Q}) = \min_{T} \{ depth(T) \} ,$$

where the minimum is taken over all possible probe strategy trees T, and the depth is the number of nodes on the longest path from the root to a leaf node in T (not counting the leaf node itself).

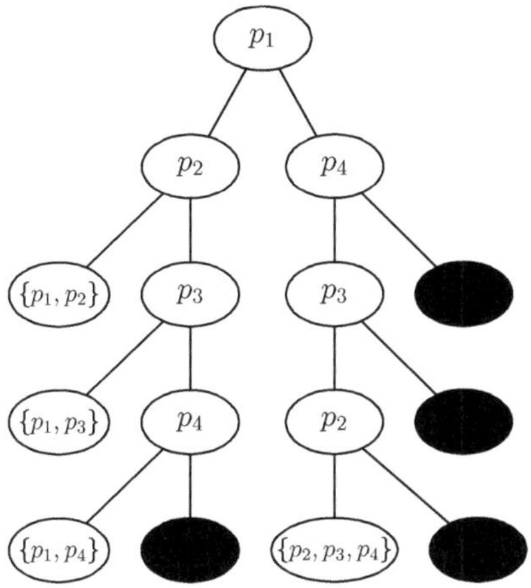

Figure 4.4: Example of a probe strategy tree. The tree [Peleg and Wool, 2002] models a probe strategy for the coterie $\mathscr{Q} = \{\{p_1, p_2\}, \{p_1, p_3\}, \{p_1, p_4\}, \{p_2, p_3, p_4\}\}$. The label of an inner node gives the process to probe. A white leaf node indicates that a quorum of noncrashed processes – given in the label – has been found. A black leaf node denotes that no quorum of noncrashed processes remains.

Example 4.11 (Probe Complexity [Peleg and Wool, 2002])
The tree shown in Fig. 4.4 models a probe strategy for the coterie

$$\mathscr{Q} = \{\{p_1, p_2\}, \{p_1, p_3\}, \{p_1, p_4\}, \{p_2, p_3, p_4\}\}$$

and has a depth of 4. This turns out to be the minimum for all probe strategies for $\mathscr{Q}$ and, therefore, equals the probe complexity of $\mathscr{Q}$.

No quorum set can have a probe complexity larger than the number of processes in the system, because it is not necessary to probe a process more than once to find a quorum of noncrashed processes. Unfortunately, many static coteries indeed meet this worst-case probe complexity [Peleg and Wool, 2002] and, therefore, are called *evasive*. For example, majority coteries and tree coteries are evasive. For nondominated coteries, Peleg and Wool [2002] found some lower bounds on the probe complexity:

Proposition 4.1 (Lower Bounds [Peleg and Wool, 2002])
If $\mathscr{Q}$ is a nondominated static coterie, then

$$\mathrm{PC}(\mathscr{Q}) \geq 2 \cdot \min\{|Q| : Q \in \mathscr{Q}\} - 1 \quad \text{and} \quad \mathrm{PC}(\mathscr{Q}) \geq \log_2(|\mathscr{Q}|) + 1.$$

Algorithm 1: RPC($\mathscr{Q}, \mathscr{S}, B, W$). Computes the minimal number of remaining probes for probing a quorum system $\mathscr{Q}$ under the sequence-based failure model $\mathscr{S}$ in the worst case, where B is a set of processes that are known to be crashed, and W is a set of processes that are known to be noncrashed.

1 $\mathscr{C} \leftarrow \{C \subseteq \Pi : \exists \langle q_1, \ldots, q_i, q_{i+1}, \ldots, q_k \rangle \in \mathscr{S} : \wedge\, C = \{q_1, \ldots, q_i\}$
2 $\qquad \wedge\, C \cap W = \emptyset$
3 $\qquad \wedge\, B \subseteq C\}$
4 $\mathscr{Q}_R \leftarrow \{Q \in \mathscr{Q} : \exists C \in \mathscr{C} : Q \cap C = \emptyset\}$
5 **if** $\mathscr{Q}_R = \emptyset \vee \exists Q \in \mathscr{Q}_R : \forall C \in \mathscr{C} : Q \cap C = \emptyset$ **then**
6 $\quad$ **return** *0*
7 **else**
8 $\quad \Pi_R \leftarrow (\bigcup_{C \in \mathscr{C}} C) \setminus (B \cup \bigcap_{C \in \mathscr{C}} C)$
9 $\quad$ **return** $1 + \min_{p \in \Pi_R} \max\{\text{RPC}(\mathscr{Q}, \mathscr{S}, B \cup \{p\}, W), \text{RPC}(\mathscr{Q}, \mathscr{S}, B, W \cup \{p\})\}$

We show below that the additional knowledge provided by sequence-based structural failure models can be exploited to reduce the probe complexity and, in particular, allows to go below these lower bounds.

Note that Peleg and Wool [2002] define the probe complexity independently of a specific structural failure model. Their probe complexity gives the minimal worst-case number of probes over all possible structural failure model including the worst possible one (e.g., all processes may fail in an arbitrary order). Such a fault assumption is not reasonable in the context of fault-tolerant systems as no system can tolerate such faults. Furthermore, probing requires less probes than indicated by the probe complexity for most structural failure models. In contrast, we define the probe complexity depending on a sequence-based structural failure model. The probe complexity gives a tight bound in the sense that indeed a number of probes as given by the probe complexity is required for probing the quorum set in some trace.

We define the probe complexity of a static quorum set $\mathscr{Q}$ for a sequence-based structural failure model $\mathscr{S}$ operationally by an algorithm RPC that computes the minimal number of remaining process probes in the worst case given some knowledge of currently crashed and noncrashed processes. The algorithm is given as Algorithm 1 and works as follows. The knowledge about currently crashed and noncrashed processes is represented by two process sets B and W:

- B (for *black*) gives a set of processes known to be currently crashed, and
- W (for *white*) gives a set of processes known to be currently noncrashed.

In line 1 – 3, the algorithm computes every process set C that may exactly describe the set of currently crashed processes. These sets are determined by three conditions:

- The sequence-based structural failure model must permit that precisely the processes in C are crashed at some point in time:

$$\exists \langle q_1, \ldots, q_i, q_{i+1}, \ldots, q_k \rangle \in \mathscr{S} : C = \{q_1, \ldots, q_i\}.$$

- No process that is known to be noncrashed can be in C: $C \cap W = \emptyset$.
- All processes that are known to be crashed must be in C: $B \subseteq C$.

In line 4, the quorum set is reduced to all those quorums that possibly contain only noncrashed processes. Only these quorums allow to perform further competitive operations. In line 5, the algorithm checks whether probing is finished. This is the case, if no quorum of noncrashed processes remains or if there is a quorum of definitely noncrashed processes. In both cases, no further probes are required, indicated by returning 0 (line 6). Otherwise, in line 8, the algorithm computes the set of *candidate processes* that are worth to be probed. A process is a candidate process iff it is not known whether the process is crashed or not. This is the case iff the process is possibly crashed (i.e., is in some $C \in \mathscr{C}$), but is not known to be crashed (i.e., is not in B and is not in every $C \in \mathscr{C}$). The remaining probe complexity is computed as the minimum (incremented by 1) taken over all maximal remaining probe complexities taken by assuming that each candidate process is either crashed or noncrashed (line 9).

We use this algorithm for an operational definition of the probe complexity of a static quorum set under a sequence-based failure model.

Definition 4.13 (Refined Probe Complexity)
The refined probe complexity $\mathrm{PC}(\mathscr{Q}, \mathscr{S})$ of a static coterie $\mathscr{Q}$ under a sequence-based failure model $\mathscr{S}$ is defined as the result of $\mathtt{RPC}(\mathscr{Q}, \mathscr{S}, \emptyset, \emptyset)$.

In principle, this algorithm corresponds to the probe complexity definition of Peleg and Wool [2002] except for additionally considering a failure model. In particular, $\mathrm{PC}(\mathscr{Q})$ equals $\mathrm{PC}(\mathscr{Q}, \mathscr{S})$ if $\mathscr{S}$ equals the worst possible sequence-based failure model.

Corollary 4.2
For a system with n processes, $\Pi = \{p_1, \ldots, p_n\}$, and a static quorum set $\mathscr{Q}$,

$$\mathrm{PC}(\mathscr{Q}) = \mathrm{PC}(\mathscr{Q}, \mathscr{S}),$$

if

$$\mathscr{S} = \bigcup_{1 \le k \le |\Pi|} \{\langle q_1, \ldots, q_k \rangle \in \Pi^* : \forall 1 \le i < j \le k : q_i \neq q_j\}.$$

We consider our notion of probe complexity reasonable as it gives a tight bound for a particular structural failure model as shown below.

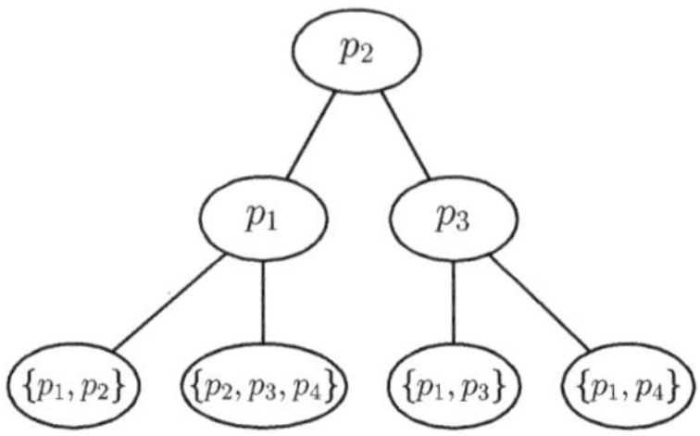

Figure 4.5: A tree that models a probe strategy for the coterie of Fig. 4.4 under the assumption that the coterie is highly available.

Theorem 4.5
Let P be a distributed system property and assume a sound and complete sequence-based failure model given by $\mathscr{S}$. For a quorum set $\mathscr{Q}$, the refined probe complexity $\mathrm{PC}(\mathscr{Q}, \mathscr{S})$ gives a tight bound on the number of probes.

PROOF:
$\langle 1 \rangle 1$. There is no trace in P such that a process requires more probes than indicated by $\mathrm{PC}(\mathscr{Q}, \mathscr{S})$ to find a quorum of noncrashed processes or to reveal that no such quorum exists.
PROOF: By Theorem 4.7 given below: We present a strategy that never requires more probes than indicated by $\mathrm{PC}(\mathscr{Q}, \mathscr{S})$.
$\langle 1 \rangle 2$. There is a trace $\tau \in P$ such that a process needs a number of probes equal to $\mathrm{PC}(\mathscr{Q}, \mathscr{S})$ in τ to find a quorum of noncrashed processes or to reveal that no such quorum exists.
PROOF: With step $\langle 1 \rangle 1$, it suffices to obtain a contradiction under the assumption that, for any trace, a number of probes $k < \mathrm{PC}(\mathscr{Q}, \mathscr{S})$ suffices.
Without loss of generality, choose k such that, for some trace, indeed k probes are necessary. Assume that the processes $q_1, \ldots, q_k$ are probed in ascending order. By induction on this sequence, it can be shown that $\mathrm{RPC}(\mathscr{Q}, \mathscr{S}, \emptyset, \emptyset) = k$, a contradiction.
$\langle 1 \rangle 3$. Q.E.D.
PROOF: By $\langle 1 \rangle 1$ and $\langle 1 \rangle 2$.

In contrast to the refined probe complexity, the original one is significantly larger than the number of probes actually required under many failure models.

Example 4.12 (Probe Complexity vs. Number of Probes)
Consider the coterie $\mathscr{Q}$ of Fig. 4.4. This coterie has a probe complexity $\mathrm{PC}(\mathscr{Q}) = 4$. However, if we assume that the coterie is highly available for some sequence-based failure model $\mathscr{S}$, the probe complexity $\mathrm{PC}(\mathscr{Q}, \mathscr{S})$ is less than or equal to 2.

For example, consider the Didep model

$$\mathscr{D} = \kappa_M(\{\{p_1\},\{p_2,p_3\},\{p_2,p_4\},\{p_3,p_4\}\}),$$

where κ_M denotes the monotone closure. $\mathscr{Q}$ is highly available for $\mathscr{D}$ and, therefore, also highly available for an equivalent sequence-based model $\mathscr{S}$. Figure 4.5 shows a corresponding probe strategy tree for $\mathscr{Q}$ and $\mathscr{S}$ with a depth of 2. In particular, the probe complexity is even below the lower bounds given in Proposition 4.1.

For another example, consider a set of processes, $\Pi = \{p_1,\ldots,p_7\}$ and a coterie $\mathscr{Q}$ built from subsets of cardinality 4. The probe complexity PC($\mathscr{Q}$) equals 7 as majority coteries are evasive. If $\mathscr{Q}$ is highly available, the probe complexity is considerably smaller: Under the fault assumption that at most three processes may crash, the probe complexity is 6. If at most two processes may crash, the probe complexity is 5; for one crashed process at most, it is 4.

Note that a lower refined probe complexity is not an artefact of highly available coteries: Consider a fault assumption that an arbitrary number of processes may crash, but only in a fixed sequence: Any p_j only crashes if all $p_i, 1 \leq i < j$, have crashed already. In this case, the probe complexity reduces to 1, because only p_4 needs to be probed. If p_4 has crashed, at most p_5, p_6, and p_7 are noncrashed and no quorum of correct processes remains. If p_4 has not crashed, p_4, p_5, p_6, and p_7 are noncrashed and form a quorum. While this example is a special case, the probe complexity generally becomes lower with more restrictions on the sequence of process failures.

The examples illustrate that the probe complexity strongly depends on the actual fault assumption. In particular, the lower bounds found by Peleg and Wool [2002] do not hold under many fault assumptions. While finding lower bounds for dominated and nondominated coteries that consider the current fault assumption is a topic for future work, we turn towards an optimal probe strategy next.

An Optimal Probe Strategy A probe strategy defines in which order processes are probed to find a quorum of noncrashed processes or to reveal that no such quorum exists. Of particular interest are probe strategies that (i) are *universal* in the sense that they are defined for all quorum sets and (ii) require as few probes as possible. Strategies presented so far have shortcomings in fulfilling these requirements: Peleg and Wool [1996] have presented a strategy that does not require more probes than necessary, but is only defined for nondominated coteries. While the strategy has been subsequently generalised to dominated coteries by Neilsen [1997] and Peleg and Wool [2002], these strategies require more probes than indicated by the (original) probe complexity if a coterie is dominated. Below we present a new probe strategy that is universal and never requires more probes than indicated by the refined notion of probe complexity.

Algorithm 2: PWProbe($\mathscr{Q}$). A universal dynamic probe strategy for a quorum system $\mathscr{Q}$ (adopted from Peleg and Wool [2002]).

```
1  B ← ∅
2  W ← ∅
3  while TRUE do
4      choose Q ∈ 𝒬 : (Q ∩ B = ∅ ∧ Q ⊈ W) ∨ (Q ∩ W = ∅ ∧ Q ⊈ B)
5      foreach p ∈ Q \ (B ∪ W) do
6          probe p
7          if p is crashed then
8              B ← B ∪ {p}
9          else
10             W ← W ∪ {p}

11     if ∃Q ∈ 𝒬 : Q ⊆ W ∨ Q ⊆ B then
12         choose Q ∈ 𝒬 : Q ⊆ W ∨ Q ⊆ B
13         if Q ⊆ W then
14             return Q
15         else
16             return ∅
```

Before we present our strategy, we will illustrate the shortcomings of the strategy for coteries of Peleg and Wool [2002], which is given by Algorithm 2. The algorithm maintains two variables B and W that contain sets of processes: B (for *black*) contains the set of processes whose crashes have been detected by the algorithm and initially equals the empty set (line 1); W (for *white*) contains the set of processes that have been detected to be noncrashed and also initially equals the empty set (line 2). The algorithm operates in rounds. In each round, a *candidate quorum* – a quorum that may consist of only crashed or of only noncrashed processes – is picked (line 4). All processes with unknown status in the candidate quorum are probed (lines 5–6) while maintaining B and W (lines 7–10). Note that, in case of coteries, it suffices that a process finds a quorum of either, crashed or noncrashed, processes. If the process finds a quorum of crashed processes, no quorum of noncrashed processes remains (i.e., the redundancy required for fault tolerance is exhausted) due to the intersection condition of coteries. If a quorum of crashed or of noncrashed processes is found (line 11), the algorithm terminates and returns a quorum of noncrashed processes (line 14) or the empty set (line 16) to indicate that no such quorum exists.

Example 4.13 (Probe Strategy for Coteries [Peleg and Wool, 2002])
Consider a distributed system with four processes, $\Pi = \{p_1, \dots, p_4\}$ and a coterie

$$\mathscr{Q} = \{\{p_1, p_2\}, \{p_1, p_3\}, \{p_1, p_4\}, \{p_2, p_3, p_4\}\}$$

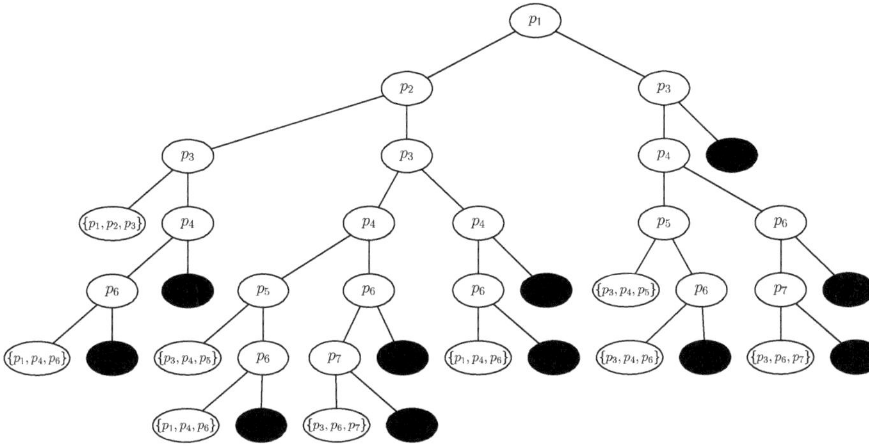

Figure 4.6: A probe strategy tree for a dominated coterie $\mathscr{Q}$. The tree has a depth of 6, which is optimal for all probe strategies for $\mathscr{Q}$.

(the same as in Fig. 4.4). If the processes p_2 and p_3 are crashed, the algorithm proceeds as follows. B and W are set to $\emptyset$ initially. In the first round, each quorum in $\mathscr{Q}$ is a candidate quorum. The algorithm may pick the candidate quorum $Q_1 = \{p_1, p_2\} \in \mathscr{Q}$. As no process is in B or in W, both processes are probed, which reveals that p_1 is noncrashed while p_2 is crashed. Hence, $B = \{p_2\}$ and $W = \{p_1\}$ after the first round. As no quorum only contains known-to-be-crashed or known-to-be-noncrashed processes, the second round is started. All quorums except Q_1 are candidate quorums at the beginning of the second round. Thus, the algorithm may pick the candidate quorum $Q_2 = \{p_1, p_3\} \in \mathscr{Q}$. As p_1 is known to be noncrashed (i.e., $p_1 \in W$), only p_3 is probed. This reveals that p_3 is crashed. Hence, the set $B = \{p_2, p_3\}$ after the second round. Still, no quorum only contains known-to-be-crashed or known-to-be-noncrashed processes. Thus, a third round is needed. Both, $Q_3 = \{p_1, p_4\} \in \mathscr{Q}$ and $Q_4 = \{p_2, p_3, p_4\} \in \mathscr{Q}$ remain as candidate quorums. The algorithm may choose Q_3 as a candidate quorum. As p_1 is known to be noncrashed, only p_4 is probed and detected to be noncrashed. Hence, $W = \{p_1, p_4\}$ after the third round. In particular, the algorithm found that Q_3 only contains noncrashed processes and, therefore, returns Q_3. Overall, the algorithm probed 4 processes, which equals the probe complexity of $\mathscr{Q}$.

The algorithm has three major limitations. First, it requires more probes than necessary under many structural failure models. In the example above, $\mathscr{Q}$ has a refined probe complexity ≤ 2 if $\mathscr{Q}$ is highly available as illustrated in Fig. 4.5. The algorithm, however, requires 4 probes – twice the refined probe complexity – as illustrated above. Second, the algorithm is only defined for coteries (which allows to stop if a quorum of failed processes has been found), but not for quorum sets.

Third, the algorithm requires more probes than indicated by the probe complexity for dominated coteries (even under the worst possible sequence-based structural failure model). For example, consider the dominated coterie

$$\mathscr{Q} = \{\{p_1, p_2, p_3\}, \{p_1, p_4, p_6\}, \{p_3, p_4, p_5\}, \{p_3, p_4, p_6\}, \{p_3, p_6, p_7\}\}$$

for a distributed system with seven processes, $\Pi = \{p_1, \ldots, p_7\}$. A probe strategy tree for $\mathscr{Q}$ is given in Fig 4.6. This tree has a depth of 6 and, as it turns out, no probe strategy tree for this coterie has a smaller depth. The strategy of Peleg and Wool [2002], however, requires 7 probes in the worst case: Consider that the processes p_2, p_5, and p_7 are crashed, while the others are noncrashed. The algorithm may choose $\{p_3, p_4, p_5\}$ as the first candidate quorum. As B and W initially equal the empty set, all three processes must be probed, which reveals that p_3 and p_4 are noncrashed while p_5 is crashed. Subsequently, the algorithm may choose $\{p_1, p_2, p_3\}$ as the next candidate quorum. Only p_1 and p_2 must be probed as p_3 has already been probed. As no quorum of crashed or noncrashed processes has been found yet, the algorithm starts another round and may choose $\{p_3, p_6, p_7\}$ as the next candidate quorum. Both, p_6 and p_7 are probed. Hence, all seven processes of the systems are probed before the algorithm finishes. The algorithm requires one probe more than indicated by the (original notion of) probe complexity.

Our adaptive probe strategy – given as Algorithm 3 – avoids these three limitations by additionally considering a sequence-based failure model $\mathscr{S}$. Like the strategy of Peleg and Wool [2002], the algorithm has two variables, B and W, for maintaining sets of processes that have been detected to be crashed and noncrashed, respectively. It additionally maintains two variables, $\mathscr{C}$ and $\mathscr{Q}_R$. The variable $\mathscr{C}$ holds all sets of process that may be currently crashed. Initially, it contains all sets that correspond to some prefix of some sequence in $\mathscr{S}$ (line 3). The variable $\mathscr{Q}_R$ holds all quorums of $\mathscr{Q}$ that possibly contain noncrashed processes only, initially $\mathscr{Q}$ (line 4). The algorithm operates in rounds. The algorithm starts another round if some quorum of possibly noncrashed processes remains (i.e., $\mathscr{Q}_R \neq \emptyset$), but each of these quorums possibly contains a crashed process (i.e., $\forall Q \in \mathscr{Q}_R : \exists C \in \mathscr{C} : Q \cap C \neq \emptyset$, line 5). Otherwise, the algorithm terminates, because either no possible quorum remains or a quorum of known-to-be-noncrashed processes has been found. In a round, the algorithm first determines all *candidate processes* that are worth to be probed. A process p is a candidate process iff it may be crashed (i.e., $\exists C \in \mathscr{C} : p \in C$), but the crash has not been detected yet (i.e., $p \notin B$) and cannot be deduced from $\mathscr{C}$ (i.e., $p \notin \bigcap_{C \in \mathscr{C}} C$). Overall, the set of all processes with unknown status is the union of all $C \in \mathscr{C}$ without processes in B and without processes in $\bigcap_{C \in \mathscr{C}} C$ (line 6). For each of these processes, the

Algorithm 3: Probe($\mathscr{Q}$,$\mathscr{S}$). A universal probe strategy for a quorum set $\mathscr{Q}$ and a sequence-based failure model $\mathscr{S}$. The strategy is optimal in the sense that it performs as few probes as possible without further knowledge. In the worst case, it performs a number of probes equal to the refined probe complexity $PC(\mathscr{Q},\mathscr{S})$.

1 $B \leftarrow \emptyset$

2 $W \leftarrow \emptyset$

3 $\mathscr{C} \leftarrow \{C \subseteq \Pi : \exists \langle q_1,\ldots,q_i,q_{i+1},\ldots,q_k\rangle \in \mathscr{S} : C = \{q_1,\ldots,q_i\}\}$

4 $\mathscr{Q}_R \leftarrow \mathscr{Q}$

5 **while** $\mathscr{Q}_R \neq \emptyset \wedge \forall Q \in \mathscr{Q}_R : \exists C \in \mathscr{C} : Q \cap C \neq \emptyset$ **do**

6     $\Pi_R \leftarrow (\bigcup_{C \in \mathscr{C}} C) \setminus (B \cup \bigcap_{C \in \mathscr{C}} C)$

7     $m \leftarrow \min_{p \in \Pi_R} \max\{\mathrm{RPC}(\mathscr{Q},\mathscr{S},B \cup \{p\},W), \mathrm{RPC}(\mathscr{Q},\mathscr{S},B,W \cup \{p\})\}$

8   **choose** $p \in \Pi_R$ **:** $m = \max\{\mathrm{RPC}(\mathscr{Q},\mathscr{S},B \cup \{p\},W), \mathrm{RPC}(\mathscr{Q},\mathscr{S},B,W \cup \{p\})\}$

9   probe p

10   **if** *p is crashed* **then**

11         $B \leftarrow B \cup \{p\}$

12   **else**

13         $W \leftarrow W \cup \{p\}$

14     $\mathscr{C} \leftarrow \{C \in \mathscr{C} : B \subseteq C \wedge C \cap W = \emptyset\}$

15     $\mathscr{Q}_R \leftarrow \mathscr{Q}_R \setminus \{Q \in \mathscr{Q} : \forall C \in \mathscr{C} : Q \cap C \neq \emptyset\}$

16 **if** $\mathscr{Q}_R = \emptyset$ **then**

17   **return** $\emptyset$

18 **else**

19   **choose** $Q \in \mathscr{Q}_R$ **:** $\forall C \in \mathscr{C} : Q \cap C = \emptyset$

20   **return** Q

algorithm determines the maximal remaining probe complexity taken under the assumption that (i) the process is crashed and (ii) the process is noncrashed. It sets the minimum of these values to the variable m (line 7) and chooses a corresponding process p (line 8). Probing this process yields the minimal number of further probes without further knowledge. Subsequently, this process is probed (line 9) and, depending on the results, p is added to B or W (lines 10–13). At the end of a round, the algorithm maintains $\mathscr{C}$ and $\mathscr{Q}_R$. In particular, a C is removed from $\mathscr{C}$ if it contains a process known to be noncrashed or if does not contain a process that is known to be crashed (line 14). A quorum Q is removed from $\mathscr{Q}_R$ if Q contains a known to be crashed process (line 15). After the last round, either no quorum of possibly noncrashed processes remains or some quorum exists that only contains known to be noncrashed processes. The algorithm returns the empty set in the first case (line 19) and a quorum of noncrashed processes in the latter case (line 20).

We continue with firstly proving that the algorithm indeed gives a correct probe strategy and secondly showing that the algorithm is efficient in the sense that it never requires more probes than given by the refined probe complexity.

Theorem 4.6
The adaptive probe strategy given in Alg. 3 returns a quorum of noncrashed processes or the empty set if no such quorum exists.

PROOF:
$\langle 1 \rangle 1$. After the last round, some $C \in \mathscr{C}$ equals the set of currently crashed processes.
PROOF: Initially, $\mathscr{C}$ contains all sets of processes that may be crashed at some point in time. A set is only removed from $\mathscr{C}$ if it does not contain a process that is detected to be crashed or if it does contain a process that is detected to be noncrashed. Hence, the set that equals the set of currently crashed processes remains in $\mathscr{C}$.
$\langle 1 \rangle 2$. If the algorithm terminates, it returns a $Q \in \mathscr{Q}$ or an empty set.
PROOF: If the while-loop terminates, $\mathscr{Q}_R = \emptyset$ or $\exists Q \in \mathscr{Q}_R : \forall C \in \mathscr{C} : Q \cap C = \emptyset$. In the former case, the algorithm returns an empty set via line 17; in the latter case, a $Q \in \mathscr{Q}_R$ via line 20. As each Q in $\mathscr{Q}_R$ is also in $\mathscr{Q}$, the algorithm returns a $Q \in \mathscr{Q}$ in this case.
$\langle 1 \rangle 3$. If the algorithm returns a $Q \in \mathscr{Q}$, all processes in Q are noncrashed.
PROOF: If the algorithm returns a quorum $Q \in \mathscr{Q}$, Q is in $\mathscr{Q}_R$ after the last round and, for each $C \in \mathscr{C}$, Q does not share a process with C. As some $C \in \mathscr{C}$ equals the set of currently crashed processes by $\langle 1 \rangle 1$, Q does not contain a crashed process.
$\langle 1 \rangle 4$. If the algorithm returns the empty set, each quorum in $\mathscr{Q}$ contains a crashed process.
PROOF: If the algorithm returns the empty set, $\mathscr{Q}_R$ is empty after the last round. Before the first round, $\mathscr{Q}_R$ contains all quorums of $\mathscr{Q}$. A quorum Q is removed from $\mathscr{Q}_R$ iff Q contains a known to be crashed process. Hence, if $\mathscr{Q}_R$ is empty, no quorum contains only noncrashed processes.
$\langle 1 \rangle 5$. The algorithm terminates.
PROOF: Probing a process terminates. If the algorithm does not terminate, infinitely many rounds are executed. In each round, a process that has not been probed yet is probed. As the number of processes in the system is finite, only finitely many rounds are executed.
$\langle 1 \rangle 6$. Q.E.D.
PROOF: By $\langle 1 \rangle 2 - \langle 1 \rangle 5$.

Theorem 4.7
The adaptive probe strategy given in Alg. 3 requires less than or equal to $\mathrm{PC}(\mathscr{Q}, \mathscr{S})$ probes for a static quorum set $\mathscr{Q}$ and a sequence-based structural failure model $\mathscr{S}$.

PROOF:
$\langle 1 \rangle 1$. In each round between line 7 and 8, m equals $\mathtt{RPC}(\mathscr{Q}, \mathscr{S}, B, W) - 1$.

PROOF: By the definition of RPC.

$\langle 1\rangle 2$. In the first round, m equals PC$(\mathscr{Q},\mathscr{S}) - 1$ after line 7.

PROOF: By $\langle 1\rangle 1$ and as B and W equal empty sets in the first round.

$\langle 1\rangle 3$. In round $r+1$, m (after executing line 7) is strictly less than the value of m in round r.

PROOF: Let m^r, B^r, W^r, and Π_R^r denote the values of m, B, W, and Π_R in round r between executing line 7 and 8. By $\langle 1\rangle 1$, m^r equals $\mathrm{RPC}(\mathscr{Q},\mathscr{S},B^r, W^r)$ -1. Assume that process $p^r \in \Pi_R^r$ is probed in round r. Then, m^{r+1} either equals $\mathrm{RPC}(\mathscr{Q},\mathscr{S},B^r \cup \{p^r\}, W^r) - 1$ or $\mathrm{RPC}(\mathscr{Q},\mathscr{S},B^r, W^r \cup \{p^r\}) - 1$ such that

$$m^{r+1} < \max\{\mathrm{RPC}(\mathscr{Q},\mathscr{S},B^r \cup \{p^r\}, W^r), \mathrm{RPC}(\mathscr{Q},\mathscr{S},B^r, W^r \cup \{p^r\})\}.$$

By the definition of RPC,

$$max\{\mathrm{RPC}(\mathscr{Q},\mathscr{S},B^r \cup \{p^r\}, W^r), \mathrm{RPC}(\mathscr{Q},\mathscr{S},B^r, W^r \cup \{p^r\})\}$$

is less or equal than $\mathrm{RPC}(\mathscr{Q},\mathscr{S},B^r, W^r) - 1$, which completes the proof.

$\langle 1\rangle 4$. In the last round, $m \geq 0$ after executing line 7.

PROOF: As Alg. 1 only returns values greater than or equal to 0.

$\langle 1\rangle 5$. If the algorithm executes more than PC$(Q,\mathscr{S})$ rounds, the value of m in the first round is greater than or equal to PC$(\mathscr{Q},\mathscr{S})$.

PROOF: By $\langle 1\rangle 4$, $m \geq 0$ in the last round (after executing line 9). With $\langle 1\rangle 3$, $m \geq r-1$ in the first round (after executing line 9) if the algorithm executes overall r rounds. Hence, if the algorithm executes PC$(\mathscr{Q},\mathscr{S})$ rounds, the value of $m \geq$ PC$(\mathscr{Q},\mathscr{S}) - 1$ in the first round. If the algorithm executes more than PC$(\mathscr{Q},\mathscr{S})$ rounds, the value of $m \geq$ PC$(\mathscr{Q},\mathscr{S})$.

$\langle 1\rangle 6$. Q.E.D.

PROOF: By $\langle 1\rangle 2$ and $\langle 1\rangle 5$, the algorithm executes PC$(\mathscr{Q},\mathscr{S})$ rounds at most. In each round, one process is probed.

Example 4.14

To illustrate that our algorithm does not require more probes than indicated by the refined probe complexity, let us reconsider the dominated coterie of Fig. 4.6. Under the sequence-based structural failure model that allows all processes to fail in arbitrary orders, the algorithm probes the processes as specified by the strategy tree in the figure. In contrast to the probe strategy of Peleg and Wool [2002], the algorithm, therefore, requires only 6 probes as given by the refined probe complexity.

4.6 Summary

Implementing a fault-tolerant distributed system often requires to realise some coordination and agreement among the participating processes. Coteries are a valuable tool to realise such coordination and agreement. Their popularity stems from their flexibility of allowing different trade-offs among qualities such as load, capacity, and availability. The question of how to construct coteries for different trade-offs has stimulated a significant amount of research over the past thirty years.

With this chapter, we contribute to this line of research by giving necessary and sufficient conditions for highly available coteries in terms of Didep models. The results are constructive in the sense that, if a highly available coterie exists, we show how to derive a highly available coterie from a Didep model. The results cover the two extremes of functional failure models, crash and Byzantine failures, as well as static and dynamic coteries. The results show that dynamic coteries allow to improve the availability in the presence of crash failures, but not in the presence of Byzantine failures. In this case, however, dynamic coteries may allow to improve other qualities, for example, the performance, as shown by Alvisi et al. [2000].

Besides high availability, we additionally considered the quality of probe complexity. We refined the notion of probe complexity used in the literature by considering sequence-based structural failure models. While the original notion is defined for the worst-case structural failure model, the refined notion gives tight bounds for a given failure model. Additionally, we have presented a universal probe strategy that never requires more probes than indicated by the refined probe complexity for all kinds of quorum sets. This strategy is, therefore, more efficient for many coteries than the strategies in the literature.

Our discussion on coteries in this chapter is for the most part independent of a particular application. Possible applications include concurrency control in replicated databases, directory services, and mutual exclusion. We will consider such an application, namely the problem of consensus, in the next chapter and, in particular, present solutions to consensus that rely on coteries.

5 Reaching Consensus

Reaching consensus is a fundamental problem for theory and practice of fault-tolerant distributed computing. In the consensus problem, each process initially *proposes* a value and is supposed to eventually *decide* a value. The processes are supposed to agree on a proposed value; that is, the decision values must be the same and equal one of the values that were actually proposed. Historically, the consensus problem originates from the SIFT project [Wensley et al., 1978] on building a highly reliable fault-tolerant computer for aircraft control applications. In these applications, critical tasks were executed redundantly, and consensus on the results was reached before further using them.

The practical relevance of consensus stems from being fundamental for agreement and coordination in distributed systems. If processes cooperate or compete in a system, they are required to coordinate and agree on their actions and, thereby, often face problems that are variants of consensus. For example, in a replicated database, the processes are required to reach agreement on whether to commit or abort a transaction. Or, in a sensor network, the processes must agree on the values measured by all sensors. At the heart of these problems, known as *atomic commit* and *interactive consistency*, and other agreement problems is the consensus problem. Being able to solve consensus is, therefore, a good indicator whether other relevant problems can be solved as well. Hence, consensus is a good candidate for fundamental research on distributed systems.

The relevance of consensus for theory stems from being very sensitive to fault and synchrony assumptions: Even small changes in the assumptions make the consensus problem harder or even impossible to solve. Consequently, consensus has often been used as a "benchmark" problem to compare different system models and to assess new ones. Generally, such studies address the questions whether consensus can be solved at all and, if this is the case, which efficiency and resilience can be achieved.

For example, the seminal FLP impossibility result (named after its authors Fischer, Lynch, and Patterson) states that consensus cannot be solved deterministically in an asynchronous system in the presence of crash failures. This result is widely regarded as one of the most important results in distributed computing. Dolev et al. [1987] and Dwork et al. [1988] have shown how to solve consensus despite crash failures in partially synchronous systems and have identified the minimal synchrony conditions to do so. Aguilera et al. [2000] adapted the failure detector model to crash-recovery failures and have shown how to solve consensus under this model. Santoro and Widmayer [2005] introduced a new system model for dynamic and transient failures and assess the model using the consensus problem. The relevance of consensus also extends to related domains like multiprocessor programming, where synchronisation primitives are compared by their ability to solve different variants of consensus [Herlihy and Shavir, 2008].

The consensus problem is of particular importance for fault-tolerant distributed computing, because a consensus algorithm can be used as a universal building block for implementing fault-tolerant distributed systems. For example, such an algorithm allows to apply the approach of *state-machine replication* for implementing a fault-tolerant system. Originally introduced by Lamport [1978b] and surveyed by Schneider [1990], the basic idea of state-machine replication is to implement a fault-tolerant service by replicating a server and coordinating the client interactions with the server replicas. The coordination of the client interactions can be implemented using a consensus algorithm.

Contribution We use the consensus problem as an example to demonstrate that Didep models are indeed tractable. That is, our intention is to show that designing and evaluating fault-tolerant distributed systems is still possible with Didep models although they are more expressive than previous models and, therefore, allow to specify faults more accurately. In particular, we show how to solve consensus under Didep models by reusing and transforming existing algorithms, which illustrates that using Didep models does not impose the need for completely new solutions. Quite the contrary, tractable adaptions of existing solutions suffice to solve problems under Didep models. For example, some of the algorithms that we rely on are quorum-based. Thus, we can reuse the construction of highly available quorum systems from the previous chapter.

Another aspect to demonstrate is that Didep models are universal in the sense that they can be combined with different functional failure models and different synchrony assumptions. Covering a wide range of possible assumptions, we exemplarily consider benign as well as malicious failures, transient and permanent failures, and synchrony assumptions ranging from asynchronous systems with unreliable failure detectors to synchronous systems.

If a less expressive model (e.g., a threshold model) "under-approximates" a fault assumption, using a Didep model allows to obtain a higher assumption coverage and, therefore, a more resilient solution. If a less expressive model "over-approximates" a fault assumption, using a Didep model allows to obtain a more efficient solution. We address both aspects by evaluating the resilience and the efficiency of our solutions to consensus and find that certain Didep models allow more efficient and/or more resilient consensus algorithms. In particular, this is the case when a Didep model describes directed dependent failures. Our results obtained under Didep models can be considered strict generalisations of previous results obtained under less expressive classes of structural failure models. As a very special case, we demonstrate that some Didep models even allow to circumvent the FLP impossibility result. More precisely, this is the case if there is a single process that all others depend upon. While such a structural failure model is of little practical relevance, the result is interesting from a theoretical perspective as it opens another dimension to circumvent the FLP result.

Overview This chapter is organised as follows. We distinguish related work from our contributions in Section 5.1 and give a brief introduction to the consensus problem and its solutions in Section 5.2. Section 5.3 presents two approaches to solve consensus in asynchronous systems with failure detectors despite benign crash failures under adversary structures and under Didep models. Section 5.4 shows how to solve consensus in partially synchronous systems despite permanent crash failures and transient send omission failures. In Section 5.5, we present solutions to consensus for synchronous systems despite malicious Byzantine failures, before we conclude in Section 5.6.

5.1 Related Work

Due to the relevance of consensus, a vast amount of research has been spent on studying the problem and its solutions. Different surveys summarise this area of research [Fischer, 1983, Turek and Shasha, 1992, Barborak et al., 1993, Guerraoui et al., 1999] and basically every book on distributed computing includes a chapter on consensus (e.g., the books from Lynch [1996], Coulouris et al. [2005], Ben-Ari [2006], Guerraoui and Rodrigues [2006], Ghosh [2006]).

We use consensus as a "benchmark" problem for different failure models and for different timing models. In particular, we consider different structural failure models. Closely related to our results, Junqueira [2006] has shown how to solve consensus under core / survivor sets models. He combined these models with crash and Byzantine failures and has presented consensus algorithms for synchronous systems and systems augmented with failure detectors. These algorithms are not completely new, but are based on previously known principles from algorithms for threshold models. Analogous results – while not that extensive – have been obtained for other classes of structural failure models, for example, for adversary structures by Fitzi and Maurer [1998].

In contrast, we apply more expressive Didep models and consider different functional failure models and timing models including combinations thereof that have not been addressed for less expressive structural failure models so far. For example, we consider send omission failures and partially synchronous systems, which only has been addressed for threshold models so far. Furthermore, as far as we know, we are the first to present a failure-detector-based algorithm for crash failures and adversary structures. In particular, we are able to reuse some results of the previous chapter on coteries as some of the algorithms rely on quorums.

Similarly to related work, we do not develop completely new algorithms from scratch, but build on previous consensus algorithms. This serves our purpose to illustrate that Didep models are tractable. Note that adapting previous algorithms has been a common approach in the literature. For example, the algorithms of Junqueira [2006] are inspired by algorithms from Lamport et al. [1982], Chandra and Toueg [1996], Doudou et al. [2002], Kihlstrom et al. [2003], and Charron-Bost and Schiper [2004]. In contrast, our algorithms are based on the ones from Hurfin et al. [2002], Bar-Noy et al. [1987], Charron-Bost and Schiper [2007]. Some of these algorithms meet lower bounds on efficiency and resilience for threshold models. We generalise such results by using Didep models and, in some cases, are able to improve on bounds obtained under less expressive failure models.

We reuse previous algorithms using three different approaches. First, we directly apply known algorithms under minor modifications and specific parameter settings. For crash failures, we reuse a *versatile* algorithm from Hurfin et al. [2002], which by itself unifies different consensus algorithms. Such an approach has, for example, also been used by Keidar and Rajsbaum [2001] using the closely related algorithm of Mostéfaoui and Raynal [1999]. While Keidar and Rajsbaum [2001] use a flexible algorithm to prove upper and lower bounds under the threshold model, we configure a flexible algorithm to be used for another system model. For Byzantine failures and synchronous systems, we adapt the algorithm of Bar-Noy et al. [1987] to Didep models. Second, we transfer an algorithm from a completely different system model, the *Heard-Of model*, to our system model and adapt it to Didep models. Third, we present a consensus algorithm that invokes an existing one. Such an approach has, for example, been used by Brasileiro et al. [2001] to implement *one-step consensus* under threshold models. While their implementation only invokes the underlying consensus algorithm if unanimity is not reached in an initial communication phase, our implementation always invokes the underlying algorithm and is designed for Didep models.

In particular, the latter algorithm allows to identify different roles of processes. The processes that are directed dependent on other processes do not participate in reaching agreement on a decision value, but are only informed later about the final decision value. Lamport [1998] has identified three different roles, of processes, *proposers*, *acceptors*, and *learners*, for his *Paxos* algorithm. Proposers propose initial values. Acceptors decide on proposed values while coordinating with other acceptors. Learners are only informed about the decision value. As required by the consensus problem, all processes are proposers in our case. The processes that are directed dependent on others are learners. Processes that are not directed dependent on others are acceptors. While Lamport [1998] assumes a given assignment of roles to processes, our results show how a role assignment can be derived from a structural failure model.

5.2 Introduction to Consensus

To solve consensus under different failure models, we need to understand how the problem is specified precisely. Having a look at the underlying principles how to solve consensus and how solutions are evaluated will ease the understanding of actual algorithms that are presented subsequently.

5.2.1 Specifying Consensus

As a fundamental problem of fault-tolerant distributed computing, consensus is given by a property (i.e., a set of traces). Usually, this property is given by one liveness property and two safety properties that are defined as follows:

Uniform Termination Every process eventually decides on some value.

Uniform Agreement No two processes decide differently.

Validity If a process decides a value v, then v was proposed by some process.

These properties define a variant of the consensus problem for fault-free systems. Without faults, the consensus problem has simple solutions and is of limited theoretical interest. Note that none of the properties refers to faults in any way, which makes the specification hard and in most cases impossible to implement in the presence of faults: For example, if a process crashes before it decides a value, it cannot decide anymore and, therefore, violates the termination property. For the sake of fault tolerance, the overall problem must be *weakened* by allowing further traces. In the presence of crash failures, uniform termination and uniform agreement are usually substituted by the weaker properties of *termination* and *agreement*.

Termination Every correct process eventually decides on some value.

Agreement No two correct processes decide differently.

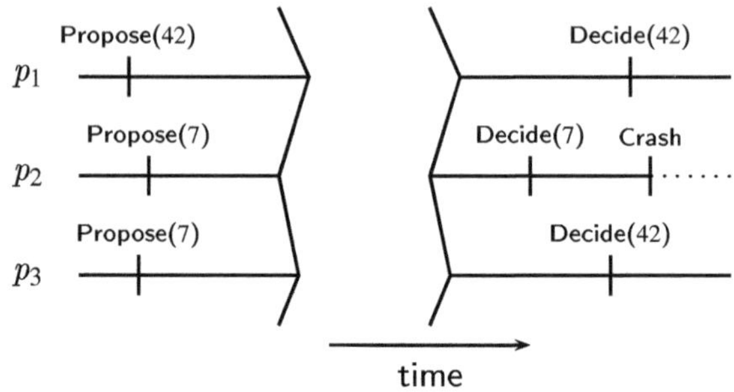

Figure 5.1: Possible trace of consensus in the presence of crash failures.

The intersection of termination, agreement, and validity defines the consensus problem that can be solved in partially synchronous systems or with the help of failure detectors in the presence of crash failures. Note that implementing the termination and the agreement property alone is trivial: A system that lets each process decide a common predetermined value implements agreement and termination. The validity property prohibits such trivial solutions.

Definition 5.1 (Consensus)
The *consensus* problem is the property defined by the intersection of the properties termination, agreement, and validity.

Figure 5.1 illustrates a trace of a solution to consensus. Each process proposes a value, for example, p_1 proposes 42. Eventually, every correct process decides and no two correct processes decide differently. Note that this notion of consensus allows a faulty process to decide differently. In the figure, process p_2 is faulty and, therefore, is allowed to decide a different value than the other processes.

TLA specification of consensus A formal TLA specification of the consensus problem is given in Fig. 5.2. The formula *Spec* specifies the consensus problem on a high-level of abstraction in terms of the output variables $proposal_p$, $decision_p$, and $failed_p$ for each process $p \in \Pi$. Each process p has $proposal_p$, $decision_p$, and $failed_p$ as output variables and all other variables as environment variables. The specification does not include any hidden variables. As an abbreviation, we write e_p for the environment variables of p and $vars$ for all variables of the system.

The $proposal_p$ and $decision_p$ variables hold the proposal and decision values of process p. Initially, they are set to a "nonvalue" $\perp$ to denote that no value has been proposed or decided. The $failed_p$ variable – initially equal to FALSE – is used to denote whether the process is currently failed or not.

$$
\begin{aligned}
Init \triangleq\ & \forall p \in \Pi : \land\ proposal_p = \bot \\
& \qquad\quad\ \land\ decision_p = \bot \\
& \qquad\quad\ \land\ failed_p = \text{FALSE} \\
Propose_p(v) \triangleq\ & \land \neg failed_p \\
& \land proposal_p = \bot \\
& \land proposal'_p = v \\
& \land \text{UNCHANGED } \langle e_p, decision_p, failed_p \rangle \\
Decide_p(v) \triangleq\ & \land \neg failed_p \\
& \land proposal_p \neq \bot \land decision_p = \bot \\
& \land \exists q \in \Pi : proposal_q = v \\
& \land \forall q \in \Pi : decision_q = v \lor decision_q = \bot \\
& \land decision'_p = v \\
& \land \text{UNCHANGED } \langle e_p, proposal_p, failed_p \rangle \\
Next \triangleq\ & \exists p \in \Pi, v : Propose_p(v) \lor Decide_p(v) \\
L \triangleq\ & WF_{\langle vars \rangle}(Next) \\
Crash_p \triangleq\ & \land \neg failed_p \\
& \land failed'_p = \text{TRUE} \\
& \land \text{UNCHANGED } \langle e_p, proposal_p, decision_p \rangle \\
Fault \triangleq\ & \exists p \in \Pi : Crash_p \\
Spec \triangleq\ & Init \land \Box[Next \lor Fault]_{vars} \land L
\end{aligned}
$$

Figure 5.2: A TLA specification of the consensus problem.

A process p proposes a value v by the $Propose_p(v)$ action. This action can only be taken if p is not failed and if p has not proposed any value yet. The proposed value v is recorded in $propose_p$.

A process p decides a value v by the $Decide_p(v)$ action. This action can only be taken if

1. p is not failed,
2. p has already proposed a value,
3. p has not decided any value yet,

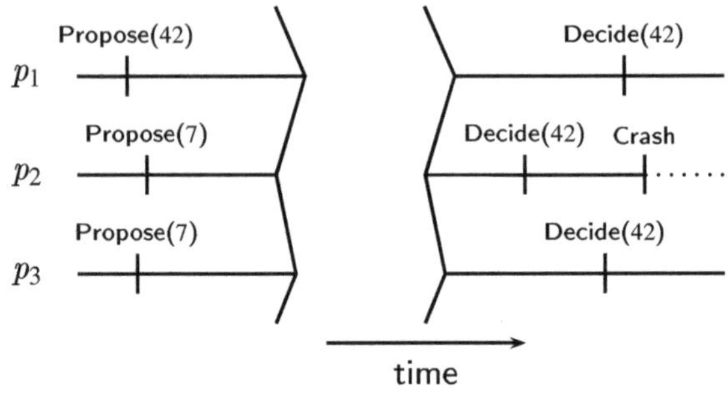

Figure 5.3: Possible trace of uniform consensus.

4. some process has proposed v, and

5. no other process has decided another value yet.

If the action is taken, the decision value v is recorded in $decision_p$.

Besides proposal and decision steps, p is allowed to perform a fault step by the $Crash_p$ action if it is not failed yet. This action marks the process as failed and, thereby, disables all further actions of the process.

Uniform Consensus Another – stronger – variant of consensus is also common in the literature: the problem of *uniform consensus* that, in contrast to consensus, only substitutes uniform termination by termination, but leaves uniform agreement. Figure 5.3 illustrates a trace of a solution to uniform consensus. In this case, a faulty process that decides is required to decide the same value as a correct process. In particular, the trace of consensus shown in Figure 5.1 is not a trace of uniform consensus.

While the consensus problem is strictly weaker than the uniform consensus problem, this difference is of minor importance under many system models. As shown by Guerraoui [2000], any *indulgent* algorithm that solves consensus also solves uniform consensus. An indulgent algorithm is an algorithm that can cope with unreliable failure detection: The algorithm is indulgent towards the failure detector. However, uniform consensus is strictly harder to solve in synchronous systems [Charron-Bost and Schiper, 2004].

Byzantine Consensus For Byzantine failures, the definition of uniform consensus is too strict: As as Byzantine process may behave arbitrarily, it may decide a value although some other process has decided another value already, which violates uniform agreement. Moreover, even the weaker form of consensus is too strict. Byzantine processes may consistently lie about their proposal value and behave as they would have proposed a different value. This value may become the decision value. Hence, a value is decided that was not proposed by any process, which violates validity. Furthermore, a Byzantine process may decide a value that was not proposed at all, which also violates validity. Therefore, consensus is further weakened by substituting *weak validity* for validity:

Weak Validity If a correct process p decides and all correct processes propose v, then p decides v.

We call the problem defined by agreement, weak validity, and termination the *Byzantine consensus* problem.

While such weakenings prevent trivial violations of a property due to a failure model, a weakened property may still be impossible to implement under a given system model. For example, the FLP impossibility result shows that this is the case for asynchronous systems and crash failures.

5.2.2 The FLP Impossibility Result

As one of the most seminal results in fault-tolerant distributed computing, Fischer et al. [1985] have shown that

> no consensus protocol is totally correct in spite of one [crash] fault

in asynchronous systems with deterministic protocols. This result is also known as the FLP impossibility result named after the authors, Fischer, Lynch, and Patterson.

We will later refine the FLP result and show that special structural failure models allow to circumvent the FLP result. Let us briefly sketch its proof to understand later on why this is possible. In principle, the proof of the FLP result can be summarised as follows. Without loss of generality, consider binary consensus, that is, only the values 0 and 1 can be proposed and decided. A system state has a decision value v iff some processes already decided v. A system state s is *bivalent* iff both, 0 and 1, are decision values of states reachable from s. It is univalent iff either 0 or 1 is the only decision value of all states reachable from s. A trace τ is a deciding trace iff some processes decide in τ.

Fischer et al. [1985] proof that the following three properties hold for each system that solves consensus:

1. There is a trace with a bivalent initial state.

2. Whenever a system is in a bivalent state, a (nonstuttering) step to another bivalent state can be taken.

3. Any deciding trace from a bivalent initial state includes a step from a bivalent to a univalent state.

Due to property 1 and 2, a system may never reach a univalent state. With property 3, the system has a trace that is not a deciding one. In this case, the system does not implement the termination property of consensus.

Circumventing the FLP Result Due to the relevance of the consensus problem, the FLP result stimulated a vast amount of research how to circumvent the result [Rabin, 1983, Dolev et al., 1987, Ben-Or et al., 1988, Dwork et al., 1988, Chandra and Toueg, 1996, Cristian and Fetzer, 1999, Veríssimo and Casimiro, 2002]. In principle, such approaches can be classified according to whether they further weaken the problem specification, strengthen the system model, or do both.

For example, Rabin [1983] and Ben-Or et al. [1988] do both: They strengthen the system model by allowing processes to make random choices and weaken the problem specification by requiring termination with probability 1. Another approach is to strengthen the timing assumptions. For example, Dolev et al. [1987] and Dwork et al. [1988] show how to solve consensus in partially synchronous systems despite crash failures. Another approach that strengthens the system model is to augment a system with failure detectors as introduced in Section 2.6. Let us have a look at the underlying principles of many consensus implementations.

5.2.3 Principles of Solving Consensus

Many algorithms that solve consensus are based on the same fundamental principles: They proceed in *(a)synchronous rounds* and assign a coordinator to each round using the *rotating coordinator* paradigm. The coordinator of a round tries to impose its estimate value to become the decision value. All processes follow a certain *message exchange pattern* that determines the communication costs and the latency incurred by the algorithm.

(A)synchronous Rounds Many approaches to solve consensus structure the execution of an algorithm into rounds. Each process proceeds sequentially from round to round and, usually, annotates the messages it sends with the current round number. While synchronous systems allow to synchronise entering and leaving a round among the processes, processes rely on *asynchronous rounds* in asynchronous systems. In this case, *asynchronous* means that (i) there is no upper bound for the number of (nonstuttering) steps that a process remains in a round and (ii) different processes may be in different rounds at the same time (i.e., they proceed asynchronously from round to round).

Usually, each process sends one or more messages within a round and awaits messages from some other processes before moving to the next round. To avoid that a process waits forever for a message from a crashed process, each process uses time-outs in synchronous systems or only waits for messages from processes that are currently not suspected by a failure detector. In this case, the completeness property of the failure detector ensures that no process blocks permanently.

Rotating Coordinator Paradigm If an algorithm relies on the rotating coordinator paradigm, each round r is coordinated by a predetermined round coordinator $\text{coord}(r)$. The function $\text{coord}()$ must be deterministic to avoid that multiple processes try to coordinate the same round. The aim of a round is to let the coordinator of the round impose a decision value. The basic idea is that the coordinator multicasts its current estimate of the decision value in a first phase. In a second phase, the processes exchange messages to support the coordinator. As a process may crash while being coordinator, the role of the coordinator must be rotated among the processes. While a coordinator of a round undertakes a centralised role during the round, the system remains truly distributed due to the rotation.

Usually, the coordinator succeeds in imposing a decision value if it remains noncrashed and, in case of an asynchronous system, is not suspected by others during the round. The accuracy property of a failure detector guarantees that (eventually) a correct process p is not suspected by any process. If the $\text{coord}()$ function returns this process for infinitely many rounds, p will eventually become the coordinator when not suspected by any process and, therefore, succeeds in imposing a decision value. In a synchronous system, a nonfailed process usually succeeds in imposing a decision value as soon as it becomes coordinator.

The two central requirements on coord, being deterministic and returning every process for infinitely many rounds, are easily met by defining $\text{coord}(r) = p_{(r \bmod n)+1}$, where $\Pi = \{p_1, \ldots, p_n\}$.

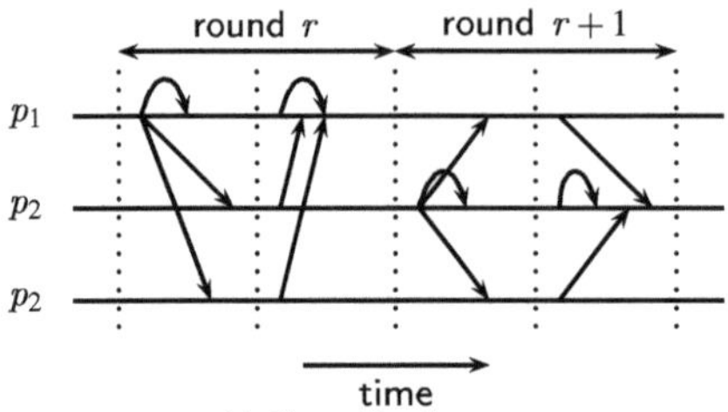

(a) Centralised pattern.

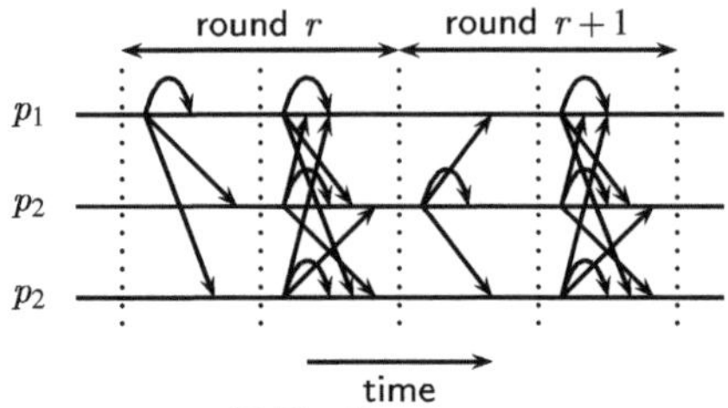

(b) Distributed pattern.

Figure 5.4: Illustration of message exchange patterns. With a centralised pattern, the processes only communicate with the coordinator of a round during the round. With a distributed pattern, all processes communicate with each other during each round.

Message Exchange Pattern The message exchange pattern describes how the processes support the coordinator to impose a decision value. It determines the message costs of a system and has an impact on when processes are able to decide. Patterns range from *centralised* to *distributed* with various patterns in between.

With a centralised pattern, the processes only communicate with the coordinator of a round as illustrated in Fig. 5.4a. For solving consensus, the processes usually acknowledge the estimate sent by the coordinator in this case. The coordinator waits for these acknowledgments and, if enough processes sent them, can decide the estimation value. For example, the $\diamond\mathscr{S}$-based consensus algorithm of Chandra and Toueg [1996] uses a centralised message exchange pattern.

With a distributed pattern, all processes communicate with each other during a round as illustrated in Fig. 5.4b. For solving consensus, a process relays the estimate value received from the coordinator to all other processes. If a process receives enough relay messages with the same estimate value, it can decide the estimation value. For example, the consensus algorithms of Schiper [1997] and Mostéfaoui and Raynal [1999] use a distributed message exchange pattern.

5.2.4 Quality of Consensus Algorithms

Distributed systems are usually assessed by two quality measures: time and communication complexity [Lynch, 1996]. The *time complexity* measures how long a system takes to reach a final state. A final state is reached when the system has produced all the required outputs or when all processes have halted. The *communication complexity* measures how many messages are sent until a final state is reached.

In case of consensus, time complexity is measured by *the number of rounds* and by the *number of communication phases* in a round that yields the decision. In a failure-free trace (i.e., no process crashes), consensus can be reached in a single round. This is the common case in many real-world systems, because failures are rare in such systems. The number of communication phases measures how long it takes to reach a decision within a round that yields the decision. It, therefore, measures the time complexity for the common case. The communication complexity of consensus algorithms is measured by the number of message that are sent in a round.

Another important measure with respect to fault tolerance is the *resilience* of a distributed system. The resilience of a system measures to which extent faults can be tolerated by a system. Given a functional failure model, the resilience is given as a predicate that specifies which structural failure models of a certain class can be tolerated. The form of this predicate depends on the class of structural failure models that is used. For example, in case of threshold models, the resilience predicate is stated in terms of thresholds (e.g., "less than one-third of all processes may fail"). In case of set-based models, a predicate is most likely given in terms of process sets.

Let us briefly summarise upper and lower bounds on these measures, which helps to assess the consensus algorithms for Didep models later on.

Number of Rounds The worst-case number of rounds of a consensus algorithm that tolerates crash failures in a synchronous system grows linearly with the number of failures that are tolerated: If an algorithm tolerates at most t crash failures, there is some trace that requires $t+1$ rounds [Dolev and Strong, 1982]. This lower bound also holds for Byzantine failures [Fischer and Lynch, 1982] and is tight: Pease et al. [1980] present an algorithm that never requires more than $t+1$ rounds. However, in case of crash failures, $t+1$ rounds are only required if indeed t processes crash. In a trace with $f \leq t$ faulty processes, $f+1$ rounds are necessary and sufficient to solve consensus [Dolev et al., 1990, Keidar and Rajsbaum, 2001, Charron-Bost and Schiper, 2004]. To solve uniform consensus, an additional round (i.e., $f+2$ overall rounds), is necessary and sufficient if $f < t-1$. If $f = t-1$ or $f = t$, the bound of $t+1$ rounds holds. Charron-Bost and Schiper [2004] use this result to show that, in synchronous systems, uniform consensus is harder than consensus.

In an asynchronous system with a $\diamond\mathcal{S}$ failure detector, the situation is worse. There is no upper bound on the number of rounds required to solve consensus despite crash failures, because the failure detector is allowed to make mistakes for an arbitrary (but finite) amount of time. As long as the coordinator of each round is suspected by all processes, no coordinator is able to impose a decision value. As each consensus algorithm that is indulgent to a $\Diamond\mathscr{S}$ also solves uniform consensus, the lower bounds of uniform consensus for synchronous systems from above apply.

Fortunately, the lack of an upper bound is not a severe limitation in real-world systems. The common case in such systems is that processes and channels are timely while failures are rare. Hence, a failure detector gives accurate information most of the time. Therefore, a decision is reached within a round with a nonfailed coordinator, often the very first round. From a practical point of view, it is therefore interesting to consider the number of communication phases within the deciding round to reach a decision.

Number of Communication Phases Within a decision round, one communication phase suffices to reach consensus in a synchronous system if no failure occurs in the round [Dolev et al., 1990]. Charron-Bost and Schiper [2004] show that uniform consensus requires two communication phases in this case.

The results for uniform consensus also hold in the asynchronous system model. In an asynchronous system with a $\Diamond\mathscr{S}$ failure detector, two communication phases are necessary for uniform consensus. Two communication phases are also necessary for consensus as any algorithm that solves consensus under such a system model also solves uniform consensus. As for synchronous systems, this bound is tight: Schiper [1997] and Mostéfaoui and Raynal [1999] present algorithms that allow decisions after two communication phases in the deciding round. In contrast, the algorithm of Chandra and Toueg [1996] requires three communication phases in the deciding round. The former are also known as *early-decision* algorithms.

For special cases, the number of communication phases can fall below the lower bounds. For example, Brasileiro et al. [2001] give an algorithm that requires only one communication phase in the deciding round if at most $n/3$ processes may crash and $n-f$ processes propose the same value. They additionally show that the $n/3$ bound can be weakened to $n/2$ if some value is privileged in the sense that this value will be decided if the majority of processes propose this value.

Note that the message exchange pattern has a significant impact on the number of communication phases required by an algorithm. The early-decision algorithms of Schiper [1997] and Mostéfaoui and Raynal [1999] use distributed message exchange patterns; the algorithm of Chandra and Toueg [1996] with 3 communication phases uses a centralised pattern. Despite the number of communication phases, the message exchange pattern also has an impact on the number of messages per round, which measures the communication complexity.

Number of Messages The number of messages sent in a round depends on the message exchange pattern that is used by an algorithm. With a centralised pattern, the round coordinator sends a message to every process, which reply to the coordinator with one message each. Consequently, the number of messages per round is at least in $O(n)$, where n denotes the number of processes. With a distributed pattern, the round coordinator sends a message to every process, which communicate among each other: Each process sends a message to every other process. In this case, the number of messages per round is in $O(n^2)$. Both patterns are two extremes of a range of possible communication patterns. In fact, there is a communication pattern for every k, $1 \leq k \leq n$, such that the number of messages in a round are in $O(kn)$ [Hurfin et al., 2002].

In summary, a centralised message exchange pattern incurs message costs in $O(n)$, but makes three communication phases necessary. A distributed pattern incurs message costs in $O(n^2)$ and only requires two communication steps. Hence, the pattern used determines a trade-off between time and communication complexity.

Resilience The resilience that a system can achieve depends on the respective system model and, therefore, on the underlying system assumptions. The failure model and the timing model are of particular relevance. Chandra and Toueg [1996] have shown that $t < n/2$ is a necessary and sufficient condition to solve consensus despite crash failures in an asynchronous system with a $\diamond\mathscr{S}$ failure detector under threshold models, where t gives the threshold and n is the number of overall processes. They additionally have shown that consensus can be solved for any number of crashes using a failure detector in $\mathscr{S}$.

These results have been generalised by Junqueira [2006] for the same system model except for using core / survivor sets instead of thresholds. He introduced a resilience predicate, called *crash partition*, which states that for any partitioning of the process set Π with two partitions, there is some core that is a subset of one of the partitions. This predicate generalises the $t < n/2$ predicate as, whenever $t < n/2$ is satisfied for a threshold model, crash partition is satisfied by a corresponding core model, but not vice versa. The crash partition predicate is equivalent to an adversary structure being 2-well-formed: A core model satisfies the crash partition predicate iff the corresponding adversary structure is 2-well-formed. For adversary structures, resilience is described in terms of a $Q^{(k)}$ predicate [Hirt and Maurer, 1997, Fitzi and Maurer, 1998], which is equivalent to being k-well-formed.

Many results obtained for asynchronous systems with unreliable failure detectors can be transferred to partially synchronous systems. This is, for example, the case for resilience predicates and crash failures: $t < n/2$ is necessary and sufficient to solve consensus in a partially synchronous system [Dwork et al., 1988].

In synchronous systems, consensus can be reached for any number of process crashes [Lynch, 1996, Chapter 6]. In this case, using more expressive structural failure models does not yield any advantages with respect to resilience (but with respect to efficiency). In the Byzantine failure model, Pease et al. [1980] have shown that $3t < n$ is necessary and sufficient under threshold models. This result has been generalised by Hirt and Maurer [1997] using adversary structures: A 3-well-formed adversary structure is necessary and sufficient to solve consensus despite Byzantine failures. For core / survivor sets, Junqueira [2006] have introduced the *Byzantine partition* predicate stating that for any partition of the process set with three partitions, there is some core that is a subset of some partition. This resilience predicate is equivalent to a 3-well-formed adversary structure.

With this overview of the problem of consensus, we are now ready to look at actual solutions and to evaluate them.

5.3 Consensus in Asynchronous Systems with Unreliable Failure Detectors

Let us have a look on implementations of consensus in asynchronous systems that tolerate crash failures. Due to the FLP impossibility result, no such implementation exists at all. Chandra and Toueg [1996] propose to augment a system with failure detectors and present different deterministic algorithms that solve consensus. Further consensus algorithms for this system model with different trade-offs between time and communication complexity can be found in the literature [Schiper, 1997, Mostéfaoui and Raynal, 1999, Hurfin et al., 2002]. In this section, we adopt an algorithm that is derived from the algorithm of Hurfin et al. [2002]. The advantages of this algorithm lie in its versatility with respect to the message exchange pattern and the failure detector used. In particular, the algorithm allows to adapt the message exchange patterns for each round. Our algorithm is essentially equal to the original one except for some adaptations for set-based failure models.

For now, we only consider crash, but not Byzantine failures. While crash failures are rather easy to detect by failure detectors using heartbeat techniques in a sufficiently synchronous system, Byzantine failures are significantly harder to detect. For example, Byzantine failures permit a failed process to always respond correctly in time when being diagnosed but otherwise to respond arbitrarily when accessed. Different approaches on Byzantine failure detection [Masum, 2000, Alvisi et al., 2001, Doudou et al., 2002, Kihlstrom et al., 2003] focus on failures that are as severe as possible (i.e., "as Byzantine as possible"), but remain detectable. For example, Kihlstrom et al. [2003] subclassified Byzantine failures and introduced the class of *detectable* Byzantine failures. Additionally, they have shown how to implement a failure detector for these failures and how to solve consensus using these detectors. In general, however, it is impossible to detect all kinds of Byzantine failures.

5.3.1 A Versatile Consensus Algorithm

Hurfin et al. [2002] have presented a generic failure-detector-based consensus algorithm that is versatile in two dimensions: the message exchange pattern used during each round and the underlying failure detector. The algorithm allows to define a different message exchange pattern for each round and allows to use either, an $\mathcal{S}$ or a $\diamond\mathcal{S}$ failure detector. In this section, we will restrict ourselves to a variant of the algorithm that relies on a $\diamond\mathcal{S}$ failure detector. The relevance of the algorithm stems from unifying several previous approaches to solve consensus. In particular, the algorithms of Chandra and Toueg [1996], Schiper [1997], and Mostéfaoui and Raynal [1999] can be considered special instances of the versatile algorithm.

A variant of the algorithm is presented in Fig. 4. It differs from the original algorithm of Hurfin et al. [2002] in the definition of the good function. Hurfin et al. [2002] defined it as a function from a set of processes to an integer depending on the failure detector used. In contrast, we define it as a predicate on a set of processes. For threshold failure models considered by Hurfin et al. [2002], this is only a difference in syntax, but will be of convenience for set-based failure models.

The algorithm proceeds in asynchronous rounds and uses the rotating coordinator paradigm. At the beginning of a consensus execution, each process p_i calls Consensus(v_i) with v_i being the proposal value. The local state of p_i includes three variables:

r_i the current round number,

est_i the current estimate of the decision value, and

ts_i a timestamp that gives the last round during which est_i has been updated.

A process decides by executing the **decide** statement with the decision value (lines 22 and 28). After a decision, a process quits executing the algorithm by a **return** statement (lines 23 and 29).

Each round consists of two communication phases as described above. During the first phase, the current coordinator broadcasts its current estimate of the decision value to all processes by a PROP(r, est) message (line 9). Each process waits

Algorithm 4: VersatileConsensus(v_i). A versatile failure-detector-based consensus algorithm of Hurfin et al. [2002].

```
1  cobegin
2      task T1
3          r_i ← 0
4          est_i ← v_i
5          ts_i ← 0
6          while TRUE do
7              r_i ← r_i + 1
8              p_cc ← coord(r_i)                        // determine current coordinator
               // Phase 1 of round r_i:  from p_cc to Π
9              if p_i = p_cc then foreach p ∈ Π do send PROP(r_i, est_i) to p
10             wait until PROP(r_i, v) has been received from p_cc or p_cc ∈ Suspects(p_i)
11             if PROP(r_i, v) has been received from p_cc then
12                 est_i ← v
13                 ts_i ← r_i
               // Phase 2 of round r_i:  from Π to D ∪ A
14             D ← decider(r_i)                         // determine decision makers
15             A ← agr_keeper(r_i)                      // determine agreement keepers
16             foreach p ∈ D ∪ A do send ECHO(r_i, est_i, ts_i) to p
17             if p_i ∈ D ∪ A then
18                 wait until ∃Q_i ⊆ Π : P(Q_i) ∧ ECHO(r_i, est, ts) received from all
                   p ∈ Q_i
19                 if p_i ≠ p_cc then est_i ← choose est : est received with highest ts
20                 if p_i ∈ D ∧ good({p ∈ Q_i : ECHO message from p has ts = r_i}) then
21                     foreach p ∈ Π \ {p_i} do send DECISION(est_i) to p
22                     decide est_i
23                     return
24     end task
25     task T2
26         wait until DECISION(est) has been received from p_j
27         foreach p ∈ Π \ {p_i, p_j} do send DECISION(est) to p
28         decide est
29         return
30     end task
31 coend
```

for this message or stops waiting if the coordinator becomes suspected (line 10). If a process receives such a message, it adopts the sent estimate from the coordinator as its own estimate and remembers the round number of this update (lines 11 – 13).

In the second phase, the processes support the coordinator in imposing a decision value depending on the message exchange pattern. The message exchange pattern of a round is represented by two process sets, D and A. The processes in

D (for *decision makers*) check whether they can decide during the round (line 20). Only processes in D can decide during the second phase of a round in line 22. Others are informed about a decision by a DECISION message (line 21) and decide as soon as such a message is received (lines 26–28). With a centralised message exchange pattern, only the round coordinator checks whether to decide, that is, $D = \{p_{cc}\}$. With a distributed pattern, all processes check whether to decide (i.e., $D = \Pi$) and, therefore, allow for early decisions. The processes in A (for *agreement keepers*) guarantee that no other value can be decided if a value was decided already. If a value is decided during a round r, the processes in A adopt this value as their own estimate (line 19). In particular, if the coordinator of the next round is in A, no other value can be decided during the next round.

At the beginning of the second phase, all processes send their current estimate with the associated timestamp (i.e., a ECHO(r, est, ts) message) to all processes in $D \cup A$ (line 16). Hence, the set $D \cup A$ determines the message exchange pattern of the round. The processes in this set wait for ECHO(r_i, est, ts) messages from all processes of a quorum (line 18). The decision whether such messages have been received from a quorum is formalised by checking a predicate P that depends on the failure detector used. Within a round, the predicate must ensure that two quorums Q_i and Q_j do intersect and that each quorum Q contains all but possibly crashed processes. Hurfin et al. [2002] show that, for a threshold model based on $t \in \mathbb{N}$, it suffices to have P(Q) is true if Q contains $n - t$ processes under a $\diamond\mathscr{S}$ failure detector.

All processes in D test whether enough messages with a timestamp equal to the round number have been received to decide the decision value (line 20). The value of "enough" is formalised by a good predicate that depends on the used failure detector. It must ensure that at least one message with a timestamp equal to the round number has been received from a correct process (i.e., a process that will not crash). For a failure detector in $\diamond\mathscr{S}$ and a threshold model based on $t \in \mathbb{N}$, it suffices that such a message is received from at least $t+1$ processes. If a process is able to decide, it informs the others about its decision (line 21) before it decides itself (line 22).

We now give a lemma that asserts the correctness of the algorithm.

Lemma 5.1

Assume a crash failure model for processes. Algorithm 4 solves the consensus problem deterministically if

1. `coord` implements the rotating coordinator paradigm,
2. `decider` and `agr_keeper` are deterministic,
3. `coord`$(r) \in$ `decider`(r) for all rounds r,
4. `coord`$(r+1) \in$ `agr_keeper`(r) for all rounds r,

5. $\forall p_i, p_j \in \Pi : Q_i^r \cap Q_j^r \neq \emptyset$ for all rounds r, where Q_i^r and Q_j^r are the quorums of the processes p_i and p_j in round r, respectively,
6. for all rounds r, $\forall p_i \in \Pi : Q_i^r$ contains all but possibly crashed processes, and
7. $\texttt{good}(Q)$ is true iff Q contains a correct process.

PROOF: We only sketch the proof here. See Hurfin et al. [2002] for a rigorous proof.

⟨1⟩1. (Validity) If a process decides a value v, then v was proposed by some process.

PROOF: Validity is guaranteed, because each round coordinator tries to impose its own proposal value or a value that was previously sent by another coordinator. The first coordinator tries to impose its own proposal value. By induction, each coordinator only tries to impose some proposed value. A value is only decided if imposed by a coordinator.

⟨1⟩2. (Agreement) No two correct processes decide differently.

PROOF: If some process decides the value v in round r, then at least one correct process sent an ECHO(r, v, r) message in round r. At this point, r is the highest timestamp in the system. If a process decides afterwards in line 22, it has received ECHO messages from all but possibly crashed processes. If a process decides in line 27, some other process sent the decision value in line 21. This process has received ECHO messages from all but possibly crashed processes. In both cases, the process has received a ECHO message with v and the highest timestamp and, consequently, adopted v as its estimate value.

⟨1⟩3. (Termination) Every correct process eventually decides on some value.

PROOF: If some correct process p_i has not decided in a round r, it will start round $r+1$, because, otherwise, it must have been blocked in line 10 or 18 (i.e., in some **wait until** statement). However, a correct process p_i cannot block in these lines, because channels are reliable, the failure detector guarantees strong completeness, `decider` and `agr_keeper` are deterministic, and Q_i does not contain crashed processes.

Due to the accuracy property of the failure detector and due to the rotating coordinator paradigm, a correct process eventually is not suspected by any process and coordinates a round. As being in D, this process succeeds in deciding in this round.

If a process decides, then all correct processes will decide, because a process that decides has sent a DECISION message to all processes.

⟨1⟩4. Q.E.D.

PROOF: By ⟨1⟩1 – ⟨1⟩3.

Note that Condition 1 (rotating coordinator) can be easily satisfied independent of further assumptions by defining $\texttt{coord}(r) = p_{(r \bmod n)+1}$. In fact, this definition is used in many consensus algorithms [Chandra and Toueg, 1996, Mostéfaoui and Raynal, 1999, Schiper, 1997]. Likewise, the Conditions 2, 3, and 4 can be easily satisfied determining the message exchange pattern: $\texttt{decider}(r) = \{\texttt{coord}(r)\}$ and $\texttt{agr\_keeper}(r) = \{\texttt{coord}(r+1)\}$ satisfy the conditions and impose a centralised message exchange pattern. Alternatively, $\texttt{decider}(r) = \Pi$ and $\texttt{agr\_keeper}(r) = \Pi$ satisfy the conditions and impose a distributed message exchange pattern. In summary, it suffices to show that the Conditions 5 – 7 hold for a given system to implement consensus using the versatile algorithm. Next, we use the versatile algorithm to solve consensus under the adversary structure model.

5.3.2 Adversary Structures

Recall from Section 3.5.4 (p. 74) that an adversary structure $\mathscr{A}$ is a monotone set of process sets. It defines a structural failure model by sets of possibly faulty processes. It can describe undirected dependent faults, but cannot describe directed dependent faults.

For solving consensus, let us investigate how to satisfy the Conditions 5–7 of Lemma 5.1. For Condition 5 and 6, we derive a quorum set $\mathscr{Q}$ from an adversary structure $\mathscr{A}$ by considering each set of all but possibly crashed processes as a quorum (which is closely related to the construction of highly available coteries from Didep models in the previous chapter):

$$\mathscr{Q} = \{Q \subseteq \Pi : \exists A_1 \in \mathscr{A} : Q = \Pi \setminus A_1 \wedge \forall A_2 \in \mathscr{A} : A_1 \not\subset A_2\}.$$

By this construction, if $\mathscr{A}$ is 2-well-formed, $\mathscr{Q}$ is not only a quorum set, but also a coterie. If, in the algorithm of Fig. 4, each process only accepts quorums of $\mathscr{Q}$, that is,

$$\forall p_i \in \Pi : Q_i^r \in \mathscr{Q}$$

for all rounds r, every two quorums do intersect, which satisfies Condition 5 of Lemma 5.1. Additionally, each quorum in $\mathscr{Q}$ contains all but possibly crashed processes satisfying Condition 6: By the construction of $\mathscr{Q}$, there is a trace for each quorum in $\mathscr{Q}$ such that all but the processes in $\mathscr{Q}$ are crashed.

For Condition 7, $\text{good}(Q)$ must be true iff Q contains a correct process for the current trace. Note that some $A \in \mathscr{A}$ precisely describes the set of faulty processes for the current trace. If it is guaranteed that Q is not a subset of A, Q contains a correct process. As A itself is unknown, Q should not be a subset of any set in $\mathscr{A}$.

This can be achieved by

$$\mathtt{good}(Q) = \begin{cases} \text{TRUE} & \text{if } \forall A \in \mathscr{A} : Q \not\subseteq A \\ \text{FALSE} & \textit{otherwise.} \end{cases}$$

With these definitions of quorums and the good function, consensus is solved by algorithm 4 given a proper implementation of the rotating coordinator paradigm and an appropriate message exchange pattern.

Theorem 5.1
The algorithm shown in Fig. 4 solves consensus despite crash failures in an asynchronous system with a $\diamond\mathscr{S}$ failure detector under a sound and complete adversary structure $\mathscr{A}$ if

1. coord implements the rotating coordinator paradigm,
2. decider and agr_keeper are deterministic,
3. $\mathtt{coord}(r) \in \mathtt{decider}(r)$ for all rounds r,
4. $\mathtt{coord}(r+1) \in \mathtt{agr\_keeper}(r)$ for all rounds r,
5. $\mathscr{A}$ is 2-well-formed.

PROOF: We use Lemma 5.1 to prove the theorem. Conditions 1 – 4 of Lemma 5.1 are satisfied by the Conditions 1 – 4 of this theorem. It suffices to show that the Conditions 5 – 7 of Lemma 5.1 hold under the definition of Q_i^r and good from above.

$\langle 1\rangle 1.$ $\forall p_i, p_j \in \Pi : Q_i^r \cap Q_j^r \neq \emptyset$ for all rounds r
PROOF: By the definition of $\mathscr{Q}$ and as $\mathscr{A}$ is 2-well-formed.

$\langle 1\rangle 2.$ $\forall p_i \in \Pi : Q_i^r$ contains all but possibly crashed processes for all rounds r
PROOF: For each $Q \in \mathscr{Q}$, there is some $A \in \mathscr{A}$ such that $Q = \Pi \setminus A$. This A may contain all crashed processes.

$\langle 1\rangle 3.$ $\mathtt{good}(Q)$ is true iff Q contains a correct process.
PROOF: By the definition of good, $\mathtt{good}(Q)$ is true iff $\forall A \in \mathscr{A} : Q \not\subseteq A$. As some $A \in \mathscr{A}$ equals the set of all faulty processes, Q contains at least one correct process.

$\langle 1\rangle 4.$ Q.E.D.
PROOF: By $\langle 1\rangle 1$ – $\langle 1\rangle 3$ and Lemma 5.1.

The algorithm bears the advantage that it is optimal with respect to resilience, that is, no algorithm can solve consensus if $\mathscr{A}$ is not 2-well-formed under an otherwise equivalent system model.

Theorem 5.2
Consensus cannot be solved deterministically using a $\diamond\mathscr{S}$ failure detector in an asynchronous system under a sound and complete adversary structure $\mathscr{A}$ in the presence of crash failures if $\mathscr{A}$ is not 2-well-formed.

PROOF: We assume that there is an algorithm given by a property C that implements consensus even if $\exists A_1, A_2 \in \mathscr{A} : A_1 \cup A_2 = \Pi$ and obtain a contradiction. To obtain the contradiction, we show that there are two traces τ_0 and τ_1 and two disjunct process sets A_0 and A_1 such that the processes in A_0 decide 0 in τ_0 and the processes in A_1 decide 1 in τ_1. Additionally, there is a third trace τ_C that is indistinguishable from τ_0 for processes in A_0 and indistinguishable from τ_1 for processes in A_1. Hence, the agreement property is violated by τ_C.

$\langle 1 \rangle 1$. There are two adversary classes $A_0, A_1 \in \mathscr{A}$ such that both cover the whole process set and do not have a common process. Formally,

$$\exists A_0, A_1 \in \mathscr{A} : (A_0 \cup A_1 = \Pi) \wedge (A_0 \cap A_1 = \emptyset).$$

PROOF: Such A_0 and A_1 exist as $\mathscr{A}$ is not 2-well-formed and is monotone.

$\langle 1 \rangle 2$. There is a trace τ_0 in C such that:

- All processes propose 0.
- All processes in A_1 crash at the beginning of τ_0.
- All processes in $A_0 = \Pi \setminus A_1$ are correct.
- All processes in A_0 suspect each process in A_1 right from the beginning.

PROOF: Such a trace exists, because A_1 is in $\mathscr{A}$ and the processes have a $\Diamond\mathscr{S}$ failure detector. The processes in A_0 are correct due to $\langle 1 \rangle 1$.

$\langle 1 \rangle 3$. Each process in A_0 eventually decides 0 in τ_0. Let t_0 be the time when the last process in A_0 decides.

PROOF: As C implements consensus.

$\langle 1 \rangle 4$. There is a trace τ_1 in C such that:

- All processes propose 1.
- All processes in A_0 crash at the beginning of τ_1.
- All processes in $A_1 = \Pi \setminus A_0$ are correct.
- All processes in A_1 suspect each process in A_0 right from the beginning.

PROOF: Such a trace exists, because A_1 is in $\mathscr{A}$ and the processes have a $\Diamond\mathscr{S}$ failure detector. The processes in A_1 are correct due to $\langle 1 \rangle 1$.

$\langle 1 \rangle 5$. Each process in A_1 eventually decides 1 in τ_1. Let t_1 be the time when the last process in A_1 decides.

PROOF: As C implements consensus.

$\langle 1 \rangle 6$. There is a trace τ_C in C such that:

- All processes in A_0 propose 0 and all processes in A_1 propose 1.
- All processes are correct.

- All processes in A_0 suspect each process in A_1 from the beginning until t_0.
- All processes in A_1 suspect each process in A_0 from the beginning until t_1.
- All messages between processes from A_0 and A_1 are delayed by the channels until $t_0 + t_1$.

PROOF: Such a trace exists, because $\emptyset$ is in $\mathscr{A}$, the processes have a $\diamond\mathscr{S}$ failure detector, and the system is asynchronous.

$\langle 1 \rangle 7$. Each process in A_0 decides 0 and each process in A_1 decides 1 in τ_C.

PROOF: By $\langle 1 \rangle 3$, each process in A_0 decides 0, because no process in A_0 can distinguish τ_C from τ_0 until t_0. By $\langle 1 \rangle 5$, each process in A_1 decides 1, because no process in A_1 can distinguish τ_C from τ_1 until t_1.

$\langle 1 \rangle 8$. Q.E.D.

PROOF: By $\langle 1 \rangle 7$, C violates agreement.

For other quality measures than resilience, the algorithm benefits from being versatile in the message exchange pattern. The number of messages can be minimised by choosing a centralised message exchange pattern, the number of communication phases by a distributed one. As for all algorithms that rely on unreliable failure detectors, the number of rounds cannot be bounded. However, the algorithm terminates at the latest in the round after the failure detector provides accurate information.

5.3.3 Didep Models

For solving consensus under Didep models, we follow a similar approach as for adversary structures: we leave the message exchange pattern open, but give a quorum construction and define a good function depending on the failure model. For the quorum construction, we reuse the construction of Lemma 4.2 (p. 112) for highly available coteries:

$$\mathscr{Q} = \left\{ Q \subseteq \Pi : \exists D_1 \in \mathscr{D}|_{\mu(\mathscr{D})} : (Q = \mu(\mathscr{D}) \setminus D_1) \wedge \left(\forall D_2 \in \mathscr{D}|_{\mu(\mathscr{D})} : D_1 \not\subset D_2\right)\right\}$$

As for adversary structures, if $\mathscr{D}$ is 2-well-formed, $\mathscr{Q}$ is not only a quorum set, but also a coterie. Additionally, we define the good function analogously as for adversary structures:

$$\mathsf{good}(Q) = \begin{cases} \text{TRUE} & \text{if } \forall D \in \mathscr{D} : Q \nsubseteq D \\ \text{FALSE} & \textit{otherwise}. \end{cases}$$

Theorem 5.3
The algorithm shown in Fig. 4 solves consensus despite crash failures in an asynchronous system with a $\Diamond\mathscr{S}$ failure detector under a sound and complete Didep model $\mathscr{D}$ if

1. `coord` implements the rotating coordinator paradigm,
2. `decider` and `agr_keeper` are deterministic,
3. $\texttt{coord}(r) \in \texttt{decider}(r)$ for all rounds r,
4. $\texttt{coord}(r+1) \in \texttt{agr\_keeper}(r)$ for all rounds r,
5. $\mathscr{D}$ is 2-well-formed.

PROOF: We use Lemma 5.1 to prove the theorem. Conditions 1 – 4 of Lemma 5.1 are satisfied by the Conditions 1 – 4 of this theorem. It suffices to show that the Conditions 5 – 7 of Lemma 5.1 hold under the definition of Q_i^r and `good` from above.

$\langle 1\rangle 1.$ $\forall p_i, p_j \in \Pi : Q_i^r \cap Q_j^r \neq \emptyset$ for all rounds r
PROOF: By the construction of $\mathscr{Q}$ and as $\mathscr{D}$ is 2-well-formed.

$\langle 1\rangle 2.$ $\forall p_i \in \Pi : Q_i^r$ contains all but possibly crashed processes for all rounds r
PROOF: For each $Q \in \mathscr{Q}$, there is some $D \in \mathscr{D}$ such that $Q = \Pi \setminus D$. This D may contain all crashed processes.

$\langle 1\rangle 3.$ $\texttt{good}(Q)$ is true iff Q contains a correct process.
PROOF: By the definition of `good`, $\texttt{good}(Q)$ iff $\forall D \in \mathscr{D} : Q \not\subseteq D$. As some $D \in \mathscr{D}$ equals the set of all faulty processes, Q contains at least one correct process.

$\langle 1\rangle 4.$ Q.E.D.
PROOF: By $\langle 1\rangle 1 - \langle 1\rangle 3$ and Lemma 5.1.

As we will see below, the algorithm is not optimal with respect to resilience in this case: Even if a sound and complete Didep model is not 2-well-formed, it may be possible to solve consensus. In principle, the number of messages and the number of communication phases again depend on the used message exchange pattern. However, for special Didep models, it can be possible to further reduce the number of messages and communication phases and even find a bound for the number of rounds (see below).

The results above illustrate that the algorithm of Hurfin et al. [2002] is versatile in another dimension, namely, in the dimension of structural failure models. Only little changes were required to use the algorithm with adversary structures or Didep models instead of threshold models, which we consider an evidence that set-based failure models are tractable. Next, we will present a different approach to solve consensus that also allows to reuse previous algorithms.

A Transformer Algorithm Above, consensus was solved under Didep models by setting the parameters of an existing algorithm and running it as it is. We will

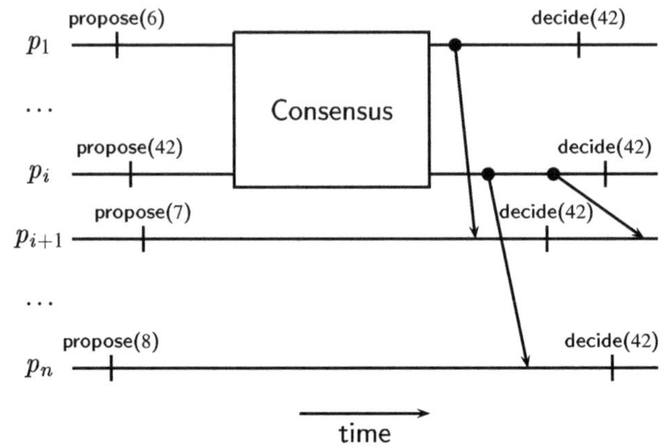

Figure 5.5: A possible trace of the transformed consensus algorithm. All processes initially propose some value. For example, p_1 proposes 6. The processes in $\mu(\mathscr{D})$ ($\{p_1,\ldots,p_i\}$ in this case) invoke an existing consensus algorithm. After the algorithm returns, each process $p \in \mu(\mathscr{D})$ informs the processes that depend on p about the decision value and decides this value. A process not in $\mu(\mathscr{D})$ waits to be informed about the decision and decides the first value it receives.

now take a different approach and transform an arbitrary existing algorithm by augmenting it with some means of reliable multicast. To understand the underlying idea of the transformation, recall that a Didep model $\mathscr{D}$ induces a set of processes $\mu(\mathscr{D})$ such that each process $q \in \Pi$ depends on a process $p \in \mu(\mathscr{D})$: If a process $p \in \mu(\mathscr{D})$ fails, so do all the processes that depend on p. If q indeed depends on a different process p, q can be omitted from finding the decision value in an algorithm as, from the perspective of fault tolerance, q does not contribute to the redundancy for tolerating faults. It suffices if p eventually informs q about the outcome. Generalising from single processes to all processes, it suffices that the processes in $\mu(\mathscr{D})$ find the decision value and inform the processes in $\Pi \setminus \mu(\mathscr{D})$ as illustrated in Fig. 5.5.

The algorithm is given in Fig. 5. A process p_i in $\mu(\mathscr{D})$ invokes a consensus algorithm for the processes on $\mu(\mathscr{D})$ with its proposal value and assigns the result to v (line 2). Before deciding v (line 7), it multicasts the result to all processes that depend on p_i (line 3 and 4) by DECISION messages. If p_i is not in $\mu(\mathscr{D})$, it waits for a DECISION(v) message from a process it depends on (line 6) and decides v (line 7).

Algorithm 5: DidepConsensus(v_i). A consensus algorithm for Didep models using a consensus algorithm for adversary structures.

if $p_i \in \mu(\mathscr{D})$ **then**
  $v \leftarrow$ `Consensus`(v_i) with Π substituted by $\mu(\mathscr{D})$
  foreach $p \in \{q \in \Pi \setminus \mu(\mathscr{D}) : \forall S \in \mathscr{D} : p_i \in S \Rightarrow q \in S\}$ **do**
    send DECISION(v) to p
else
  wait until DECISION(v) *received from* $p \in \{q \in \mu(\mathscr{D}) : \forall S \in \mathscr{D} : q \in S \Rightarrow p_i \in S\}$
decide v

Theorem 5.4
The algorithm `DidepConsensus` solves consensus despite crash failures under a Didep model $\mathscr{D}$ if consensus – restricted to $\mu(\mathscr{D})$ – is solved by `Consensus`.

PROOF: We need to show that validity, agreement, and termination are guaranteed by Algorithm `DidepConsensus`.

⟨1⟩1. (Validity) If a process decides a value v, then v was proposed by some process.
PROOF: Each value decided is a value returned by `Consensus`. As this algorithm is correct by assumption, the returned value is a value that was proposed.

⟨1⟩2. (Agreement) No two correct processes decide differently.
PROOF: It suffices to consider two arbitrary correct processes $p, q \in \Pi$ and show these processes decide the same value if they decide. We distinguish three different cases depending on which process is in $\mu(\mathscr{D})$.

⟨2⟩1. CASE: Both processes are in $\mu(\mathscr{D})$.
PROOF: Both processes decide the value returned by `Consensus`. As this algorithm is correct, both processes decide the same value.

⟨2⟩2. CASE: One process is in $\mu(\mathscr{D})$, the other one is not.
PROOF: Without loss of generality, assume that p is in $\mu(\mathscr{D})$ and q is not. q decides a value that it receives from a process in $\mu(\mathscr{D})$. By ⟨2⟩1, this process and p decide the same value. Hence, p and q decide the same value.

⟨2⟩3. CASE: None of both processes is in $\mu(\mathscr{D})$.
PROOF: Both processes decide values they received from processes in $\mu(\mathscr{D})$. By ⟨2⟩1, these processes decide the same value. Hence, p and q decide the same value as well.

⟨2⟩4. Q.E.D.
PROOF: By ⟨2⟩1 – ⟨2⟩3.

⟨1⟩3. (Termination) Every correct processes eventually decides on some value.
PROOF: It suffices to consider an arbitrary correct process p and show that it eventually decides.

⟨2⟩1. CASE: $p \in \mu(\mathscr{D})$
PROOF: As Consensus is correct by assumption and, therefore, terminates. Furthermore, p cannot block at any other point in the algorithm.

⟨2⟩2. CASE: $p \notin \mu(\mathscr{D})$
PROOF: If p is not in $\mu(\mathscr{D})$, there is a correct process $q \in \mu(\mathscr{D})$ that p depends upon. q invokes and eventually returns from Consensus. p eventually receives a value from q, because the channels are reliable.

⟨2⟩3. Q.E.D.
PROOF: By ⟨2⟩1 and ⟨2⟩2.

⟨1⟩4. Q.E.D.
PROOF: By ⟨1⟩1 – ⟨1⟩3.

In particular, the DidepConsensus algorithm allows to reuse the versatile algorithm from above. If we restrict the failure model to the processes in $\mu(\mathscr{D})$, an adversary structure can be obtained by $\kappa_M(\mathscr{D}\,|_{\mu(\mathscr{D})})$, that is, the monotone closure of the Didep model restricted to $\mu(\mathscr{D})$. Above, we already presented a consensus algorithm for adversary structures that can be reused here. However, any other algorithm for adversary structures could be used instead.

Corollary 5.1
Algorithm DidepConsensus solves consensus despite crash failures under a Didep model $\mathscr{D}$ using a $\diamond\mathscr{S}$ failure detector if

$$\forall A_1, A_2 \in \kappa_M(\mathscr{D}\,|_{\mu(\mathscr{D})}) : A_1 \cup A_2 \neq \mu(\mathscr{D}).$$

PROOF: By Theorem 5.1, VersatileConsensus solves consensus among the processes in $\mu(\mathscr{D})$ if $\kappa_M(\mathscr{D}\,|_{\mu(\mathscr{D})})$ is 2-well-formed with respect to $\mu(\mathscr{D})$. Using VersatileConsensus, DidepConsensus solves consensus by Theorem 5.4 then.

Note that algorithm DidepConsensus also implements consensus in the presence of Byzantine failures if Consensus solves consensus despite those failures among the processes in $\mu(\mathscr{D})$.

Example 5.1
Consider a system with a set of processes $\Pi = \{m_1, \dots, m_4, s_1, \dots, s_l\}$, which are subject to crash failures, and a sound and complete Didep model

$$\begin{aligned}\mathscr{D} = \{ &\{m_1, m_2, s_1, \dots, s_j\}, \{m_1, s_1, \dots, s_i\},\\ &\{m_2, s_{i+1}, \dots, s_j\}, \{m_3, s_{j+1}, \dots, s_k\},\\ &\{m_4, s_{k+1}, \dots, s_l\}\} \cup \mathscr{P}(\{s_1, \dots, s_l\}).\end{aligned}$$

The processes $m_i, 1 \leq i \leq 4$, can be considered "master" processes, the processes $s_i, 1 \leq i \leq l$, "slave" processes, because the slave processes depend on the master processes. Each combination of processes in $\{s_1,\ldots,s_l\}$ may fail in a trace. The processes m_1, m_2, m_3, and m_4 may fail without another $m_h, 1 \leq h \leq 4$, and m_1 and m_2 may fail jointly. If m_1 fails, all processes in $\{s_1,\ldots,s_i\}$ fail as well. If m_2 fails, all processes in $\{s_{i+1},\ldots,s_j\}$ fail as well. If m_3 fails, all processes in $\{s_{j+1},\ldots,s_k\}$ fail as well. If m_4 fails, all processes in $\{s_{k+1},\ldots,s_l\}$ fail as well. Therefore, each process depends on a process in $\{m_1,\ldots,m_4\}$ such that

$$\begin{aligned}\mu(\mathscr{D}) &= \{m_1,\ldots,m_4\}\\ \mathscr{D}\,|_{\mu(\mathscr{D})} &= \{\{m_1,m_2\},\{m_1\},\{m_2\},\{m_3\},\{m_4\},\emptyset\}.\end{aligned}$$

As $\kappa_M(\mathscr{D}\,|_{\mu(\mathscr{D})})$ is 2-well-formed with respect to $\mu(\mathscr{D})$, consensus can be solved among the processes of $\mu(\mathscr{D})$ by an algorithm for adversary structures. Hence, `DidepConsensus` solves consensus for $\mathscr{D}$ if it uses such an algorithm.

Quality of the Algorithm Under threshold models and under adversary structures, the number of messages per round are in $O(n)$ with a centralised message exchange pattern and in $O(n^2)$ under a distributed message exchange pattern, where n is the number of processes in the systems. The transformed algorithm above allows to improve on these bounds. For m being the number of processes in $\mu(\mathscr{D})$, the number of messages is in $O(m)$ with a centralised message exchange pattern and in $O(m^2)$ with a distributed message exchange pattern, because the invoked consensus algorithm is restricted to the processes in $\mu(\mathscr{D})$. The algorithm improves on the bounds as $m \leq n$. Hence, whenever $\mu(\mathscr{D}) \neq \Pi$, the algorithm takes strictly less messages per round. However, after the last round, the algorithm multicasts the decision value to the processes in $\Pi \setminus \mu(\mathscr{D})$. This adds an overhead of $O(m \cdot (n-m))$ messages independent of the number of rounds.

The number of communication phases per round and the overall number of rounds is determined by the invoked consensus algorithm. Analogously to the number of messages, the transformed algorithm adds an overhead of one communication phase to multicast the decision value.

Circumventing the FLP Impossibility Result Interestingly, the transformed algorithm allows to circumvent the FLP impossibility result for certain Didep models. In particular, this is the case if $\mu(\mathscr{D}) = \{p\}$ for some Didep model $\mathscr{D}$ and some process $p \in \Pi$. In this case, the invoked algorithm must solve consensus for a single process only, which is trivially implemented by having the process decide its proposal value. Note that this is possible without any failure detector in an asynchronous system. Therefore, Didep models open another condition under which the FLP result does not hold.

An intuitive reason for circumventing the FLP result is that a Didep model $\mathscr{D}$ with $\mu(\mathscr{D}) = \{p\}$ allows to predetermine a leader, namely p. Each process accepts p as a leader and either, eventually receives the decision from p or crashes. This can be considered a special case of the results of Chandra et al. [1996], which have shown that a *leader failure detector* suffices to solve consensus. Such a failure detector eventually outputs the same nonfaulty process at all nonfaulty processes.

Due to the importance of the FLP result, let us have a closer look, why the algorithm allows to circumvent the FLP result and, in particular, at which point the algorithm breaks an assumption of its proof. Recall that Fischer et al. [1985] have shown that three properties with respect to bivalent states hold for each system that solves consensus (see p. 147). The first property states that there is a trace with a bivalent initial state. The proof of Fischer et al. [1985] for this property starts as follows: Assume that a property P has no trace with a bivalent initial state. Then P must have different traces with 0 and with 1 as the only decision value as it implements validity. Two initial states are *adjacent* if they differ only in the initial value of some process p. There is an initial state with 0 as the only possible decision value adjacent to an initial state with 1 as the only possible decision value. Let q be the process such that both states differ in the proposal value of q. Then, the proof continues by considering some trace τ_0 in P in which q crashes initially, but other processes decide. Here, the proof assumes that such a trace exists in P. However, this does not hold for our algorithm: if the proposal value of q determines the outcome of the decision, then $\mu(\mathscr{D}) = \{q\}$. If q crashes initially, no process can decide, which does not violate termination as all other processes crash as well due to the failure model. In summary, the first property of the FLP proof does not hold under Didep models.

A Didep model with $\mu(\mathscr{D}) = \{p\}$ is obviously not 2-well-formed, because $\Pi \in \mathscr{D}$. The versatile algorithm `VersatileConsensus` cannot tolerate such a failure model and, therefore, is not optimal in resilience. Interestingly, such a Didep model allows improvements on other quality measures as well. The number of *overall* messages is $n-1$, because p only multicasts the decision to all other processes. As the multicast forms the only communication phase, the number of *overall* communication phases is 1. Furthermore, an execution of the algorithm requires one round at most, while the number of rounds cannot be bound under a $\diamond\mathscr{S}$ failure detector in general. While these improvements are interesting from a theoretical perspective, they are less interesting for practice. Although centralised systems (e.g., client/server systems) may have a single-point-of-failure, having a truly distributed system with all processes depending on a single process is hardly realistic.

In general, an advantage of asynchronous systems is that they are completely time-free: Their specifications do not reference time in any way, which usually reduces the complexity of a specification dramatically. However, most failure models draw it impossible to solve seminal problems like consensus under purely asynchronous systems. We continue with solving consensus under stronger synchrony assumptions, namely partially synchronous systems.

5.4 Consensus in Partially Synchronous Systems

The previous section has shown how to reach consensus in asynchronous systems with failure detectors despite crash failures, that is, permanent failures. To demonstrate that Didep models are also applicable under stronger synchrony assumptions and transient failure models, we show how to solve consensus in partially synchronous systems despite dynamic omission failures. Let us start with solving consensus in a partially synchronous system despite permanent crash failures.

Tolerating Crash Failures In the previous section, we reused the algorithm `VersatileConsensus` that was developed for threshold models and asynchronous systems and applied it to Didep models. We can further benefit from this algorithm and also use it in a partially synchronous system: Hurfin et al. [2002] have shown that the algorithm can be easily adapted to implement consensus in a partially synchronous system (without a failure detector, but with eventually synchronous processes and communication): The only reference to failure detectors is in line 10 of the algorithm,

wait until PROP(r_i, v) *has been received from* p_{cc} *or* $p_{cc} \in \text{Suspects}(p_i)$.

Hurfin et al. [2002] have shown that, if this line is replaced by

reset $timer_i$
wait until PROP(r_i, v) *has been received from* p_{cc} *or* $timer_i \leq 0$,

then the algorithm will solve consensus in a partially synchronous system (under the conditions stated in Lemma 5.1). The timer must be set depending on the bounds Δ and δ for message delivery times and relative process speeds. As the system eventually obeys these bounds, the PROP messages of a correct coordinator will be received by all correct processes before their timers reach 0. Hence, the proposal is considered by all correct processes. Hence, a decision is reached in this round.

Algorithm 6: ThreeQuorumsConsensus(v_i).

1 $r_i \leftarrow 0$
2 **while** TRUE **do**
3 $\quad r_i \leftarrow r_i + 1$
4 $\quad$ **foreach** $p \in \Pi$ **do** send EST(r_i, v_i) to p
5 $\quad$ **reset timer**
6 $\quad$ **wait until**
7 $\quad\quad \vee$ DECISION(d) *has been received*
8 $\quad\quad \vee$ EST$(r, *)$ *with* $r > r_i$ *has been received*
9 $\quad\quad \vee$ EST$(r_i, *)$ *has been received from each* $p \in \Pi$
10 $\quad\quad \vee$ *time-out occurs*
11 $\quad$ **if** DECISION(d) *has been received* **then**
12 $\quad\quad$ **foreach** $p \in \Pi$ **do** send DECISION(d) to p
13 $\quad\quad$ **decide** d if not decided yet
14 $\quad$ **else if** EST$(r, *)$ *with* $r > r_i$ *has been received* **then**
15 $\quad\quad r_i \leftarrow \max\{r : \text{EST}(r, *) \text{ has been received}\}$
16 $\quad$ **else if** $\exists Q_1 \in \mathcal{Q}$: EST$(r_i, *)$ *has been received from each* $p \in Q_1$ **then**
17 $\quad\quad$ **if** $\exists Q_2 \in \mathcal{Q}, v \in V$: EST(r_i, v) *has been received from each* $p \in Q_1 \cap Q_2$ **then**
18 $\quad\quad\quad v_i \leftarrow v$
19 $\quad\quad$ **else**
20 $\quad\quad\quad v_i \leftarrow \min\{v : \text{EST}(r_i, v) \text{ has been received}\}$
21 $\quad\quad$ **if** $\exists Q_3 \in \mathcal{Q}, d \in V$: EST(r_i, d) *has been received from each* $p \in Q_3$ **then**
22 $\quad\quad\quad$ **foreach** $p \in \Pi$ **do** send DECISION(d) to p
23 $\quad\quad\quad$ **decide** d if not decided yet

Tolerating Transient Omission Failures So far, we only addressed crash failures, that is, permanent failures. In fact, a criticism on process failure models is that they do not allow to handle transient failures well [Santoro and Widmayer, 1989, 2005, Charron-Bost and Schiper, 2007]. We illustrate that this criticism is not valid in general by showing how to implement consensus under transient send omission failures and Didep models in partially synchronous systems.

Algorithm 6 describes a consensus algorithm that is inspired by an algorithm given by Charron-Bost and Schiper [2007] for the *Heard-Of* system model. We have adapted the algorithm to our system model for partial synchrony and Didep models and transformed it into a quorum-based algorithm. Alternatively, we could have shown that the heard-of communication predicate required for the original algorithm can be implemented under our assumptions.

The algorithm proceeds in rounds, but does not use the rotating coordinator paradigm. The algorithm uses a message exchange pattern, which is related to the distributed message exchange pattern: Within a round r_i, each process p_i sends its current estimate value v_i to all other processes by an EST message (line 4). Then, the process waits for a message for round r_i from every process (line 9). If p_i is meanwhile informed about a decision by a DECISION message from another process (line 7), p_i decides itself (line 11–13). If p_i is not informed about a decision, but receives a message from a round $r > r_i$ while waiting (line 8), p_i immediately proceeds to the round with the greatest round number a message has been received for (line 14–15).

The algorithm is quorum-based and relies on a static coterie $\mathcal{Q}$. If EST messages for round r_i have been received from all processes of a quorum $Q_1 \in \mathcal{Q}$ (line 16), p_i proceeds by updating its estimate value and possibly decides. First, p_i checks whether there is a quorum Q_2 such that the same value v has been received from each process in $Q_1 \cap Q_2$ in round r_i (line 17). If this is the case, p_i sets its own estimate value v_i to v (line 18). Otherwise, it sets v_i to the minimum value received for round r_i (line 20). Furthermore, p_i decides a value if it has received the same value from a quorum $Q_3 \in \mathcal{Q}$ in round r_i (line 21–23). Before deciding, p_i informs all other processes about its decision (line 12 and 22).

To detect lost messages, each process starts a timer (line 6) whose time-out indicates that possibly no further messages for round r_i will be received. The bound on relative process speeds δ and on message delivery times Δ can be used to calculate a time-out value that eventually guarantees that no further messages for the round will be received after the system obeys the bounds. In particular, this can be achieved by setting the time-out to the maximal time it takes a process to

- receive a sent message (from the sending process that starts the timer),
- proceed immediately to another round (if the receiver of the message is in a round behind the sender), and
- send and receive a message (from the receiver back to the original sender).

We construct the static coterie $\mathcal{Q}$ from a Didep model $\mathcal{D}$ as before (see p. 112):

$$\mathcal{Q} = \{Q \subseteq \Pi : \exists D_1 \in \mathcal{D}|_{\mu(\mathcal{D})} : (Q = \mu(\mathcal{D}) \setminus D_1) \wedge (\forall D_2 \in \mathcal{D}|_{\mu(\mathcal{D})} : D_1 \not\subset D_2)\}$$

Lemma 5.2
If a Didep model $\mathcal{D}$ is 3-well-formed and the static coterie $\mathcal{Q}$ is constructed as above, then $\mathcal{Q}$ is highly available and

$$\forall Q_1, Q_2, Q_3 \in \mathcal{Q} : Q_1 \cap Q_2 \cap Q_3 \neq \emptyset.$$

PROOF: Analogously to Theorem 4.1.

Theorem 5.5
Algorithm 6 solves consensus despite transient send omission failures in a partially synchronous system if $\mathcal{D}$ is 3-well-formed.

PROOF: We prove that the algorithm even solves the stricter uniform consensus. We prove each of its properties separately.

⟨1⟩1. (Validity) If a process decides a value v, then v was proposed by some process.

PROOF: If a process p decides a value v, it has received v by a DECISION message or by some EST messages. If p has received v by a DECISION message, another process has decided v already. It suffices to consider the first process that decides v. This process has received v by an EST message from a process p_i. When p_i sent the message, v is equal to v_i. Either p_i has received v itself by an EST message or v is equal to p_i proposal value. By induction, v was proposed by some process.

⟨1⟩2. (Uniform Agreement) No two processes decide differently.

PROOF: We assume that two processes p_1, p_2 decide differently and obtain a contradiction.

⟨2⟩1. Without loss of generality, we can assume that both processes decide at line 23.

PROOF: If a process decides a value d at line 13, it has received a DECISION message with d from another process. This process has either decided d at line 23 or received a DECISION message with d itself. By induction, some process must have decided d at line 23. If p_1 and p_2 decide differently, two processes decided differently at line 23. Without loss of generality, we can consider these processes as p_1 and p_2.

⟨2⟩2. If both processes decide at different rounds, they decide the same value.

PROOF: Without loss of generality, p_1 decides at round r and p_2 at round r' with $r < r'$. By ⟨2⟩1, both decide at line 23. If p_1 decides d_1, it has received d_1 from a quorum Q. In this case, no process p_i can assign a different value than d_1 to v_i at line 18 in any round $\geq r$, because, whenever p_i has received EST messages from a quorum Q_i, all processes in $Q \cap Q_i$ sent d_1. This is not the case for any another quorum $Q' \in \mathcal{Q}$ with a different value $d' \neq d_1$: As $Q \cap Q_i \cap Q' \neq \emptyset$ by Lemma 5.2, the value d' must be equal to d_1.

When p_2 decides d_2 at r' at line 23, it has received the same value d_2 from a quorum. In this case, it did assign d_2 to v_2 at round r' in line 18 and, as $r' > r$, $d_2 = d_1$.

⟨2⟩3. Both processes do not decide at the same round.

PROOF: Otherwise, each process has received an EST message with its decision value from a quorum in the same round. However, both quorums do intersect. Thus, both processes have received and, therefore, decide the same value.

⟨2⟩4. Q.E.D.

PROOF: By $\langle 2 \rangle 2$ and the assumption that both processes decide differently, both processes do not decide at different rounds. By $\langle 2 \rangle 3$, they neither decide at the same round. We have obtained a contradiction.

$\langle 1 \rangle 3$. (Uniform Termination) Every process eventually decides on some value.

PROOF: Eventually, the system obeys known bounds on relative process speed and message delay, a quorum of (then nonfailed) processes permanently succeed to, and all other (then failed) processes permanently fail to send messages. Consider a round strictly greater than all current rounds at that instance. Eventually, a nonfailed process starts this round and is the first to send messages for the round. All nonfailed processes receive the same set of messages in this round, because they immediately proceed to the round and all failed processes fail to send messages at all. Hence, all nonfailed processes adapt the same value, which enables a decision in the next round, if a decision has not been possible yet. Note that the failed processes are informed about any decision and decide as well.

$\langle 1 \rangle 4$. Q.E.D.

PROOF: By $\langle 1 \rangle 1 - \langle 1 \rangle 3$.

Quality of the Algorithm As failures are transient and as the system is partially synchronous, the number of rounds cannot be bounded: Processes may fail to send messages for an arbitrary but finite amount of time. Analogously, it may take an arbitrary but finite amount of time for processes to receive sent messages in a timely manner even when no further failures do occur. Within a round, the algorithm uses two communication phases: one for broadcasting the EST messages and, in case of a decision, one for broadcasting the decision. Hence, each process sends at least n EST messages and, in case of a decision, another n DECISION messages. Therefore, the number of messages per round is in $O(n^2)$.

The algorithm solves consensus correctly despite transient send omission failures (and also permanent crash failures) if $\mathscr{D}$ is 3-well-formed. Hence, a 3-well-formed Didep model is sufficient for solving consensus in a partially synchronous system despite such failures. As our purpose was to show that Didep models are also applicable to transient failures, we leave it as an open question whether a 3-well-formed Didep model is also necessary. For permanent crash failures, a 2-well-formed Didep model is already necessary and sufficient as we have seen above.

5.5 Consensus in Synchronous Systems

Let us now have a look at the most strict synchrony assumptions and consider synchronous systems. The algorithms we presented above for weaker system models also solve consensus in synchronous systems, because synchronous systems allow to implement failure detectors and are special cases of partially synchronous systems (the bounds on relative process speeds and message delivery times are known and hold initially). Hence, the possibility to solve consensus is out of question for the functional failure models we considered so far.

Nevertheless, synchronous systems may allow more resilient and/or more efficient solutions than possible under weaker system models. For example, synchronous systems allow to bound the number of rounds, which is impossible under partially synchronous and asynchronous system models. Likewise, high resilience is possible. In case of crash failures, consensus can even be solved for an arbitrary number of failures [Lynch, 1996]. Hence, synchronous systems allow optimal resilience, which cannot be improved further by using more expressive failure models. We, therefore, consider a more severe – actually the most severe – functional failure mode now, Byzantine failures.

Byzantine Failures Distributed consensus and its variants have been studied extensively for Byzantine failures in synchronous systems [Pease et al., 1980, Lamport et al., 1982, Bar-Noy et al., 1987, Lynch, 1996]. In this section, we reuse the algorithm of Bar-Noy et al. [1987] that is based on a strategy known as *exponential information gathering (EIG)*. With this strategy, the processes gather information by sending and relaying their proposal values for a fixed number of rounds and by recording the incoming values. After this information gathering phase, they use a common procedure to decide a value based on the recorded values.

The sending, relaying, and recording of messages is organised around a labelled-tree data structure called *EIG tree* [Bar-Noy et al., 1987]. Each edge represents a process of the system. A path from the root to a leaf node represents a sequence of processes along which proposal values are sent and relayed. No such sequence contains a process more than once (i.e., the processes in a sequence are distinct). Every node is labelled with the sequence of processes that corresponds to the edges of the path from the root to the node. For example, if the edges of the path from the root node to a node n are labelled by $p_{i_1}, \ldots, p_{i_k}$, then the node is labelled with $\langle p_{i_1}, \ldots, p_{i_k} \rangle$. The root node is labelled with the empty sequence.

While Bar-Noy et al. [1987] presented a construction of EIG trees for threshold models, we construct an EIG tree from a Didep model. Key to this construction is the observation that, for reasonable EIG trees, each label of a leaf node must

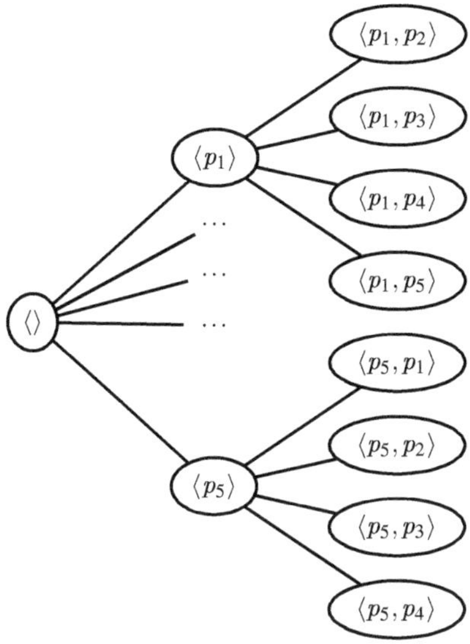

Figure 5.6: EIG tree for five processes and a threshold model with $t = 1$.

contain at least one correct process. An EIG tree is constructed from a Didep model $\mathscr{D}$ starting with an empty tree by the following steps:

1. Add a root node labelled with the empty sequence.
2. If there is a leaf node that is labelled with a sequence $\langle p_{i_1}, \ldots, p_{i_k} \rangle$ and

$$\exists D \in \mathscr{D} : \{p_{i_1}, \ldots, p_{i_k}\} \subseteq D,$$

   then add $|\Pi| - k$ children with labels $\langle p_{i_1}, \ldots, p_{i_k}, p \rangle$, where p ranges over all elements in $\Pi \setminus \{p_{i_1}, \ldots, p_{i_k}\}$.
3. Repeat step 2 as long as it allows to add new nodes.

Hence, whenever it is not guaranteed that a leaf node contains a correct process, it receives new children adding all remaining processes. This requires the assumption that at least one process is correct, that is, $\Pi \notin \mathscr{D}$.

Example 5.2 (EIG tree for threshold models)
Consider a distributed system with five processes, $\Pi = \{p_1, \ldots, p_5\}$, and a threshold model describing that at most one process may be faulty. The corresponding EIG tree is illustrated in Fig. 5.6. It has the empty sequence as the label of the root node. The five children of

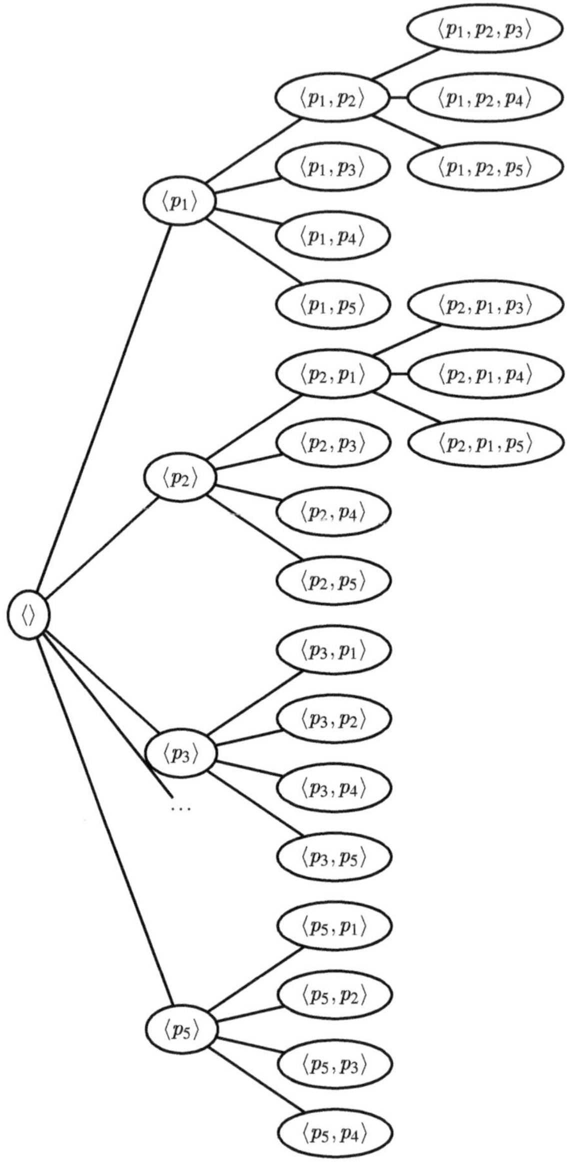

Figure 5.7: EIG tree for the Didep model $\mathscr{D} = \{\emptyset, \{p_1\}, \ldots, \{p_5\}, \{p_1, p_2\}\}$.

the root are labelled with sequences containing a single process, one node for each process. Their children are labelled with sequences of two processes, one node for each remaining process. As at most a single process is faulty in a trace, no further nodes are added.

For Didep models that correspond to threshold models, our construction yields EIG trees that are equal to EIG trees constructed by the method of Bar-Noy et al. [1987]. They construct EIG trees as trees of depth $t+1$ considering all possible sequences of distinct processes, where t describes the threshold model.

Example 5.3 (EIG tree for Didep models)
For the same system and a Didep model

$$\mathscr{D} = \{\emptyset, \{p_1\}, \ldots, \{p_5\}, \{p_1, p_2\}\}$$

instead of the threshold model, the construction yields the EIG tree shown in Fig. 5.7. The Didep model is equivalent to the threshold model except for additionally allowing that p_1 and p_2 are faulty in the same trace. Consequently, the EIG tree for the Didep model equals the tree for the threshold model except for additional children of the nodes labelled with p_1 and p_2 to ensure that each leaf node has at least one correct process in its label.

Besides the EIG tree data structure, Bar-Noy et al. [1987] have also presented a consensus algorithm for Byzantine failures that relies on an EIG tree. We adapt this algorithm and use it for EIG trees constructed from Didep models. Note that the algorithm is closely related to the algorithm from Pease et al. [1980].

The algorithm `EIGConsensus` – given as Alg. 7 – relies on an EIG tree. Each process p_i has its own copy of the EIG tree, which is annotated during the computation. Each node gets two annotations, a "value" and a "new value." Formally, we define the value and new value annotations by the mappings v_i and n_i, respectively. Both mappings map a node's label l to a value v. Intuitively, a value annotation has the following meaning: If a node with label $l = \langle p_{i_1}, \ldots, p_{i_k} \rangle$ in the EIG tree of p_i is annotated with $v_i(l) = x$, this annotation represents that p_{i_k} has told p_i in round k that $p_{i_{k-1}}$ has told p_{i_k} in round $k-1$ that ... that p_{i_1} has told p_{i_1} in round 1 that its proposal value is x. The new value annotations are used to determine the final decision value as described below.

Both annotations are initialised with some predetermined default value v_0 for each EIG tree node label (lines 1 – 3). Each process p_i then sets the value annotation of the root node to its own proposal value $prop_i$ (line 4).

The information gathering phase of the algorithm is round-based. Process p_i maintains its current round number in a variable r_i, which is initialised by 0 (line 5). Over the rounds, each process p_i sends, relays, and records proposal values along the paths of its EIG tree – proceeding from the root node down to the leaf nodes. The current level of the tree is encoded by the round number, which gives the length of node labels that are to be considered for the current round.

Algorithm 7: EIGConsensus($prop_i$). An EIG consensus algorithm for Didep models derived from Lynch [1996].

```
1  foreach label l of an EIG tree node do                    // initialise all annotations
2      v_i(l) ← v_0
3      n_i(l) ← v_0
4  v_i(⟨⟩) ← prop_i                                            // annotate root with proposal
5  r_i ← 0
   // information gathering rounds
6  while r_i < depth of the EIG tree do
7      r_i ← r_i + 1
8      foreach EIG tree node label l of length r_i − 1 that does not contain p_i do
9          foreach p ∈ Π do send RELAY(r_i, l, v_i(l)) to p
10     reset timer
11     wait until time-out occurs
12     foreach RELAY(r_i, l, v) message received from a process p do
13         if exactly one message received from p for round r_i then
14             v_i(l ∘ ⟨p⟩) ← v                     // annotate node with relayed value
   // determine decision value
15 foreach label l of an EIG tree leaf node do
16     n_i(l) ← v_i(l)
17 while r_i > 0 do
18     r_i ← r_i − 1
19     foreach label l with length r_i of some EIG tree node n do
20         if ∃v ∈ V, D ∈ 𝒟 : ∀ node label l′ :
21                 (l′ = l ∘ ⟨p_{i_{r+1}}⟩) ⇒ (n_i(l′) = v ∨ p_{i_{r+1}} ∈ 𝒟)
22         then
23             n_i(l) ← x
24 decide n_i(⟨⟩)
```

Hence, the algorithm runs for a fixed number of rounds equal to the depth of the EIG tree (line 6).

At the beginning of a round, p_i increases its round number variable (line 7). Then, p_i relays the values received at the previous round (and its own proposal value in the first round) along the edges of the EIG tree: p_i sends a message RELAY$(r_i, l, v_i(l))$ for each label l of length $r_i - 1$ to all processes if l does not contain p_i yet (lines 8 and 9). Each process sets a timer such that all messages sent by correct processes for the current round are guaranteed to be received (lines 10 and 11). For each RELAY(r_i, l, v) message that has been received from a process p, p_i records the value by setting the value annotation $v_i(l \circ \langle p \rangle) = v$, where $\circ$ denotes concatenation of sequences (line 14). However, as failed processes may send malformed or multiple messages for round r_i, p_i performs some sanity checks. It only considers proper RELAY messages and discards other messages. If a process sent multiple messages for round r_i all of them are discarded (line 13). Such an approach requires the assumption that a process can determine the actual sender of a message.

After these rounds of information gathering, each process p_i evaluates the EIG tree – from the leaf nodes up to the root node – to reach a decision. For this evaluation, p_i updates the new value annotations. Initially, the value annotation of each leaf node is copied to the new value annotation (lines 15 and 16). The round number variable is decremented step-by-step to work up from the leaf nodes to the root. For each label l of length r_i, $n_i(l)$ is set to x if all of the corresponding node's children except possibly faulty ones have the new value annotation of x (lines 19–23). Process p_i eventually decides the new value annotation of the root node $n_i(\langle\rangle)$.

Example 5.4 (EIG Consensus Algorithm)
Consider the distributed system from the previous example and the corresponding EIG tree given in Fig. 5.7. Consider a default value $v_0 = 0$ and a trace, where p_3 proposes the value 0 and p_4 and p_5 propose the value 1. Furthermore, assume that p_1 and p_2 initially fail and misbehave as follows: Whenever they are supposed to send a RELAY message to another process, they do so with value 0 for p_3, but with value 1 for p_4 and p_5. In other words, they try to convince p_3 to decide 0 and try to convince p_4 and p_5 to decide 1. Therefore, the annotated EIG trees of p_4 and p_5 are equal, but the EIG tree of p_3 differs. For illustration, these trees are given in Fig. 5.8 and Fig. 5.9, respectively.

The value annotations for nodes with labels that end in a correct process are equal in both trees. This is not surprising as all correct processes receive the same message from a correct process. The value annotations differ for labels that end in faulty processes. For example, p_3 has received RELAY$(1,\langle\rangle,0)$ messages at round 1 from p_1 and p_2. Hence, $v_3(\langle p_1\rangle) = v_3(\langle p_2\rangle) = 0$. In contrast, p_4 and p_5 have received RELAY$(1,\langle\rangle,1)$ messages at round 1 from p_1 and p_2. Hence, $v_4(\langle p_1\rangle) = v_4(\langle p_2\rangle) = v_5(\langle p_1\rangle) = v_5(\langle p_2\rangle) = 1$.

After the information gathering phase, the processes evaluate the EIG tree. For the leaf nodes, the new value annotation equals the value annotation. Consider the (inner) node with label $l = \langle p_1, p_2\rangle$ in Fig. 5.8. Process p_3 sets $n_3(l)$ to 1 although p_2 has told p_3 that p_1 has told p_2 that p_1 has 0 as the proposal value. Note that the labels of the children of the corresponding nodes end in p_3, p_4, and p_5. The latter ones informed p_3 that they have received the value 1. As $\exists D \in \mathscr{D} : \{p_3\} \subseteq D$, p_3 is possibly faulty. Hence, p_3 adopts 1 as the new value annotation for the node.

A new value annotation is not necessarily derived from the majority of a node's children (as is the case for the original EIG algorithm). For example, consider the node with label $l = \langle p_4\rangle$ in Fig. 5.8. Process p_3 sets $n_3(l)$ to 1 although no proper majority of the node's children has 1 as the new value annotation and although 1 is not the default value. However, the children whose labels end in p_1 and p_2 have 0 as their new value annotation and p_1 and p_2 are possibly faulty (and indeed are faulty in this case). Hence, p_3 adopts 1 as the new

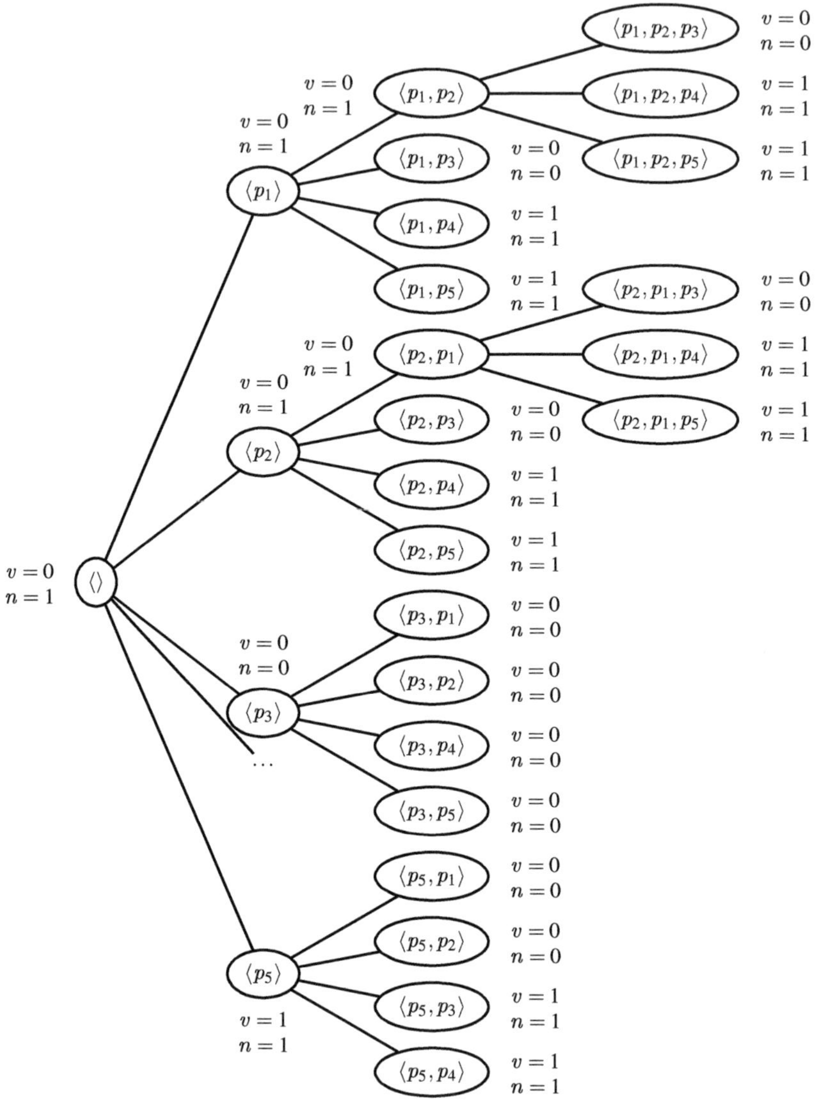

Figure 5.8: The annotated EIG tree of p_3 for Example 5.4. Process p_1 and p_2 are assumed to be faulty: they only send and relay value 0 to p_3, but value 1 to p_4 and p_5.

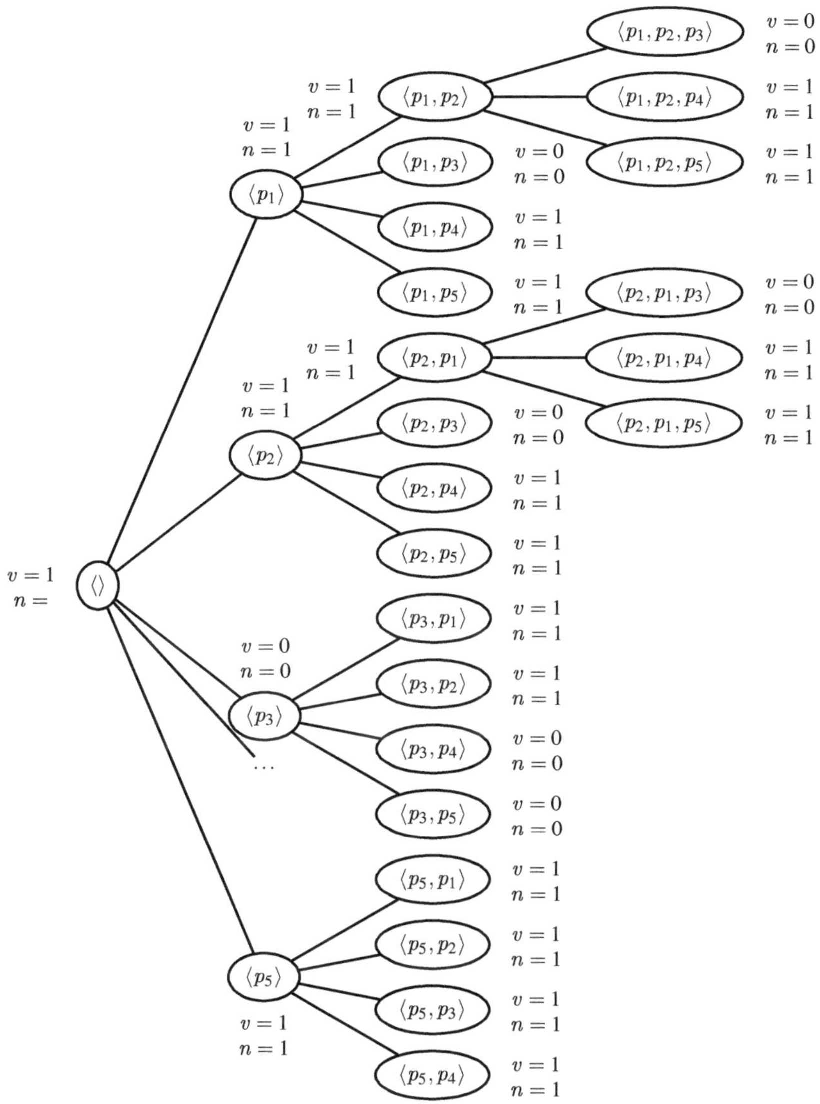

Figure 5.9: The annotated EIG tree of p_4 and p_5 for Example 5.4. Process p_1 and p_2 are assumed to be faulty: they only send and relay value 0 to p_3, but value 1 to p_4 and p_5.

value annotation. Note that the other labels of the children end in p_4 and p_5, which cannot be faulty in the same trace.

We now prove the correctness of the algorithm. In principle, the proof follows the presentation of Lynch [1996, Sect. 6.3.2]. It is adapted for covering Didep models instead of threshold models.

Theorem 5.6
The algorithm `EIGConsensus` solves Byzantine consensus despite Byzantine failures in a synchronous system under a (sound and complete) Didep model $\mathcal{D}$ if $\mathcal{D}$ is 3-well-formed.

PROOF: We prove each property (weak validity, agreement, termination) of Byzantine consensus separately.
As an abbreviation, let $d = \max\{|D| \in \mathbb{N} : D \in \mathcal{D}\}$.

$\langle 1 \rangle 1.$ (Weak validity) If a correct process p decides and all correct processes propose v, then p decides v.

PROOF: Note that the algorithm runs for $d+1$ rounds.

$\langle 2 \rangle 1.$ After $d+1$ rounds of the algorithm, for all correct processes $p_i, p_j \in \Pi$, $v_i(l) = v_j(l)$ for every label l of an EIG tree node that ends in a correct process p_k.

PROOF: As p_k is correct, it sends the same RELAY message to p_i and p_j. As p_i and p_j are correct as well, both record the same value.

$\langle 2 \rangle 2.$ Let l be any label of an EIG tree node that ends in a correct process. After $d+1$ rounds of the algorithm, there is a value v such that, for all correct processes $p_i \in \Pi$, $v_i(l) = n_i(l) = v$.

PROOF: The proof is by induction on the length of labels, with the base case proved in step 1 and the induction step in step 2.

$\langle 3 \rangle 1.$ Let l be a label of an EIG tree node that ends in a correct process and has length $|l| = d+1$. After $d+1$ rounds, there is a value v such that, for all correct processes $p_i \in \Pi$, $v_i(l) = n_i(l) = v$.

PROOF: Step $\langle 2 \rangle 1$ implies that all correct processes p_i have the same annotation $v_i(l) = x$. By the construction of the EIG tree, l is the label of a leaf node. By the construction of the new value annotations for leaf nodes, x is the required value v.

$\langle 3 \rangle 2.$ Let l be a label of an EIG tree node that ends in a correct process and has length $|l| = k$, $1 \leq k < d+1$. After $d+1$ rounds, there is a value v such that, for all correct processes $p_i \in \Pi$, $v_i(l) = n_i(l) = v$.

PROOF:

$\langle 4 \rangle 1.$ CASE: l is the label of a leaf node

PROVE: Q.E.D.

PROOF: Step $\langle 2\rangle 1$ implies that all correct processes p_i have the same annotation $v_i(l) = x$. By the construction of the new value annotations for leaf nodes, x is the required value v.

$\langle 4\rangle 2$. CASE: l is not the label of a leaf node

PROVE: Q.E.D.

As abbreviations, let L be the set of all processes in l and let C be the set $\Pi \setminus L$. Note that C is the set of all processes p such that there is an EIG tree node that has the label $l \circ \langle p\rangle$ (i.e., C is the set of all last processes in a label of a child of the node with label l), because l is not a leaf node.

PROOF:

$\langle 5\rangle 1$. For all correct processes p_i, p_j, $v_i(l \circ \langle p_j\rangle) = v$.

PROOF: By $\langle 2\rangle 1$, there is a value v such that $v_j(l) = v$ for each correct process p_j and all correct processes send the same value v to all processes at round $k+1$.

$\langle 5\rangle 2$. For all correct processes p_i, p_j, $n_i(l \circ \langle p_j\rangle) = v$.

PROOF: By $\langle 5\rangle 1$ and the inductive hypothesis.

$\langle 5\rangle 3$. There is a $D \in \mathscr{D}$ such that $\Pi \setminus D \subseteq C$.

PROOF: By the construction of the EIG tree, there is a $D \in \mathscr{D}$ such that $L \subseteq D$ as l is not the label of a leaf node.

$\langle 5\rangle 4$. There is a $D_1 \in \mathscr{D}$ such that all processes in $C \setminus D_1$ are correct.

PROOF: By the definition of $\mathscr{D}$.

$\langle 5\rangle 5$. $\forall D_2 \in \mathscr{D} : ((\Pi \setminus D) \setminus D_1) \cap ((\Pi \setminus D) \setminus D_2) \neq \emptyset$

PROOF: By $\langle 5\rangle 4$ and as $\mathscr{D}$ is 3-well-formed.

$\langle 5\rangle 6$. $\forall D_2 \in \mathscr{D} : (C \setminus D_1) \cap (C \setminus D_2) \neq \emptyset$

PROOF: By $\langle 5\rangle 3$ and $\langle 5\rangle 5$.

$\langle 5\rangle 7$. Q.E.D.

PROOF: Step $\langle 2\rangle 1$ implies that $v_i(l) = v$ for all correct processes p_i. By $\langle 5\rangle 2$, all correct processes have the same new value annotation for children of the node with label l, whose label ends in a correct process. By $\langle 5\rangle 4$ and $\langle 5\rangle 6$, the new value annotation for the node with label l is assigned v.

$\langle 4\rangle 3$. Q.E.D.

PROOF: By $\langle 4\rangle 1$ and $\langle 4\rangle 2$.

$\langle 3\rangle 3$. Q.E.D.

PROOF: By $\langle 3\rangle 1$ and $\langle 3\rangle 2$.

$\langle 2\rangle 3$. Q.E.D.

PROOF: If all correct processes propose v, then all correct processes send v in the first round. Then, for all correct processes $p_i, p_j \in \Pi$, $v_i(\langle p_j\rangle) = v$.

Step $\langle 2\rangle 2$ implies that also $n_i(\langle p_j\rangle) = v$. Due to the decision procedure and as $\mathscr{D}$ is 3-well-formed, $n_i(\langle\rangle) = v$. Hence, each correct process decides v.

$\langle 1\rangle 2$. (Agreement) No two correct processes decide differently.

PROOF: For the agreement property, we adopt further definitions from Lynch [1996].

A subset C of the nodes of an EIG tree is a *path covering* iff every path from the root to a leaf contains at least one node in C.

A tree node with label l is *common* iff, after $d+1$ rounds, all correct processes p_i have the same $n_i(l)$.

A set of tree nodes is *common* iff all the nodes in the set are common.

$\langle 2\rangle 1$. After $d+1$ rounds of the algorithm, there is a path covering that is common.

PROOF:

LET: C is the set of all nodes whose label ends in a correct process.

PROVE: C is a path covering that is common.

$\langle 3\rangle 1$. C is common.

PROOF: By step $\langle 2\rangle$ 2 of the proof for weak validity above, each node in C is common.

$\langle 3\rangle 2$. C is a path covering.

PROOF: Consider an arbitrary path from the root to a leaf node. By the construction of the EIG tree, the leaf node has a label that contains at least one correct process. By the definition of EIG tree node labels, the path has a node with a label that ends in a correct process. This node is in C.

$\langle 3\rangle 3$. Q.E.D.

PROOF: By $\langle 3\rangle 1$ and $\langle 3\rangle 2$.

$\langle 2\rangle 2$. Let l be the label of an arbitrary EIG tree node. After $d+1$ rounds of the algorithm, the node n with label l is common if there is a common path covering of the subtree with root n.

PROOF: The proof is by induction on the length of labels, with the base case proved in step 1 and the induction step in step 2.

$\langle 3\rangle 1$. Let l be a label of an EIG tree node with length $|l| = d+1$. After $d+1$ rounds, the node n with label l is common if there is a common path covering of the subtree with root n.

PROOF: By the construction of the EIG tree, n is a leaf node. The only common path covering of n's subtree contains only n. Hence, n is common if there is a common path covering of the subtree.

$\langle 3\rangle 2$. Let l be a label of an arbitrary EIG tree node n with length $|l| = k$, $1 \leq k < d+1$. After $d+1$ rounds, n is common if there is a common path covering of the subtree with root n.

PROOF:

$\langle 4 \rangle 1$. CASE: n is a leaf node
PROVE: Q.E.D.
PROOF: The only common path covering of n's subtree contains only n. Hence, n is common if there is a common path covering of the subtree.
$\langle 4 \rangle 2$. CASE: n is not a leaf node
PROVE: Q.E.D.
PROOF:
ASSUME: C is a common path covering of the subtree with root n.
PROVE: n is common
$\langle 5 \rangle 1$. CASE: $n \in C$
PROVE: Q.E.D.
PROOF: As C is common.
$\langle 5 \rangle 2$. CASE: $n \notin C$
PROVE: Q.E.D.
PROOF: Consider an arbitrary child n' of n As $n \notin C$, there is a subset of C that is a common path covering for the subtree with root n'. By the inductive hypothesis, n' is common. As the choice of n' was arbitrary, all children of n are common. As the new value annotation is computed deterministically, n is common.
$\langle 5 \rangle 3$. Q.E.D.
PROOF: By $\langle 5 \rangle 1$ and $\langle 5 \rangle 2$.
$\langle 4 \rangle 3$. Q.E.D.
PROOF: By $\langle 4 \rangle 1$ and $\langle 4 \rangle 2$.
$\langle 3 \rangle 3$. Q.E.D.
PROOF: By $\langle 3 \rangle 1$ and $\langle 3 \rangle 2$.
$\langle 2 \rangle 3$. Q.E.D.
PROOF: By $\langle 2 \rangle 1$ and $\langle 2 \rangle 2$, the root node of the EIG tree is common after $d+1$ rounds. As each correct process decides on the value of the new value annotation of the root node, no two correct processes decide differently.
$\langle 1 \rangle 3$. (Termination) Every correct process eventually decides on some value.
PROOF: Every correct process decides after $d+1$ rounds. No process does permanently block.
$\langle 1 \rangle 4$. Q.E.D.
PROOF: By $\langle 1 \rangle 1$ – $\langle 1 \rangle 3$.

Quality of the Algorithm As the system is synchronous, all bounds on relative process speeds and message delivery times hold initially. This guarantee allows to bound the number of rounds in contrast to partially synchronous or asynchronous systems: The algorithm runs for a fixed number of rounds equal to $d+1$, where

$d = \max\{|D| \in \mathbb{N} : D \in \mathscr{D}\}$ gives the maximal number of faulty processes in a trace. The number of rounds corresponds to the number of rounds obtained under threshold models: The variant of the algorithm for threshold models runs for $t+1$ rounds (which is optimal under threshold models [Fischer and Lynch, 1982]), where t describes the threshold model. Hence, using a Didep model to describe a fault assumption more accurately does not yield advantages for the efficiency in terms of the number of rounds: A threshold model that over-approximates the fault assumption yields the same number of rounds.

Each round consists of a single communication phase, which is trivially optimal. However, as the number of rounds is fixed, the number of communication phases is of minor importance.

The number of messages sent in a round is in $O(n^2)$, where n is the number of processes, as each process potentially multicasts a message to each other process in a round. In principle, this number corresponds to the number for the variant for threshold models. However, the expressiveness of Didep models allows to reduce the communication costs if dependent faults are involved. In this case, not all processes are required to multicast message in late rounds. For example, compare the EIG tree for a threshold model in Fig. 5.6 with the EIG tree for a Didep model in Fig. 5.7. With the former tree, all processes multicast messages in the last round; with the latter tree, p_1 and p_2 do not multicast messages in the last round (if they are correct). Hence, dependent faults allow to reduce the overall number of messages in this case. The extent of such a reduction depends on the extent of dependent faults.

The variant of the algorithm for threshold models is optimal with respect to resilience (under the assumption that message authentication is not available). More precisely, the algorithm solves Byzantine consensus if $3t < n$, which is an upper bound for resilience in this case. The adapted algorithm solves Byzantine consensus if the Didep model is 3-well-formed. This resilience predicate is not optimal as we have seen already by the transformer algorithm presented in Section 5.3, which also tolerates Byzantine failures. However, for Didep models of practical relevance (e.g., $\mu(\mathscr{D}) \neq \{p\}, p \in \Pi$), the algorithm achieves the best possible resilience.

5.6 Summary

The problem of consensus is fundamental for fault-tolerant distributed computing. It lies at the core of agreement and coordination in distributed systems and a solution can be used as a basic building block for fault-tolerant systems. Due to its relevance, it has been studied most intensively and extensively and has often been used as a benchmark problem for new system models.

In this chapter, we have shown how to solve consensus under Didep models in combination with different functional failure models and different synchrony assumptions. Although Didep models are more expressive than previous failure models and, therefore, allow to describe fault assumptions more accurately, they did not require completely new approaches to implement consensus. Quite the contrary, it was possible to reuse already existing algorithms, which we take as an indication that Didep model are tractable. To demonstrate that this is not an artefact of a certain functional failure model or certain synchrony assumptions, we have combined Didep models with permanent and transient failures, with benign and malicious failures, and with synchrony models ranging from synchronous to asynchronous systems covering a broad range of assumptions.

To achieve our aim, we have mainly reused and adapted already known algorithms that were originally designed for threshold models. More precisely, we reused the versatile algorithm of Hurfin et al. [2002] for crash failures in asynchronous systems augmented with failure detectors and in partially synchronous systems. Reusing this algorithm was particularly simple as it was already based on quorums, which allowed to build upon the results from the previous chapter. Additionally, we have presented a new transformer algorithm that invokes an underlying consensus algorithm for processes that are directly dependent on other processes. This algorithm tolerates benign crash as well as malicious Byzantine failures depending on the underlying algorithm.

For transient send omission failures, we adapted an algorithm from a completely different system model, the Heard-Of model [Charron-Bost and Schiper, 2007]. In particular, the adaptation included turning the algorithm into a quorum-based algorithm, which again allowed to use the quorum construction from the previous chapter. To complement these results, we have adapted a well-known synchronous algorithm [Bar-Noy et al., 1987, Lynch, 1996] for Byzantine failures that does not (explicitly) rely on quorums.

Our results additionally demonstrate that using more expressive structural failure model classes allows to obtain more efficient and/or more resilient solutions. Intuitively, Didep models provide more information on faults that can be exploited when designing fault-tolerant systems. From a theoretical point of view, certain Didep models even allow to circumvent impossibility results and to go below lower bounds on efficiency obtained under less expressive model classes. For example, the number of required messages per round is in $O(|\mu(\mathscr{D})|)$ for the versatile algorithm and a centralised message exchange pattern. In contrast, for threshold models, it is in $O(n)$, where n gives the number of overall processes, and $n > |\mu(\mathscr{D})|$ in case of directed dependent faults. Likewise, $3t < n$ is an upper bound on resilience for solving Byzantine consensus under threshold models, which is strictly generalised by a 3-well-formed Didep model.

6 Conclusion and Future Work

The topic of this thesis was to identify and evaluate models that describe the extent of faults. Of particular interest were models that cover dependent and propagating faults in the context of fault-tolerant distributed computing.

As distributed systems more and more pervade our daily life, we increasingly depend on these systems to provide their service as expected. However, each system is composed from components that are bound to fail eventually. Means of fault tolerance allow to cope with such faults: A fault-tolerant system is able to provide its service as expected despite component failures.

Unfortunately, no fault-tolerant system can tolerate arbitrary severe faults. Engineering a fault-tolerant system, therefore, requires to make an assumption on the faults to be tolerated. A fault model must be accurate for the relevant details of the fault assumption but must also be tractable. Empirical studies have shown that propagation and, in particular, dependence are relevant details of faults. If a fault model does not cover dependent and propagating faults, it may result in a system that is less efficient and/or less resilient than possible.

This thesis has contributed to the studies of the fundamentals of fault-tolerant distributed computing. Modelling faults by functional and structural failure models, we have identified classes of structural failure models that cover dependent and propagating faults. Thereby, the thesis has narrowed the gap between simple fault models and complex fault assumptions. To demonstrate that the new classes are tractable, we have developed solutions to some fundamental problems of fault-tolerant distributed computing. In particular, these solutions are hardly more complex than solutions for less expressive classes.

Modelling faults using more expressive classes turned out to be beneficial for accuracy, efficiency, and resilience. More expressive fault models allow more accurate system models and, thereby, lead to more realistic evaluation results. With more expressive models, a design can rely on more knowledge about faults than with a less expressive model. Such knowledge can be exploited to improve efficiency and resilience. For example, a system with lower message overhead can be designed. Moreover, the same degree of resilience can be achieved with less redundancy, or a higher resilience with the same level of redundancy.

Chapter 2: System Model Chapter 2 has introduced our system model and related definitions. In particular, the chapter has addressed the aspects that are fundamental for fault-tolerant distributed computing: interprocess communication, timing, and faults. The chapter has laid out the foundation for the rest of the thesis.

While the system model is fairly general, it does not cover some aspects covered by other system models. For example, we have restricted ourselves to nonprobabilistic systems, interleaving semantics, and message passing. Possible extensions of the model include probabilistic steps, noninterleaving semantics, and interprocess communication via shared memory. Moreover, our system model considers distributed systems on an abstraction level, where a system is "flatly" composed from process and channel components. A hierarchical composition remains a topic for future work. In our system model, the concerns of timing and faults are separated. In recent work, Charron-Bost and Schiper [2007] have proposed a different system model that aims to unify these concerns. Relating our system model to their model is another direction for future research.

Chapter 3: Structural Failure Models Chapter 3 has addressed the question of how to model fault assumptions. We have identified two basic building blocks, namely functional and structural failure models, for different variants of fault models. Contrasting previous claims, we have shown that any fault model for our system model can be represented by a process failure model, which does not hold for channel failure models.

Functional and structural failure models hardly impose any restrictions. They are, therefore, not tractable in general. While abstract classes of functional models have been studied extensively, structural models had received less attention. In Chapter 3, we have investigated abstract classes of structural models for dependent and propagating faults: set-based models for dependent faults and sequence-based models for dependent and propagating faults. These considerations include a detailed investigation of the expressiveness of different structural failure model classes. For example, the classes of adversary structures, core / survivor sets, and fail-prone systems turned out to be equivalent. All of these classes are strictly less expressive than the new class of Didep models, which is strictly less expressive than the class of sequence-based models.

The new classes close a gap between previous nonprobabilistic models (e.g., adversary structures or core / survivor sets) and probabilistic models that cover dependent and propagating faults (e.g., Copula and CASCADE models). The new classes cover dependent and propagating faults, but abstract from probabilistic assumptions. Chapter 3 has finished with a mapping from probabilistic models to set- and sequence-based models that relies on the notion of assumption coverage. This mapping abstracts away the associated probabilities. Hence, the resulting models are not amenable to stochastic evaluations.

The relation between stochastic and nonprobabilistic fault models deserves further attention. For example, different stochastic models incorporate different notions of dependence. The relationships between these notions and our notion of dependence is an open issue. Furthermore, we have covered eight different set-based classes of structural failure models. This variety can be explained by different application domains. For example, some classes are especially dedicated to multi-site systems. In contrast to set-based classes, we have only considered a single sequence-based class of structural failure models. Identifying and evaluating other sequence-based classes, presumably for special application domains, remains a topic for future work.

Chapter 4: Coteries As the new classes allow to describe dependent and propagating faults, they allow more accurate fault models than possible with previous classes. It remained to be shown that, despite higher accuracy, the new classes are tractable. We have illustrated that this is the case by showing how to solve some fundamental problems under the new model classes.

For many problems of fault-tolerant distributed computing, there are solutions that rely on quorums. Sets of quorums and, as a special case, coteries are fundamental means to achieve fault tolerance. Their quality is assessed, for example, by the measures of high availability and probe complexity. Both measures are of particular relevance for fault-tolerant systems: Many solutions can cope with all assumed faults if relying on a highly available coterie. Using a quorum at runtime often requires probing processes to find a quorum of nonfailed processes. In Chapter 4, we have investigated highly available coteries and the probe complexity under the new structural failure model classes.

With respect to high availability, we have given constructive characterisations of highly available coteries. The characterisations are constructive in the sense that, if a highly available coterie exists, it has been shown how to derive such a coterie from the failure model. With such constructions, previous fault-tolerant solutions can be reused under the new failure model classes, which illustrates the tractability of the classes. These considerations have covered crash as well as Byzantine failures and static as well as dynamic coteries.

With respect to probe complexity, we have refined the original notion of probe complexity by explicitly considering a sequence-based structural failure model. In contrast to the original probe complexity, the refined one gives a tight bound on the number of required probes. Additionally, we have introduced a new probe strategy that is more general in the input domain and more efficient in the number of required probes than previous strategies. The strategy is defined for all quorum sets and is not limited to coteries like previous strategies are. The strategy never requires more probes than given by the refined probe complexity for every quorum set. Previous strategies meet the original probe complexity for nondominated coteries, but require more probes for dominated ones.

There remain several directions for future work. The question of how to construct coteries that are highly available despite Byzantine failures and that are not dominated by any other such coterie has not been answered yet. While we have focussed on highly available coteries, the mapping of probabilistic fault models to Didep models (as discussed in the previous chapter) opens another approach to assess the (probabilistic) availability of a system. For crash failures, we conjecture that the maximal assumption coverage that results in a 2-well-formed Didep model equals the maximal availability that can be obtained using a static coterie. Using mappings from probabilistic fault models to Didep models, previous results obtained under probabilistic fault models can be confirmed and possibly extended to stochastically dependent faults.

For the original probe complexity, lower bounds have been found for nondominated coteries. These bounds are easy to compute as they are given in terms of the number of quorums and the minimal quorum cardinality. Such lower bounds for quorum sets under a sequence-based structural failure model are a question of future work.

Following the literature on probe strategies, we have restricted ourselves to sequential probing of processes. Another approach would be to probe all processes in parallel. While sequential probing generally requires less messages than parallel probing, it incurs a higher latency. Other approaches that limit the number of parallel probes lie in between and, thereby, allow trade-offs among the number of required messages and the latency. Constructing probe strategy trees for parallel probes and evaluations of the resulting trade-offs have not been addressed yet.

Chapter 5: Consensus Our considerations of quorums have been independent of a particular fault tolerance problem to solve. To demonstrate the tractability of Didep models for a concrete problem, Chapter 5 has addressed the seminal problem of reaching consensus. Consensus is among the most well-studied problems of distributed computing and, in particular, has been frequently used to assess new system models in the past.

The bottom line of this chapter is that using Didep models does not require to develop new solutions from scratch, but allows to reuse previous solutions for less expressive structural failure models. Solutions that rely on quorums have been particularly simple to reuse: With the construction of highly available coteries from the previous chapter, reusing such solutions hardly requires any adaptation. Nevertheless, modelling faults with Didep models turned out to be beneficial as it allowed to achieve more resilient and/or more efficient solutions if faults are directed dependent. For a special case, it even allowed to circumvent the well-known FLP impossibility result. Covering a wide range of possible assumptions, we have presented solutions for benign as well as malicious failures, for permanent and transient failures, and for asynchronous, partially synchronous, and synchronous timing models.

There remain several directions for future work. For example, we have focused on Didep models in this chapter, but did not consider sequence-based failure models. Considering these models could address the construction of the round coordinator assignment from a sequence-based model: A process that fails late – if at all – should become coordinator early, because a nonfailed coordinator is able to impose a decision value if time bounds hold or the failure detectors provides accurate information. Another direction could be to optimise the exponential-information-gathering tree construction based on knowledge of the order of failures.

On a more general note, the consensus algorithms we have presented do not solve the same problem, but different variants of consensus. Weakening the original problem (defined for fault-free systems) was necessary to make solutions possible at all and depends on the fault model under consideration. The weakenings that we presented are specific to consensus, but, in general, weakenings are necessary for many problems that need to be solved in a fault-tolerant way. It is still an open question how to weaken a specification systematically such that the resulting problem is as strong as possible, but as weak as necessary to allow the existence of solutions.

Bibliography

M. Abadi and L. Lamport. The existence of refinement mappings. *Theoretical Computer Science*, 82(2):253–284, 1991. Citations on pages 10 and 13.

M. Abadi and L. Lamport. Conjoining specifications. *ACM Transactions on Programming Languages and Systems*, 17(3):507–535, 1995. Citations on pages 10, 14, 22, and 23.

M. Abadi and S. Merz. On TLA as a logic. In M. Broy, editor, *Deductive Program Design*, NATO Advanced Science Institutes Series, pages 235–271. Springer, 1996. Citations on pages 19 and 21.

H. Abu-Amara and J. Lokre. Election in asynchronous complete networks with intermittent link failures. *IEEE Transactions on Computers*, 43(7):778–788, 1994. Citation on page 56.

D. Agrawal and A. E. Abbadi. The generalized tree quorum protocol: An efficient approach for managing replicated data. *ACM Transactions on Database Systems*, 17(4):689–717, Dec. 1992. Citations on pages 92, 100, 106, and 107.

M. K. Aguilera, W. Chen, and S. Toueg. Failure detection and consensus in the crash-recovery model. *Distributed Computing*, 13(2):99–125, 2000. Citation on page 140.

M. Ahamad, M. H. Ammar, and S. Y. Cheung. Multidimensional voting. *ACM Transactions on Computer Systems*, 9(4):399–431, Nov. 1991. Citation on page 102.

B. Alpern and F. B. Schneider. Defining liveness. *Information Processing Letters*, 21:181–185, Oct. 1985. Citation on page 15.

L. Alvisi, E. T. Pierce, D. Malkhi, M. K. Reiter, and R. N. Wright. Dynamic Byzantine quorum systems. In *Proceedings of the 2000 International Conference on Dependable Systems and Networks (DSN '00)*, pages 283–294. IEEE Press, 2000. Citations on pages 99, 116, and 138.

L. Alvisi, D. Malkhi, E. Pierce, and M. K. Reiter. Fault detection for Byzantine quorum systems. *IEEE Transactions on Parallel and Distributed Systems*, 12 (9):996–1007, Sept. 2001. Citations on pages 124 and 154.

Y. Amir and A. Wool. Evaluating quorum systems over the Internet. In *Proceedings of the 26th International Fault-Tolerant Computing Symposium (FTCS-26)*, pages 26–35. IEEE Press, 1996. Citations on pages 4, 39, and 60.

Y. Amir and A. Wool. Optimal availability quorum systems: Theory and practice. *Information Processing Letters*, 65(5):223–228, 1998. Citations on pages 92 and 100.

A. Arora and M. Gouda. Closure and convergence: A foundation of fault-tolerant computing. *IEEE Transactions on Software Engineering*, 19(11):1015–1027, Nov. 1993. Citations on pages 26 and 30.

A. Arora and S. S. Kulkarni. Component based design of multitolerant systems. *IEEE Transactions on Software Engineering*, 24(1):63–78, Jan. 1998a. Citations on pages 26 and 30.

A. Arora and S. S. Kulkarni. Detectors and correctors: A theory of fault-tolerance components. In *Proceedings of the 18th International Conference on Distributed Computing Systems (ICDCS '98)*, pages 436–443. IEEE Press, 1998b. Citation on page 30.

E. A. Ashcroft. Proving assertions about parallel programs. *Journal of Computer and System Sciences*, 10(1):110–135, Feb. 1975. Citation on page 16.

A. Avižienis, J.-C. Laprie, B. Randell, and C. E. Landwehr. Basic concepts and taxonomy of dependable and secure computing. *IEEE Transactions on Dependable and Secure Computing*, 1(1):11–33, 2004. Citation on page 1.

M. H. Azadmanesh and R. M. Kieckhafer. Exploiting omissive faults in synchronous approximate agreement. *IEEE Transactions on Computers*, 49(10): 1031–1042, 2000. Citation on page 58.

M. Bakkaloglu, J. J. Wylie, C. Wang, and G. R. Ganger. Modeling correlated failures in survivable storage systems. In *Proceedings of the 2002 International Conference on Dependable Systems and Networks (DSN '02)*. IEEE Press, 2002. Fast Abstract. Citations on pages 4, 39, 60, and 94.

A. Bar-Noy, D. Dolev, C. Dwork, and H. R. Strong. Shifting gears: Changing algorithms on the fly to expedite Byzantine agreement. In *Proceedings of the 6th Annual ACM Symposium on Principles of Distributed Computing (PODC '87)*, pages 42–51. ACM Press, 1987. Citations on pages 142, 174, 177, and 187.

D. Barbara and H. Garcia-Molina. Mutual exclusion in partitioned distributed systems. *Distributed Computing*, 1(2):119–132, June 1986. Citations on pages 101, 102, and 105.

D. Barbara and H. Garcia-Molina. The reliability of voting mechanisms. *IEEE Transactions on Computers*, 36(10):1197–1208, Oct. 1987. Citations on pages 92 and 100.

M. Barborak, A. Dahbura, and M. Malek. The consensus problem in fault-tolerant computing. *ACM Computing Surveys*, 25(2):171–220, June 1993. Citations on pages 46 and 141.

R. A. Bazzi. Synchronous Byzantine quorum systems. *Distributed Computing*, 13 (1):45–52, Jan. 2000. Citation on page 77.

M. Ben-Ari. *Principles of Concurrent and Distributed Programming*. Prentice Hall, 2nd edition, 2006. Citation on page 141.

M. Ben-Or, S. Goldwasser, and A. Wigderson. Completeness theorems for non-cryptographic fault-tolerant distributed computation. In *Proceedings of the 20th Annual ACM Symposium on Theory of Computing (STOC '88)*, pages 1–10. ACM Press, 1988. Citations on pages 75 and 148.

J. Benaloh and J. Leichter. Generalized secret sharing and monotone functions. In *Advances in Cryptology – CRYPTO '88*, volume 403 of *Lecture Notes in Computer Science*, pages 27–35. Springer, 1988. Citation on page 75.

P. A. Bernstein, V. Hadzilacos, and N. Goodman. *Concurrency Control and Recovery in Database Systems*. Addison-Wesley, 1987. Citations on pages 37, 97, and 101.

M. Biely, J. Widder, B. Charron-Bost, A. Gaillard, M. Hutle, and A. Schiper. Tolerating corrupted communication. In *Proceedings of the 26th Annual ACM Symposium on Principles of Distributed Computing (PODC '07)*, pages 244–253. ACM Press, 2007. Citation on page 41.

J. C. Bioch and T. Ibaraki. Generating and approximating nondominated coteries. *IEEE Transactions on Parallel and Distributed Systems*, 6(9):905–914, Sept. 1995. Citation on page 105.

W. J. Bolosky, J. R. Douceur, and J. Howell. The farsite project: A retrospective. *ACM SIGOPS Operating Systems Review*, 41(2):17–26, 2007. Citation on page 2.

F. V. Brasileiro, F. Greve, A. Mostéfaoui, and M. Raynal. Consensus in one communication step. In *Proceedings of the 6th International Conference on Parallel Computing Technologies (PaCT '01)*, volume 2127 of *Lecture Notes in Computer Science*, pages 42–50. Springer, 2001. Citations on pages 142 and 152.

C. Cachin. Distributing trust on the Internet. In *Proceedings of the 2001 International Conference on Dependable Systems and Networks (DSN '01)*, pages 183–192. IEEE Press, 2001. Citation on page 75.

T. D. Chandra and S. Toueg. Unreliable failure detectors for reliable distributed systems. *Journal of the ACM*, 43(2):225–267, Mar. 1996. Citations on pages 33, 34, 35, 36, 37, 43, 48, 50, 51, 52, 124, 142, 148, 150, 152, 153, 154, 155, and 159.

T. D. Chandra, V. Hadzilacos, and S. Toueg. The weakest failure detector for solving consensus. *Journal of the ACM*, 43(4):685–722, July 1996. Citation on page 168.

B. Charron-Bost and A. Schiper. Uniform consensus is harder than consensus. *Journal of Algorithms*, 51(1):15–37, 2004. Citations on pages 142, 146, 151, and 152.

B. Charron-Bost and A. Schiper. Harmful dogmas in fault tolerant distributed computing. *SIGACT News*, 38(1):53–61, 2007. Citations on pages 41, 53, 95, 142, 170, 187, and 190.

B. Charron-Bost, R. Guerraoui, and A. Schiper. Synchronous system and perfect failure detector: solvability and efficiency issues. In *Proceedings of the 2000 International Conference on Dependable Systems and Networks (DSN '00)*, pages 523–532. IEEE Press, 2000. Citations on pages 31 and 37.

W. Chen, S. Toueg, and M. K. Aguilera. On the quality of service of failure detectors. *IEEE Transactions on Computers*, 51(1):13–32, Jan. 2002. Citation on page 124.

S. Y. Cheung, M. H. Ammar, and M. Ahamad. The grid protocol: A high performance scheme for maintaining replicated data. *IEEE Transactions on Knowledge and Data Engineering*, 4(6):582–592, 1992. Citations on pages 92, 100, 102, 106, and 113.

G. Coulouris, J. Dollimore, and T. Kindberg. *Distributed Systems: Concepts and Design*. Addison-Wesley, 4th edition, 2005. Citation on page 141.

F. Cristian. A rigorous approach to fault-tolerant programming. *IEEE Transactions on Software Engineering*, 11(1):23–31, 1985. Citation on page 25.

F. Cristian. Understanding fault-tolerant distributed systems. *Communications of the ACM*, 34(2):56–78, Feb. 1991. Citation on page 42.

F. Cristian and C. Fetzer. The timed asynchronous distributed system model. *IEEE Transactions on Parallel and Distributed Systems*, 10(6):642–657, June 1999. Citations on pages 31, 33, and 148.

F. Cristian, H. Aghili, R. Strong, and D. Dolev. Atomic broadcast: From simple message diffusion to Byzantine agreement. In *Proceedings of the 15th International Fault-Tolerant Computing Symposium (FTCS-15)*, pages 1–7. IEEE Press, June 1985. Citations on pages 42, 46, and 49.

E. W. Dijkstra. Self-stabilizing systems in spite of distributed control. *Communications of the ACM*, 17(11):643–644, 1974. Citation on page 31.

E. W. Dijkstra. Guarded commands, nondeterminacy and formal derivation of programs. *Communications of the ACM*, 18(8):453–457, Aug. 1975. Citation on page 14.

I. Dobson, B. A. Carreras, and D. E. Newman. Probabilistic load-dependent cascading failure with limited component interactions. In *Proceedings of the 2004 International Symposium on Circuits and Systems (ISCAS '04)*, volume 5, pages 912–915, May 2004. Citations on pages 3, 39, 89, and 94.

I. Dobson, B. A. Carreras, and D. E. Newman. A loading-dependent model of probabilistic cascading failure. *Probability in the Engineering and Informational Sciences*, 19(1):15–32, 2005. Citations on pages 3, 39, 89, and 94.

D. Dolev and H. R. Strong. Polynomial algorithms for multiple processor agreement. In *Proceedings of the 14th Annual ACM Symposium on Theory of Computing (STOC '82)*, pages 401–407. ACM Press, 1982. Citation on page 151.

D. Dolev, C. Dwork, and L. Stockmeyer. On the minimal synchronism needed for distributed consensus. *Journal of the ACM*, 34(1):77–97, Jan. 1987. Citations on pages 33, 139, and 148.

D. Dolev, R. Reischuk, and H. R. Strong. Early stopping in Byzantine agreement. *Journal of the ACM*, 37(4):720–741, Oct. 1990. Citations on pages 151 and 152.

S. Dolev. *Self-Stabilization*. MIT Press, 2000. Citations on pages 31 and 49.

A. Doudou, B. Garbinato, and R. Guerraoui. Encapsulating failure detection: From crash to Byzantine failures. In *Proceedings of the 7th Ada-Europe International Conference on Reliable Software Technologies*, volume 2361 of *Lecture Notes in Computer Science*, pages 24–50. Springer, 2002. Citations on pages 124, 142, and 154.

C. Dwork, N. Lynch, and L. Stockmeyer. Consensus in the presence of partial synchrony. *Journal of the ACM*, 35(2):288–323, Apr. 1988. Citations on pages 33, 34, 48, 139, 148, and 154.

K. Echtle. *Fehlertoleranzverfahren*. Springer, 1990. Citation on page 41.

C. Fetzer, U. Schmid, and M. Süsskraut. On the possibility of consensus in asynchronous systems with finite average response times. In *Proceedings of the 25th International Conference on Distributed Computing Systems (ICDCS '05)*, pages 271–280. IEEE Press, 2005. Citation on page 33.

M. J. Fischer. The consensus problem in unreliable distributed systems (a brief survey). In *Proceedings of the International Conference on Fundamentals of Computation Theory (FCT 1983)*, volume 158 of *Lecture Notes in Computer Science*, pages 127–140. Springer, 1983. Citation on page 141.

M. J. Fischer and N. A. Lynch. A lower bound for the time to assure interactive consistency. *Information Processing Letters*, 14(4):183–186, June 1982. Citations on pages 151 and 186.

M. J. Fischer, N. A. Lynch, and M. S. Paterson. Impossibility of distributed consensus with one faulty process. *Journal of the ACM*, 32(2):374–382, Apr. 1985. Citations on pages 32, 43, 48, 51, 52, 147, 148, and 168.

M. Fitzi and U. M. Maurer. Efficient Byzantine agreement secure against general adversaries. In S. Kutten, editor, *Proceedings of the 12th International Symposium on Distributed Computing (DISC '98)*, volume 1499 of *Lecture Notes in Computer Science*, pages 134–148. Springer, 1998. Citations on pages 49, 75, 113, 141, and 153.

M. Fitzi, M. Hirt, and U. M. Maurer. General adversaries in unconditional multi-party computation. In K.-Y. Lam, E. Okamoto, and C. Xing, editors, *Proceedings of Advances in Cryptology (ASIACRYPT '99)*, volume 1716 of *Lecture Notes in Computer Science*, pages 232–246. Springer, 1999. Citations on pages 60 and 75.

F. C. Freiling, R. Guerraoui, and P. Kouznetsov. The failure detector abstraction. Technical Report 2006-003, University of Mannheim, Faculty of Mathematics and Computer Science, Feb. 2006. Citation on page 31.

H. Garcia-Molina and D. Barbara. How to assign votes in a distributed system. *Journal of the ACM*, 32(4):841–860, Oct. 1985. Citations on pages 102, 104, and 105.

F. C. Gärtner. Specifications for fault tolerance: A comedy of failures. Technical Report TUD-BS-1998-03, Darmstadt University of Technology, Darmstadt, Germany, 1998. Citation on page 26.

F. C. Gärtner. Fundamentals of fault-tolerant distributed computing in asynchronous environments. *ACM Computing Surveys*, 31(1):1–26, Mar. 1999. Citations on pages 2 and 30.

F. C. Gärtner. A survey of transformational approaches to the specification and verification of fault-tolerant systems. Technical Report TUD-BS-1999-04, Darmstadt University of Technology, 1999. Citations on pages 25 and 26.

F. C. Gärtner. *Formale Grundlagen der Fehlertoleranz in verteilten Systemen*. PhD thesis, Fachbereich Informatik, Technische Unversität Darmstadt, 2001. Citations on pages 30 and 31.

F. C. Gärtner. Fehlermodellierung ohne explizite Fehlerzustände. In U. Brinkschulte, K.-E. Großpietsch, C. Hochberger, and E. Mayr, editors, *Workshop Proceedings of the International Conference on Architecture of Computing Systems (ARCS 2002)*, pages 71–80. VDE Verlag, 2002. Citation on page 25.

S. Ghosh. *Distributed Systems – An Algorithmic Approach*. CRC Press, 2006. Citation on page 141.

D. K. Gifford. Weighted voting for replicated data. In *Proceedings of the 7th ACM Symposium on Operating Systems Principles (SOSP' 79)*, pages 150–162. ACM Press, 1979. Citations on pages 106 and 109.

S. Gorender, R. J. de Arújo Macedo, and M. Raynal. An adaptive programming model for fault-tolerant distributed computing. *IEEE Transactions on Dependable and Secure Computing*, 4(1):18–31, 2007. Citation on page 51.

R. Guerraoui. Indulgent algorithms (preliminary version). In *Proceedings of the 19th Annual ACM Symposium on Principles of Distributed Computing (PODC '00)*, pages 289–297. ACM Press, 2000. Citation on page 146.

R. Guerraoui. Non-blocking atomic commit in asynchronous distributed systems with failure detectors. *Distributed Computing*, 15(1):17–25, 2002. Citation on page 37.

R. Guerraoui and L. Rodrigues. *Introduction to Reliable Distributed Programming*. Springer, 2006. Citation on page 141.

R. Guerraoui, M. Hurfin, A. Mostéfaoui, R. Oliveira, M. Raynal, and A. Schiper. Consensus in asynchronous distributed systems: A concise guided tour. In *Advances in Distributed Systems – Advanced Distributed Computing: From Algorithms to Systems*, pages 33–47. Springer, 1999. Citation on page 141.

T. Harada and M. Yamashita. Transversal merge operation: A nondominated coterie construction method for distributed mutual exclusion. *IEEE Transactions on Parallel and Distributed Systems*, 16(2):183–192, Feb. 2005. Citation on page 105.

M. Herlihy and N. Shavir. *The Art of Multiprocessor Programming*. Morgan Kaufmann, 2008. Citation on page 140.

M. Hirt and U. Maurer. Complete characterization of adversaries tolerable in secure multi-party computation (extended abstract). In *Proceedings of the 16th Annual ACM Symposium on Principles of Distributed Computing (PODC '97)*, pages 25–34. ACM Press, 1997. Citations on pages 42, 74, 75, 76, 153, and 154.

C. A. R. Hoare. Communicating sequential processes. *Communications of the ACM*, 21(8):666–677, Aug. 1978. Citation on page 14.

C. A. R. Hoare. *Communicating Sequential Processes*. Prentice Hall International, 1985. Citation on page 14.

M. Hurfin, A. Mostéfaoui, and M. Raynal. A versatile family of consensus protocols based on chandra-toueg's unreliable failure detectors. *IEEE Transactions on Computers*, 51(4):395–408, 2002. Citations on pages 51, 142, 153, 154, 155, 156, 157, 158, 163, 169, and 187.

M. Hutle and A. Schiper. Communication predicates: A high-level abstraction for coping with transient and dynamic faults. In *Proceedings of the 2007 International Conference on Dependable Systems and Networks (DSN '07)*, pages 92–101. IEEE Press, 2007. Citation on page 41.

M. Ito, A. Saito, and T. Nishizeki. Secret sharing scheme realizing general access structure. In *Proceedings of the IEEE Global Telecommunications Conference (Globecom '87)*, pages 99–102. IEEE Press, 1987. Citation on page 75.

S. Jajodia and D. Mutchler. Dynamic voting algorithms for maintaining the consistency of a replicated database. *ACM Transactions on Database Systems*, 15 (2):230–280, June 1990. Citation on page 120.

F. P. Junqueira. *Coping with Dependent Failures in Distributed Systems*. PhD thesis, University of California, San Diego, 2006. Citations on pages 4, 79, 80, 113, 141, 142, 153, and 154.

F. P. Junqueira and K. Marzullo. Coping with dependent process failures. Technical Report CS2002-0723, University of California, San Diego, Dec. 2001. Citations on pages 78, 79, and 80.

F. P. Junqueira and K. Marzullo. Consensus for dependent process failures. Technical Report CS2003-0737, University of California, San Diego, Sept. 2002a. Citation on page 79.

F. P. Junqueira and K. Marzullo. Lower bound on the number of rounds for synchronous consensus with dependent process failures. Technical Report CS2003-0734, University of California, San Diego, Sept. 2002b. Citation on page 79.

F. P. Junqueira and K. Marzullo. On the generalization of $n > k \times t$ (brief announcement). Technical Report CS2003-0743, University of California, San Diego, Apr. 2003a. Citation on page 42.

F. P. Junqueira and K. Marzullo. Synchronous consensus for dependent process failures. In *Proceedings of the 23rd International Conference on Distributed Computing Systems (ICDCS '03)*, pages 274–283. IEEE Press, 2003b. Citations on pages 49, 60, 74, and 79.

F. P. Junqueira and K. Marzullo. Coterie availability in sites. In *Proceedings of the 19th International Symposium on Distributed Computing (DISC '05)*, volume 3724 of *Lecture Notes in Computer Science*, pages 3–17. Springer, 2005a. Citations on pages 42, 74, 81, 82, 83, 84, and 99.

F. P. Junqueira and K. Marzullo. Replication predicates for dependent-failure algorithms. In J. C. Cunha and P. D. Medeiros, editors, *Proceedings of the 11th International Euro-Par Conference (Euro-Par '05)*, volume 3648 of *Lecture Notes in Computer Science*, pages 617–632. Springer, 2005b. Citation on page 50.

F. P. Junqueira and K. Marzullo. The virtue of dependent failures in multi-site systems. In *Proceedings of the 1st IEEE Workshop on Hot Topics in System Dependability (HotDep'05)*. IEEE Press, 2005c. Citations on pages 42, 81, and 99.

F. P. Junqueira, R. Bhagwan, K. Marzullo, S. Savage, and G. M. Voelker. The phoenix recovery system: Rebuilding from the ashes of an internet catastrophe. In *Proceedings of the 9th Workshop on Hot Topics in Operating Systems (HotOS IX)*, 2003. Citation on page 79.

F. P. Junqueira, R. Bhagwan, A. Hevia, K. Marzullo, and G. M. Voelker. Surviving internet catastrophes. In *Proceedings of USENIX 2005 Annual Technical Conference (ATEC '05)*, pages 45–60. Usenix Association, 2005. Citations on pages 74 and 79.

P. F. Junqueira and K. Marzullo. Weak leader election in the receive-omission failure model. Technical Report CS2005-0829, University of California, San Diego, May 2005d. Citation on page 79.

I. Keidar and K. Marzullo. The need for realistic failure models in protocol design. In *Proceedings of 4th Information Survivability Workshop (ISW 2001/2002)*, Mar. 2002. Citations on pages 4, 60, and 73.

I. Keidar and S. Rajsbaum. On the cost of fault-tolerant consensus when there are no faults (preliminary version). *SIGACT News*, 32(2):45–63, June 2001. Citations on pages 142 and 151.

R. M. Keller. Formal verification of parallel programs. *Communications of the ACM*, 19(7):371–384, July 1976. Citation on page 16.

K. P. Kihlstrom, L. E. Moser, and P. M. Melliar-Smith. Byzantine fault detectors for solving consensus. *The Computer Journal*, 46(1):16–35, 2003. Citations on pages 124, 142, 154, and 155.

K. Kursawe and F. C. Freiling. Byzantine fault tolerance on general hybrid adversary structures. Technical Report AIB-2005-09, RWTH Aachen, 2005. Citation on page 76.

L. Lamport. Proving the correctness of multiprocess programs. *IEEE Transactions on Software Engineering*, 3(2):125–143, Mar. 1977. Citations on pages 15 and 16.

L. Lamport. The implementation of reliable distributed multiprocess systems. *Computer Networks*, 2(2):95–114, May 1978a. Citations on pages 48 and 97.

L. Lamport. Time, clocks, and the ordering of events in a distributed system. *Communications of the ACM*, 21(7):558–565, July 1978b. Citation on page 140.

L. Lamport. What good is temporal logic? In R. E. A. Mason, editor, *Information Processing 83*, pages 657–668. Elsevier, 1983a. Citations on pages 13 and 19.

L. Lamport. The weak Byzantine generals problem. *Journal of the ACM*, 30(3): 668–676, July 1983b. Citation on page 58.

L. Lamport. How to write a proof. *American Mathematical Monthly*, 102(7): 600–608, Aug./Sept. 1993. Citation on page 8.

L. Lamport. The temporal logic of actions. *ACM Transactions on Programming Languages and Systems*, 16(3):872–923, May 1994. Citations on pages 10, 16, 19, 21, and 24.

L. Lamport. The part-time parliament. *ACM Transactions on Computer Systems*, 16(2):133–169, may 1998. Citations on pages 81, 142, and 143.

L. Lamport. *Specifying Systems: The TLA+ Language and Tools for Hardware and Software Engineers*. Addison-Wesley, 2002. Citations on pages 8, 14, and 19.

L. Lamport and N. Lynch. Distributed computing: Models and methods. In J. van Leeuwen, editor, *Handbook of Theoretical Computer Science*, volume B, chapter 18, pages 1157–1199. MIT Press, 1990. Citation on page 10.

L. Lamport and S. Merz. Specifying and verifying fault-tolerant systems. In H. Langmaack, W.-P. de Roever, and J. Vytopil, editors, *Formal Techniques in Real-Time and Fault-Tolerant Systems*, volume 863 of *Lecture Notes in Computer Science*, pages 41–76. Springer, 1994. Citation on page 24.

L. Lamport, R. E. Shostak, and M. C. Pease. The Byzantine generals problem. *ACM Transactions on Programming Languages and Systems*, 4(3):382–401, July 1982. Citations on pages 43, 51, 52, 142, and 174.

I. Lee, R. K. Iyer, and D. Tang. Error/failure analysis using event logs from fault tolerant systems. In *Proceedings of the 21st International Fault-Tolerant Computing Symposium (FTCS-21)*, pages 10–17. IEEE Press, 1991. Citation on page 94.

P. Limbourg, H.-D. Kochs, K. Echtle, and I. Eusgeld. Reliability prediction in systems with correlated component failures. In *Proc. 20th Int. Conf. on Architecture of Computing Systems*, pages 55 – 62. VDE Verlag, 2007. Citations on pages 4 and 94.

P. Lincoln and J. M. Rushby. The formal verification of an algorithm for interactive consistency under a hybrid fault model. In C. Courcoubetis, editor, *Computer-Aided Verification (CAV '93)*, volume 697 of *Lecture Notes in Computer Science*, pages 292–304. Springer, 1993. Citation on page 45.

Z. Liu and M. Joseph. Transformation of programs for fault-tolerance. *Formal Aspects of Computing*, 4(5):442–469, 1992. Citation on page 26.

Z. Liu and M. Joseph. A formal framework for fault-tolerant programs. In C. M. Mitchell and V. Stavridou, editors, *Mathematics of Dependable Computing*, pages 131–148. Oxford University Press, 1995. Citation on page 26.

Z. Liu and M. Joseph. Verification of fault tolerance and real time. In *Proceedings of the 26th International Fault-Tolerant Computing Symposium (FTCS-26)*, pages 220–229. IEEE Press, 1996. Citation on page 26.

Z. Liu and M. Joseph. Specification and verification of fault-tolerance, timing, and scheduling. *ACM Transactions on Programming Languages and Systems*, 21(1):46–89, Jan. 1999. Citation on page 26.

Z. Liu and M. Joseph. Real-time and fault-tolerant systems. In A. Cavalcanti, A. Sampaio, and JimWoodcock, editors, *Refinement Techniques in Software Engineering*, volume 3167 of *Lecture Notes in Computer Science*, chapter 5, pages 156–219. Springer, 2006. Citation on page 26.

D. Long, A. Muir, and R. Golding. A longitudinal survey of internet host reliability. In *Proceedings of the 14th Symposium on Reliable Distributed Systems (SRDS '95)*, pages 2–9. IEEE Press, 1995. Citations on pages 39 and 60.

N. A. Lynch. *Distributed Algorithms.* Morgan Kaufmann, 1996. Citations on pages 11, 16, 141, 150, 154, 174, 178, 182, 184, and 187.

D. A. Mackall. Development and flight test experiences with a flight-crucial digital control system. Technical Report NASA-TP-2857, NASA Dryden Flight Research Center, Nov. 1988. Citations on pages 2 and 3.

M. Maekawa. A $\sqrt{n}$ algorithm for mutual exclusion in decentralized systems. *ACM Transactions on Computer Systems*, 3(2):145–159, May 1985. Citations on pages 97, 100, and 106.

D. Malkhi and M. K. Reiter. Byzantine quorum systems. In *Proceedings of the 29th Annual ACM Symposium on Theory of Computing (STOC '97)*, pages 569–578. ACM Press, 1997. Citations on pages 42, 74, and 77.

D. Malkhi and M. K. Reiter. Byzantine quorum systems. *Distributed Computing*, 11(4):203–213, Oct. 1998. Citations on pages 77, 99, 102, 115, 116, and 117.

Z. Manna and A. Pnueli. Verification of concurrent programs: Proving eventualities by well-founded ranking. Technical Report STAN-CS-82-915, Department of Computer Science, Stanford University, Stanford, CA, USA, May 1982. Citation on page 16.

B. Mans and N. Santoro. Optimal elections in faulty loop networks and applications. *IEEE Transactions on Computers*, 47(3):286–297, 1998. Citation on page 56.

J.-P. Martin, L. Alvisi, and M. Dahlin. Small Byzantine quorum systems. In *Proceedings of the 2002 International Conference on Dependable Systems and Networks (DSN '02)*, pages 374–388. IEEE Press, 2002. Citation on page 77.

A. Masum. *Non-Cooperative Byzantine Failures – A New Framework for the Design of Efficient Fault Tolerance Protocols*. PhD thesis, University of Essen, 2000. Citation on page 154.

F. J. Meyer and D. K. Pradhan. Consensus with dual failure modes. *IEEE Transactions on Parallel and Distributed Systems*, 2(2):214–222, 1991. Citation on page 45.

A. Mostéfaoui and M. Raynal. Solving consensus using Chandra-Toueg's unreliable failure detectors: A general quorum-based approach. In *Proceedings of the 13th International Symposium on Distributed Computing (DISC '99)*, volume 1693 of *Lecture Notes in Computer Science*, pages 49–63. Springer, 1999. Citations on pages 97, 142, 150, 152, 154, 155, and 159.

M. Naor and A. Wool. The load, capacity, and availability of quorum systems. *SIAM Journal on Computing*, 27(2):423–447, 1998. Citations on pages 102, 103, and 104.

M. L. Neilsen. A dynamic probe strategy for quorum systems. In *Proceedings of the 17th International Conference on Distributed Computing Systems (ICDCS '97)*, pages 95–99. IEEE Press, 1997. Citations on pages 101, 126, and 131.

J. Nordahl. *Specification and Design of Dependable Communicating Systems*. PhD thesis, Department of Computer Science, Technical University of Denmark, 1992. Citations on pages 26 and 41.

J. Nordahl. Design for dependability. In C. E. Landwehr, editor, *Proceedings of the 3rd IFIP Working Conference on Dependable Computing for Critical Applications (DCCA-3)*, pages 29–38. Springer, 1993. Citations on pages 26 and 41.

S. Owicki and D. Gries. An axiomatic proof technique for parallel programs. *Acta Informatica*, 6(6):319–340, 1976. Citation on page 16.

S. Owicki and L. Lamport. Proving liveness properties of concurrent programs. *ACM Transactions on Programming Languages and Systems*, 4(3):455–495, July 1982. Citation on page 16.

M. Pease, R. Shostak, and L. Lamport. Reaching agreement in the presence of faults. *Journal of the ACM*, 27(2):228–234, 1980. Citations on pages 151, 154, 174, and 177.

D. Peleg and A. Wool. The availability of quorum systems. *Information and Computation*, 123(2):210–223, Dec. 1995. Citation on page 99.

D. Peleg and A. Wool. How to be an efficient snoop or the probe complexity of quorum systems (extended abstract). In *Proceedings of the 15th Annual ACM Symposium on Principles of Distributed Computing (PODC '96)*, pages 290–299. ACM Press, 1996. Citations on pages 126 and 131.

D. Peleg and A. Wool. How to be an efficient snoop, or the probe complexity of quorum systems. *SIAM Journal on Discrete Mathematics*, 15(3):416–433, Mar. 2002. Citations on pages 100, 101, 102, 104, 126, 127, 128, 129, 131, 132, 134, and 137.

K. J. Perry and S. Toueg. Distributed agreement in the presence of processor and communication faults. *IEEE Transactions on Software Engineering*, 12(3):477–482, 1986. Citation on page 52.

A. Pnueli. The temporal logic of programs. In *Proceedings of the 18th IEEE Symposium on Foundations of Computer Science (FOCS 1977)*, pages 46–67. IEEE Press, 1977. Citations on pages 14, 16, and 19.

D. Powell. Failure mode assumptions and assumption coverage. In D. K. Pradhan, editor, *Proceedings of the 22nd International Fault-Tolerant Computing Symposium (FTCS-22)*, pages 386–395. IEEE Press, July 1992. Citations on pages 49 and 92.

M. O. Rabin. Randomized Byzantine generals. In *Proceedings of the 24th IEEE Symposium on Foundations of Computer Science (FOCS 1983)*, pages 403–409. IEEE Press, 1983. Citation on page 148.

M. Rabinovich and E. D. Lazowska. Improving fault tolerance and supporting partial writes in structured coterie protocols. In *Proceedings of the 1992 ACM SIGMOD International Conference on Management of Data*, pages 226–235, 1992. Citations on pages 107 and 109.

J. Rushby. A formally verified algorithm for clock synchronization under a hybrid fault model. In *Proceedings of the 13th Annual ACM Symposium on Principles of Distributed Computing (PODC '94)*, pages 304–313. ACM Press, 1994. Citation on page 58.

N. Santoro and P. Widmayer. Time is not a healer. In *Proceedings of the 6th Annual Symposium on Theoretical Aspects of Computer Science (STACS '89)*, volume 349 of *Lecture Notes in Computer Science*, pages 304–313. Springer, 1989. Citations on pages 40, 41, 95, and 170.

N. Santoro and P. Widmayer. Majority and unanimity in synchronous networks with ubiquitous dynamic faults. In A. Pelc and M. Raynal, editors, *Proceedings of the 12th International Colloquium on Structural Information and Communication Complexity (SIROCCO 2005)*, volume 3499 of *Lecture Notes in Computer Science*, pages 262–276. Springer, 2005. Citations on pages 40, 41, 140, and 170.

H. M. Sayeed, M. Abu-Amara, and H. Abu-Amara. Optimal asynchronous agreement and leader election algorithm for complete networks with Byzantine faulty links. *Distributed Computing*, 9(3):147–156, 1995. Citation on page 56.

A. Schiper. Early consensus in an asynchronous system with a weak failure detector. *Distributed Computing*, 10(3):149–157, Apr. 1997. Citations on pages 150, 152, 154, 155, and 159.

A. Schiper and S. Toueg. From set membership to group membership: A separation of concerns. *IEEE Transactions on Dependable and Secure Computing*, 3 (1):2–12, 2006. Citation on page 51.

U. Schmid, B. Weiss, and J. Rushby. Formally verified Byzantine agreement in presence of link faults. In *Proceedings of the 22rd International Conference on Distributed Computing Systems (ICDCS '02)*, pages 608–616. IEEE Press, 2002. Citation on page 58.

F. B. Schneider. Implementing fault-tolerant services using the state machine approach: A tutorial. *ACM Computing Surveys*, 22(4):299–319, 1990. Citation on page 140.

F. B. Schneider. What good are models and what models are good? In S. Mullender, editor, *Distributed Systems*, chapter 2, pages 17–26. ACM Press, 2nd edition, 1993a. Citation on page 2.

M. Schneider. Self-stabilization. *ACM Computing Surveys*, 25(1):45–67, 1993b. Citations on pages 31 and 49.

H.-S. Siu, Y.-H. Chin, and W.-P. Yang. Byzantine agreement in the presence of mixed faults on processors and links. *IEEE Transactions on Parallel and Distributed Systems*, 9(4):335–345, 1998. Citations on pages 58 and 59.

D. Skeen. A quorum-based commit protocol. Technical Report TR82-483, Cornell University, Feb. 1982. Citation on page 97.

D. Tang and R. K. Iyer. Analysis and modeling of correlated failures in multicomputer systems. *IEEE Transactions on Computers*, 41(5):567–577, 1992. Citations on pages 3, 4, 39, 60, and 94.

D. Tang and R. K. Iyer. Dependability measurement and modeling of a multicomputer system. *IEEE Transactions on Computers*, 42(1):62–75, Jan. 1993. Citations on pages 4, 39, 60, 94, and 100.

P. M. Thambidurai and Y.-K. Park. Interactive consistency with multiple failure modes. In *Proceedings of the 7th Symposium on Reliable Distributed Systems (SRDS '88)*, pages 93–100. IEEE Press, 1988. Citations on pages 45 and 49.

O. Theel and H. Pagnia. Optimal replica control protocols exhibit symmetric operation availabilities. In *Proceedings of the 28th International Fault-Tolerant Computing Symposium (FTCS-28)*, pages 252–261. IEEE Press, 1998. Citation on page 92.

R. H. Thomas. A majority consensus approach to concurrency control for multiple copy databases. *ACM Transactions on Database Systems*, 4(2):180–209, June 1979. Citations on pages 106 and 113.

Z. Tong and R. Y. Kain. Vote assignments in weighted voting mechanisms. *IEEE Transactions on Computers*, 40(5):664–667, May 1991. Citation on page 100.

J. Turek and D. Shasha. The many faces of consensus in distributed systems. *Computer*, 25(6):8–17, June 1992. Citation on page 141.

P. Veríssimo and C. Almeida. Quasi-synchronism. a step away from the traditional fault-tolerant real-time system models. *Bulletin of the Technical Committee on Operating Systems and Application Environments (TCOS)*, 7(4):35–39, Dec. 1995. Citation on page 33.

P. Veríssimo and A. Casimiro. The timely computing base model and architecture. *IEEE Transactions on Computers*, 51(8):916–930, Aug. 2002. Citations on pages 33 and 148.

P. Veríssimo and M. Raynal. Time in distributed system models and algorithms. In *Advances in Distributed Systems*, volume 1752 of *Lecture Notes in Computer Science*, pages 1–32. Springer, 2000. Citation on page 31.

H. Völzer. Verifying fault tolerance of distributed algorithms formally – an example. In *Proceedings of the International Conference on Application of Concurrency to System Design (CSD '98)*, pages 187–197. IEEE Press, 1998. Citations on pages 26 and 41.

C. J. Walter and N. Suri. The customizable fault/error model for dependable distributed systems. *Theoretical Computer Science*, 290(2):1223–1251, 2003. Citation on page 52.

T. Warns, C. Storm, and W. Hasselbring. Availability of globally distributed nodes: An empirical evaluation. In *Proceedings of the 27th Symposium on Reliable Distributed Systems (SRDS '08)*, pages 279–284. IEEE Press, 2008. Citations on pages 3, 39, and 60.

H. Weatherspoon, T. Moscovitz, and J. Kubiatowicz. Introspective failure analysis: Avoiding correlated failures in peer-to-peer systems. In *Proceedings of the 21st Symposium on Reliable Distributed Systems (SRDS '02)*, pages 362–369. IEEE Press, 2002. Citations on pages 39 and 60.

J. H. Wensley, L. Lamport, J. Goldberg, M. W. Green, K. N. Levitt, P. M. Melliar-Smith, R. E. Shostak, and C. B. Weinstock. SIFT: Design and analysis of a fault-tolerant computer for aircraft control. *Proceedings of the IEEE*, 66(10): 1240–1255, Oct. 1978. Citation on page 139.

P. Yalagandula, S. Nath, H. Yu, P. B. Gibbons, and S. Sesh. Beyond availability: Towards a deeper understanding of machine failure characteristics in large distributed systems. In *Proceedings of the 1st Workshop on Real, Large Distributed Systems (WORLDS '04)*. USENIX Association, 2004. Citations on pages 4, 39, and 60.

Index

MIX
Papier aus verantwortungsvollen Quellen
Paper from responsible sources
FSC® C105338

If you have any concerns about our products,
you can contact us on
ProductSafety@springernature.com

In case Publisher is established outside the EU,
the EU authorized representative is:
Springer Nature Customer Service Center GmbH
Europaplatz 3, 69115 Heidelberg, Germany

Printed by Libri Plureos GmbH
in Hamburg, Germany